Understanding Medjugorje

Heavenly Visions
or
Religious Illusion?

By the same author

Marian Apparitions, the Bible, and the Modern World,
(Gracewing, Leominster, 2002)

Italian translation:

Il libro delle Apparizioni Mariane, (Gribaudi, Milan, 2004)

Apparitions of Mary: Their Meaning in History,
(Catholic Truth Society, London, 2000)

Forthcoming

Christian Living: The Spirituality of the Foyers of Charity

More details at: www.theotokos.org.uk

Further copies of this book can be ordered online securely using a credit card at:

www.theotokos.org.uk/pages/books/medjbook/medjbook.html

or you can order copies via online booksellers, or through your local bookseller.

Understanding Medjugorje

Heavenly Visions
or
Religious Illusion?

Donal Anthony Foley

Theotokos Books

Published by Theotokos Books
PO Box 8570, Nottingham, England

www.theotokos.org.uk
books@theotokos.org.uk

First Published in 2006

Cover photographs courtesy of Mark Waterinckx.

Cover design/implementation by Thomas Grimer/Mike Daley

ISBN 0955074606

Contents

CONTENTS

Foreword

Medjugorje has been with us now for nearly twenty-five years—but what are Catholics to make of it all? Donal Foley's book *Understanding Medjugorje* seeks to clear away the confusion surrounding this issue and give a balanced understanding of the alleged visions and their consequences.

Many sincere Catholics believe in Medjugorje, but it is questionable whether many have properly investigated or understood what has gone on in Bosnia-Herzegovina since 1981. How many Medjugorje supporters have any real idea of the historical background to the visions, or of what went on in the town during the civil war which tore Yugoslavia apart in the 1990s, or of the long-running dispute between the Franciscans and local Church authorities? Foley explores these points, and also looks at the intimate link between Medjugorje and the Charismatic Movement. He also shows how influential priests and theologians have played a large part in the worldwide promotion of Medjugorje, and have been a significant factor in its acceptance by many Catholics.

He also amasses evidence from diverse sources to show that the contents and origin of the messages of Medjugorje leave much to be desired. Ironically, even promoters of the messages have tampered with them in order to save their credibility. In particular, this book scrutinizes the transcripts of the original tapes of the visionaries' experiences. These were made shortly after they claimed to see the Blessed Virgin on 24 June 1981. A close analysis of the contents of these tapes shows that there are serious difficulties in believing that it really was the Mother of God who appeared to the visionaries.

In the same way, the subsequent activities of the visionaries are studied, with some disturbing results, especially when compared to recognized seers such as St Bernadette or the three young shepherds of Fatima. Foley also compares the events of Medjugorje with what took place during Church-approved Marian apparitions such as Lourdes or Fatima, and shows that they have very little in common. Analyzing the authoritative statements given up to now, it is clear that the Church has not given any official support to Medjugorje; rather, in effect she has given a negative judgment, but has accompanied it with a pastoral concern to avoid scandal and disillusion, and to provide for the large numbers of pilgrims going there in good faith.

Moreover, this book looks at the Church's position on alleged visions in general and how this affects Medjugorje. The arguments put forward concerning the "good fruits" experienced by many at Medjugorje are also evaluated, and it is demonstrated that while undoubtedly many people have benefited from a visit there, such positive factors cannot override the overwhelming theological objections to Medjugorje. Foley particularly focuses on the fact that Medjugorje has had a serious impact on Fatima, with profound consequences for the Church, and he argues that it is only when this situation is rectified, that we can expect a genuine worldwide Catholic renewal.

In short, *Understanding Medjugorje* raises important questions about Medjugorje, questions which no sensible Catholic can ignore.

Fr Peter Joseph STD
Chancellor of the Maronite Diocese of Australia

Preface

Donal Foley's new book represents an important and courageous step in the direction of re-posing the question of the link between truth and religious experience. As with all courageous acts, it takes up considerable dangers—those of provoking hostility as well as the danger of being misunderstood. Medjugorje has become the most popular site of Marian pilgrimage since Fatima, and a questioning of its truth is bound to generate a debate. However, it isn't necessary to agree with every aspect of his judgment on Medjugorje to realize that he is raising important points about the visions which do need to be dealt with.

Foley gained the right to address this difficult question by an extremely important book he wrote just a few years ago—*Marian Apparitions, the Bible, and the Modern World*—in which he not only summarized the story of Marian apparitions in modern times, but also connected the main apparitions, with great precision and erudition, both to historical events and biblical passages, in a way which had a considerable, stunning, even frightening coherence.

I would like to make three major points. First, whatever caused the visions at Medjugorje—which began on 24 June 1981—this happened at a place and time that gained a significance later that no living human beings could have known in advance. At that moment, Medjugorje was a provincial backwater deep in the heartland of Communist Yugoslavia, and though a highly liminal point, literally at the border zone between Croatia, Serbia and Bosnia, or Western Christianity, Eastern Christianity and Islam, this was hardly visible at that time. If anybody would have predicted then that exactly (to the day) ten years later the Yugoslavian state would have ceased to exist, this would have only provoked a combination of hilarious laughter and stunned consternation, and a serious dilemma whether a mental hospital or a high security prison is the better place for such a blasphemous fool.

Second, part of Foley's argument is concerned with the character of the visionaries as a validation of truth claims. In their behavior he quite rightly perceives a basic contrast with Fatima. While the validity of this point cannot be denied, the reasons, I believe, might be even more complex. The seers of Fatima, and almost all the other recognized seers, were not only much younger than most of the visionaries of Medjugorje, but they also did not go through the experience of Communism. Central to such experiences was not simply the suffering and deprivation under a dictatorial regime, but the utter moral and intellectual degradation undergone in a regime that made confusion and self-abandonment into the central principles of its functioning; and in this precise sense, Yugoslavia went further than most of its neighbors. Short of a detailed exposition of this Communist "experience", I can only signal that much of the perplexity related to the conduct of the visionaries can be rendered intelligible through such confusion— with the proviso that, as it can explain everything, it of course does not explain anything in particular. No other place needed more of an eruption of transcendence than a former Communist country— but for exactly the same reasons, in no other place would it have been easier to imitate or abuse genuine spirituality.

The third point moves outside the realm of human experience but—or rather exactly because of this—might be the most important of all. The irruption of the transcendental into our world is awesome, indeed overwhelming, revealing not only the presence of the divine but at the same time our radical powerlessness. It is by no means accidental or irrational that humans everywhere developed various ways to minimize the impact of this dangerous force, ranging from ignoring its existence (characteristic of the Enlightenment attitude), to attempts to control it by magic, or by the more sophisticated trick through which the unconditional acceptance and adoration of past instances of transcendence is used to "exorcise" any further divine contact, by conjuring up the image of the "hidden god" or the "last prophecy"—something which, strangely, brings out the close ties between Judaism, Protestantism and Islam.

In this context, the resurgence, even outright domination, of Marian apparitions in modern times poses all kind of puzzles. Why is it that the direct presence of various saints, or of Christ himself, is no longer experienced today? What does it mean that the figure of the Virgin Mother seems to take up an exclusive mediatory role between the divine and the human realms in our days—exactly at the moment when, in social life, including politics and increasingly even in religion, issues of gender and sexuality take up an increasingly dominant role, and in directions exactly opposed to the figure and message of Mary?

Questions like these of course cannot be answered by means of science or even philosophy; but the social sciences like anthropology, history, or sociology, could bring in a number of facts and perspectives that can help us reflect on the significance of these phenomena. And, if we do not want to stick our head into the sand, in the legendary fashion of the ostrich, but are trying to make sense of the events that take place around us, communication with the realm of the divine can only be ignored at our peril.

Whether one agrees or not with the conclusions of Donal Foley, one thing cannot be doubted: this book is the product of a serious, genuine search for the truth. And hopefully in this we can all agree: that once truth is liberated from the prison where it was enclosed by a one-sided, "routinized" mechanization misconceived as science, then this is of primary importance for any work of human thought.

Professor Arpad Szakolczai
Sociology Department, University College Cork

Introduction

The basic facts about Medjugorje can be related quite quickly. Beginning on 24 June 1981, six young people from the locality, a small village in Bosnia-Herzegovina, five of them in their mid-teens, and one aged ten, began to claim that they were seeing the Blessed Virgin Mary on a bleak hillside near their homes. Four were girls, and two boys. Very rapidly, news of this spread—initially in the village itself and then throughout still-Communist Yugoslavia. Great crowds of pilgrims congregated as the days went on and the visionaries claimed that they were still seeing Our Lady, or the *Gospa,* as she is known in Croatian. Some of the local Franciscan priests supported these claims, and even the Bishop, Msgr Zanic, was open to this possibility initially, although over a period of time, he began to have serious doubts.

Meanwhile, increasing numbers of pilgrims from further afield came to visit during the 1980s, as Medjugorje became well known throughout the Catholic Church. The civil war in Yugoslavia in the early nineties only temporarily affected its popularity, and for nearly twenty-five years now, some of the visionaries have been claiming to receive daily visitations from the Blessed Mother.

Great numbers still journey to Medjugorje, even though the present Bishop, Msgr Peric, has declared himself opposed to the visions, and despite the fact that in 1991 the Bishops' Conference of ex-Yugoslavia came to the conclusion that it could not be affirmed that "supernatural apparitions and revelations" had taken place there. In addition, the claims of the visionaries have received no official support from the Vatican. That, very briefly, is an outline of what has taken place regarding Medjugorje, but there are other aspects to these events which this work will seek to bring out.

In order to do this, it is necessary to look initially at the historical background to Medjugorje, including the local Franciscan dispute with official Church authority which has affected Bosnia-Herzegovina in recent years. This forms a backdrop to the Medjugorje visions, and without an understanding of this discord, the reader will not grasp one of the main causative factors behind the growth of Medjugorje.

Another major contributory factor has been the conjunction between the Charismatic Movement and the visions. Again, without this factor of a Charismatic network already in place around the world—and able to support the visions and the visionaries—it is doubtful if Medjugorje would have had anything like the impact it has had on the Church.

A crucial point is that most of the early books about Medjugorje were based on quite late interviews with the visionaries, and the primary source material—tapes made during the first week or so of the visions—have been for the most part ignored. On examination, these reveal some hitherto largely unknown facts about Medjugorje, and this book is thus, amongst other things, concerned with assessing the importance of the evidence found on these tapes.

Prologue - Assault on a Bishop

An angry mob breaks into a bishop's official residence. They search for him, going from room to room until they find him. They drag him outside and pressure him to agree to their demands. He refuses and says that if necessary he will suffer just as Christ had to suffer. This type of language only makes them more infuriated, and some of them press forward, tearing off his pectoral cross, ripping his cape, and then assaulting him. He tells them that automatic excommunication is the penalty for attacking a bishop, but they pay no heed, dragging him off and imprisoning him. They hold him until late at night, their mood growing uglier with every moment, his life in imminent danger. The mob thinks he has insulted some of their deceased relatives; they shout that they have plenty of weapons. Finally, a local leader manages to persuade the crowd to disperse, and the Bishop narrowly escapes their clutches.[1]

This didn't happen during the Middle Ages, or more recently, under a totalitarian regime. This incident happened in March 1995, in an at least nominally Catholic European area.

The Bishop in question was Bishop Ratko Peric, the Ordinary of Mostar in Bosnia-Herzegovina, a region which was shrouded in obscurity until the 1980s, when the events at a small village called Medjugorje started to become famous in the Catholic Church and beyond. Bishop Peric's "crime" was that as part of the restructuring of his diocese, he had asked the local Franciscan friars to stop using the church hall which had functioned as their parochial centre, and to take up some new appointments. They refused, and along with a large group of parishioners decided to take their protests directly to the Bishop. The result was the incident outlined above,[2] in which the Franciscans in question chose not to interfere because they have been involved in a lengthy dispute with the local bishops, a tragic disagreement with deep historical roots, one which has seriously affected the Catholic Church in the region, and which has now become linked with the visions at Medjugorje.

1

Medjugorje: the Historical Background

The Franciscans, the Bogomils, and Islam

It is important to become familiar with the historical background if we are to understand the root of the religious problems connected with Medjugorje. These go back as far as the fourteenth century, and even further, when Franciscan missionaries were given the task of bringing Bogomil heretics in the Bosnia-Herzegovina area back to the Church. The Bogomils were a dualistic neo-Manichaean sect who originated in tenth-century Bulgaria before spreading to Asia Minor and the Balkans. Their beliefs were related to those of the Albigensians of southern France, but in particular, they seem to have regarded both Christ *and* Satan as sons of God the Father. For them, Satan was the creator of the world, and thus we see here a type of equivalence between Christ and the devil in the Bogomil mind. Nor is this all ancient history, given that Fr Ivo Sivric, an important Medjugorje commentator, felt obliged to speak of the local Croatians as still having certain traits typical of the Bogomils.[3]

When the Franciscans arrived in the area, they were faced, apart from the Bogomils, with a religion of primitive rituals, including animal sacrifice, which aimed at appeasing powerful nature spirits, such as Gromovnik, the "spirit of thunder," who was believed to live on Mount Sipovac, the peak overlooking Medjugorje. It may well be that these rituals were somehow a part of Bogomil religion, and it certainly seems that Medjugorje itself was actually a Bogomil religious center. It transpires, too, that at this time there was a certain tension between the communities at Medjugorje and Bijakovici—the village from which the future visionaries would come—which could erupt into violence, and that the people of Bijakovici were more welcoming to the Christian missionaries.[4]

The Franciscans soon made local recruits, but disaster struck in the fifteenth century when the area was conquered by the Ottoman Turks. Only the Franciscans remained to minister to the people after the secular clergy fled, and four hundred years of persecution began. The cruelty of Turkish rule was bitterly resented and groups of "guerrilla" fighters formed to oppose this foreign domination. This in turn led to vicious reprisals, in which ordinary Croats would be tortured to reveal the whereabouts of the fighters. This method of forcing people to betray each other often led to brutal vendettas amongst the Croats.

In the early sixteenth century, the Turkish ruler, Osmok, in an effort to reduce the bloodletting caused by these revenge attacks, and the consequent loss of productivity, invited some Franciscans into his realm. Thus, in exchange "for the restoration of order and the regular payment of tribute, the priests were promised lodgings, tax exemption and a moderate extent of religious freedom, including the right to engage in missionary activities." But the old religion of the area lived on, and clan elders from Medjugorje were also allowed, for a fee, to perform their rituals in honor of Gromovnik on Mount Sipovac, despite the best efforts of the Franciscans: thus, the two religions in the Medjugorje area coexisted uneasily. The Franciscans, though, were unable to pacify the region permanently, and outbreaks of violence recurred on a regular basis up to the end of Ottoman rule.

Rome and the Church in Bosnia-Herzegovina

In 1878, Bosnia and Herzegovina were liberated from the Turkish yoke, and three years later Pope Leo XIII issued a bull establishing the authority of the secular clergy, even though there were very few of them on the ground at the time. This is the modern origin of the disputes between the Franciscans and the secular clergy, which have dominated Church life in Bosnia-Herzegovina in recent years. Regrettably, the Franciscans did not cooperate with the hierarchy installed by Rome, and their example was followed by many of the ordinary faithful. Thus, the Catholic Church in Bosnia-Herzegovina was not able to mature properly, and the area remained in many respects a missionary territory. Instead of a proper Catholic sacramental life, religious rituals in the area, in a throwback to the past, revolved around ancestor veneration and various superstitious practices, with minimal Catholic content. The authorities in Rome put pressure on the Franciscans to remedy this situation, but even in the 1920s, orthodox Catholic church services were still being performed in conjunction with traditional clan rituals at local cemeteries.[5]

When the Habsburg Empire fell in 1918, the Kingdom of the Serbs, Croats, and Slovenes was founded, and, following a coup in 1929, the Serb King enforced policies favoring his kinsmen, using *Chetnik* militants, while the kingdom was renamed Yugoslavia—the "land of the South Slavs." This meant that in Medjugorje, the Serb community was able to confiscate farmland from Croats, and individual Serbs in the area became very influential, thus inflaming an already bad situation and facilitating the rise of Croat *Ustasha* militants. During the thirties, clashes between the two groups became more and more violent: "The destruction of Serb property, mutilation of individuals and manslaughter were soon to be everyday occurrences. The Serbs responded in kind, sometimes with even greater violence, and were backed in the process by mobile units of [Chetniks]."

At this point, following a visit to Rome in 1933, when he received advice and funds from Pope Pius XI, the parish priest at Medjugorje decided to build a huge cross atop Mount Sipovac to commemorate the 1900th anniversary of the Crucifixion. The majority of the community were enthusiastic, particularly as it was a time of drought and general hardship, and the building work was welcome; within a year the cross had been completed, and the mountain was renamed Krizevac, the "Mount of the Cross." Thus, it was reclaimed from Gromovnik.[6]

In Yugoslavia as a whole, the administration of the new state was virtually monopolized by ethnic Serbs, especially in the judiciary and the military, and the combination of Serb nationalism and the Orthodox Church resulted in a policy of institutionalized discrimination against the Catholic Church in Yugoslavia. This culminated in the inability of the Yugoslav government, in 1935, to obtain parliamentary ratification of the terms of the concordat which it had agreed with the Vatican. This discriminatory policy was of great significance in the rise of the extreme right wing Ustasha, and led to many Croatians welcoming the German invaders in 1941 as liberators.

World War II and its Aftermath

The more recent history of Bosnia-Herzegovina is equally relevant if we are to understand the background to the religious phenomenon of Medjugorje. This particularly applies to the atrocities that happened in the area during the Second World War, in 1941, when a fascist state was created by Croatian Ustasha forces in alliance with the Nazi occupiers of the country. Among the Herzegovina Franciscans who collaborated with the Ustasha was a friar, Fr Filopovic, who became a concentration camp attendant at Jasenovac, the most notorious such centre, a place renowned for its brutality and the use of torture. In Medjugorje itself, the Ustasha gathered together about six hundred Serbs from western Herzegovina, and brutally murdered them at a place near the hamlet called Surmanci, not far from the village, mostly by throwing them off precipices into a mass grave. Survivors were finished off with hand grenades, or in some cases buried alive. This was almost exactly forty years before the alleged visions at Medjugorje began in June 1981.

The Croats paid dearly for this deed later on, suffering dreadfully at the hands of the Chetniks and Tito's partisans. It seems that in the region surrounding Medjugorje, the Brotnjo plateau, up to a quarter of the population, or some five thousand people, perished during this period. Apart from this "official" violence at the hands of the Serbs and the Communists, brutal clan feuds also had their effect, so that by the end of the war, in the Gomila hamlet alone, a part of Bijakovici, "approximately 20% of the 400 villagers had lost their lives in clan vendettas." Three of the Medjugorje visionaries would come from Gomila. Even after this, the local people had to endure multiple atrocities under the new Communist regime, including torture, rape, and widespread murder. Much communal bitterness was stored up, and this caused continuing trouble even in the sixties and seventies, when old clan feuds were reignited, often because of disputes over land. Murderous vendettas still plagued the region, as "private" violence held sway. Similarly, from the 1970s onwards, young Croats, resentful at their lack of basic rights, began to organize themselves into armed "Neo-Ustasha" groups in Bosnia and Herzegovina, while in response, the Serbs organized their own "Neo-Chetnik" groups.[7]

The Franciscan Problem

Returning to the religious situation, we can note that in 1923 the Vatican had facilitated an agreement between the local bishop and the Franciscans, regarding the sharing of parishes. However, at the request of one of his successors, Bishop Petar Cule, the Ordinary of Mostar-Duvno, the Holy See agreed to annul this agreement. Thereafter, the Franciscans were supposed to hand their parishes over to the jurisdiction of the Bishop, but they refused to do so, claiming that the annulment had been reached without their agreement. However, as more diocesan clergy were ordained from the 1950s onwards, the Franciscans came under increasing pressure to relinquish control over the parishes they had looked after, but they were still unwilling to do this.

By 1975, the situation had become so serious that the Holy See issued a special decree—*Romanis Pontificibus*—demanding their obedience on this matter, but the Franciscans continued their resistance, and in consequence were penalized with various disciplinary measures. Hence, at the time of the Medjugorje visions, they were in a state of active disobedience to both the local bishop and Rome, and clearly this was not a happy portent for the future.

But in fairness to the Franciscans, it should be said that they had maintained the Faith in Bosnia-Herzegovina during four hundred years of Muslim persecution, when it was cut off from the mainstream Catholic world, and so it is understandable that a spirit of self-reliance should have developed amongst them. The tragedy was that self-reliance turned into stubbornness, and stubbornness into open disobedience.

By September 1980, less than a year before the visions began, Bishop Pavao Zanic, having taken over from Bishop Cule, decided to create a new parish in Mostar, one which would be composed of three-quarters of the parishes being run by the Franciscans. This led to recriminations on the part of some Franciscans, and this defiance was not limited to the clergy: it seems that many of the local faithful, too, from 1975 onwards, were unwilling to accept secular priests in their parishes.[8]

The End of Communism

Another vital factor in this complex situation was the effect that Pope John Paul II's policies were having in Eastern Europe, particularly after his visit to Poland in 1979. Following the death of Tito in 1980, Croatian nationalism began to reawaken: after the Second World War, Tito had governed the various fractious Yugoslav states with an iron hand, but now a new era had arrived, and no one was quite sure what would happen, particularly with the advent of the Solidarity movement in Poland. When it became known, in June 1981, that teenagers in Medjugorje were claiming to have seen the Blessed Mother, the final critical element was added to an already volatile mixture, one that would see, within a decade, the eruption of a bloody civil war, as Yugoslavia tore itself apart.

For the Pope, however, the problem which would emerge as support for Medjugorje grew was that, on the one hand, he wanted to encourage a grassroots Marian movement in Croatia along the lines of traditional Marian devotion in Poland, as a way of hastening the end of Communism; but he also wanted the dispute with the Franciscans to end. It was a very difficult situation, which could have been made much worse by hasty action, although there are signs that it may finally be in the process of being resolved.[9]

It is quite certain that the vast majority of pilgrims to Medjugorje have known little or nothing about the complicated history of the region, as outlined above. We are not dealing with a normal Catholic culture here, but one with a strange and checkered history, comprised of heretical sects, pagan religion, seemingly endless violence, and a long running dispute between official Church authority and local Franciscans.

2

Medjugorje and the Charismatic Movement

The Charismatic Movement and the Franciscans

Apart from the history of the region, it is important to understand the spiritual atmosphere in parts of Bosnia-Herzegovina in the years leading up to the visions. It seems that the Charismatic Renewal had become popular, due in particular to the efforts of two Franciscan priests, Jozo Zovko and Tomislav Vlasic. But the prayer meetings organized by them were far from traditional, and often involved people wandering about with their eyes *closed*, or alternatively having them open in order to look other participants in the eyes, before confessing their sins (non-sacramentally) to each other. Some meetings could also include speaking in tongues. The whole idea was to break down barriers, and the group dynamics of these meetings were very effective, indeed too effective, in doing just that. These techniques were developed from the sensitivity-training programs promoted by W. R. Coulson, and Carl Rogers. Indeed, the process of milling around a room in a disordered way was actually known as the "milling around" exercise, while another technique was known as "boundary breakers."

These techniques have since become notorious for their ability to manipulate people, in what can be a type of "brainwashing," particularly when used in "encounter" groups. As E. Michael Jones, author of two important books on Medjugorje, says: "When combined with the normal charismatic tendency of praying for a passage or getting a word of prophecy, especially when this is done under an authority figure like a priest, they can be especially effective in producing what otherwise would be known as mystical experiences in the participants."[10]

However, it should be noted that it is not being suggested here that such encounter groups have been, or are, common amongst Charismatics—they obviously represent an aberration which is outside the mainstream of Charismatic activities. Nevertheless, it is clear that they did have quite a strong influence on certain individuals in the early days.

The above-mentioned Fr Jozo Zovko was the parish priest at St James's Church in Medjugorje in June 1981, when the visions began, and according to Marijan Pehar, another local Franciscan, had been holding similar prayer group/encounter sessions in the parish. But it doesn't seem as though any of the Medjugorje visionaries had actually attended them—rather, in some respects, they were "outsiders" before the visions began. Mary Craig, another Medjugorje author, describes Fr Zovko as, "an enthusiast for the charismatic movement, [who] was disappointed by Medjugorje's lukewarm response to the changes he was trying to bring about in its prayer-life, and was inclined to dismiss the village's spiritual state as 'stunted and anaemic'."[11]

Fr René Laurentin, the well-known mariologist and Medjugorje author, had this to say in 1998 about these Charismatic activities: "If Fr. Jozo has charisms, they have blossomed from natural gifts. That might explain why, when he lays hands on people, so many fall in the total physical, psychic and spiritual relaxation we call 'Resting in the Spirit'." However, despite this clear Charismatic activity, Fr Laurentin denied that Fr Zovko was "involved in the Charismatic Renewal," which would appear to be rather a strange statement to make. Regarding Fr Vlasic, he said that he is, "very much involved with the Charismatic Renewal," but that he "purposely avoided all interference of charismatic activities in order to dedicate himself to the spiritual awakening of the parish."[12]

Charismatic Problems

There was apparently something of a crisis in the Charismatic Movement in the late 1970s and early 1980s, prompted by the general tendency of "enthusiastic" movements like the Charismat-

ics to run out of steam. This "crisis of faith" was revealed at the
time in a number of articles in Charismatic publications such as
New Covenant magazine. Attendance at the Notre Dame Charismatic Renewal conferences from 1979 to 1981 had dropped
appreciably, and the movement seemed to be entering a period of
decline. Something was needed to give it new impetus, and that
something would come from a quite unexpected quarter—
unbeknownst to all, the Charismatic Movement and Medjugorje
were converging, and this involvement of the Charismatics would
have huge repercussions for the Church in the West.

Meanwhile, two priests, Frs George Kosicki and Gerald Farrell,
had written a book entitled, *The Spirit and the Bride Say "Come!"*
which was published in early 1981. In this work, they argued that
the Charismatic movement within Catholicism was becoming too
ecumenical, and losing its Catholic identity. Having read Fr Gobbi's
Our Lady Speaks to Her Beloved Priests, they concluded that what
was needed was an injection of his type of Marian apocalypticism, a
message they saw as, "a prophetic word to the Church in our time."
They envisioned a Charismatic mass-movement, which would
fulfill the message of Fatima: "We believe that the promise of our
Lady concerning the final triumph of her Immaculate Heart, the
conversion of Russia and the ensuing world peace is soon to be
fulfilled. ...Those who are spiritually attuned to the needs of our
time agree that only a sovereign act of God can meet our present
needs, an outpouring of the Spirit such as occurred at Guadalupe."
As for prayer, they seem to have been thinking in terms of a
mixture of the rosary and speaking in tongues.[13] It is interesting to
note that at this stage, in the very early eighties, even Charismatics
such as the authors of the above book thought in terms of Fatima as
the natural place for Catholics to turn to when thinking of prophetic Marian teachings.

This is not to suggest, though, that a conscious process of manipulation was taking place regarding the Charismatic Renewal
assuming a more Marian aspect: clearly it was, and is, far too diverse
a movement for a few individuals to have brought this about.
Rather, it is probably more accurate to see this process as part of a
more general return to Marian devotion, in the aftermath of the
upheavals which took place after Vatican II.

Be that as it may, it would be through the Charismatic Renewal that a great deal of the publicity about Medjugorje would be generated worldwide—one only has to look at the writings of Charismatic authors such as Fr Robert Faricy to appreciate this.[14] And even as vocal a supporter of Medjugorje as Denis Nolan was obliged to admit later that, "some have tried to 'create' Medjugorje in their own image. Perhaps this charge could be made in regard to some involved in the Charismatic Renewal."[15]

The fact is that the Franciscans most involved in promoting Medjugorje were undoubtedly heavily influenced by the Charismatic Renewal, and this symbiotic relationship between Medjugorje and the Charismatics would only grow stronger in succeeding years.

Once again, though, this is not meant as a general criticism of the Charismatic Movement, given that under the right conditions, it is quite possible that the Holy Spirit will grant extraordinary graces and charisms, such as healing gifts, to particular individuals. However, while acknowledging this, the *Catechism of the Catholic Church* also cautions that authentic discernment is critical, and in particular tells us that: "No charism is exempt from being referred and submitted to the Church's shepherds" (799-801). It should also be noted that there has been a degree of reticence about the Charismatic Movement from the Vatican, and while both Paul VI and John Paul II expressed support for it, concerns have been expressed about some "excesses" at Charismatic prayer services, as well as possible "abuses" at healing services.[16]

Medjugorje and the Visionaries

At the time the visions began, in June 1981, Medjugorje was a village with a population of about three thousand, situated in Bosnia-Herzegovina, in what was then Yugoslavia, about twenty-five miles from the Adriatic coast. However, most of the visionaries were born in the hamlet of Bijakovici, situated at the foot of Podbrdo, the hill where the first visions took place, which is a short distance away from Medjugorje itself. Two bigger mountains, Crnica and Krizevac, form a backdrop, and the latter was known as Sipovac until 1933, when, as we have seen, a huge concrete cross was built on its summit. Krizevac has become a focus for pilgrims to Medjugorje, while Podbrdo is a foothill of the mountain Crnica.

The visionaries were Vicka Ivankovic, aged nearly seventeen (b. 3 Sept. 1964), Mirjana Dragicevic (b. 18 March 1965), Marija Pavlovic (b. 1 April 1965), and Ivan Dragicevic (b. 25 May 1965), all aged sixteen, Ivanka Ivankovic aged fifteen (b. 21 June 1966), and Jakov Colo (6 May 1971), aged ten.[17] Thus, there were four girls and two boys, Ivan and Jakov, and although some others were present at the beginning, these six have become the focus of the worldwide attention that Medjugorje has generated.[18] An important point to note is that, apart from Jakov, we are not dealing with *children* here, but rather with *young adults,* young people who had been exposed to many of the corrupting influences of the modern world, including television. This contrasts strongly with the seers of approved Marian apparitions of the past, whose average age was about eleven and who were brought up in the generally much better moral atmosphere then prevailing.

Unlikely Marian Seers

The fact is that the seers of approved apparitions have almost invariably been very innocent in the sense of being uncorrupted by the world. Most of them have been children or very simple adults. Only the children at Beauraing and Banneux had been exposed to modern communications in the form of the cinema—and clearly, 1930s cinema cannot be compared in terms of its corrupting influence with late twentieth century television. At Medjugorje, the young people, despite Communism, had all been exposed to modern Western culture with all its power to degrade and undermine Christian values.

Compare this factor with the situation of most of the recognized seers who lived in previous centuries, often in rural areas far from cities, and most of whom were quite young children. It is true that Juan Diego of Guadalupe was an adult, but he had only been baptized a few years previously, and was spiritually childlike, while Catherine Labouré, who saw Our Lady at Rue du Bac, was a reserved young nun in her twenties. At La Salette, Mélanie was fourteen and Maximin eleven, while at Lourdes, Bernadette was fourteen. The latter three in particular came from extremely poor backgrounds, both materially and culturally. At Pontmain, the four main seers were aged between ten to twelve, while at Knock those present were mainly adults, although adults with a very simple faith. Fatima is outstanding in this respect since Lucia as the eldest was only ten, with Francisco and Jacinta only aged eight and seven respectively at the outset. At Beauraing, the eldest of the five children was about fifteen, and at Banneux, Mariette Beco was eleven.

In the majority of these cases, then, we are dealing with *very* unsophisticated seers, some of whom had not even reached puberty, and thus their testimony has been intrinsically more believable than that of many more modern visionaries, including those at Medjugorje. The latter, as young people living in the eighties, would not have escaped the serious contamination which is present in the modern world. All of this tells us that the Medjugorje visionaries were far from ideal candidates as prospective Marian seers. It would seem that they were mostly too old and too worldly, and came from a mixed culture which was influenced by both Communism and television. They also had to contend with the effect of living in a distorted Catholic culture in which the disputes between the Franciscans and the secular clergy were a significant disturbing factor, one that was bound to have an effect on the young people.

The Corrupting Influence of Communism

The point about the corrupting influence of Communism needs to be further explained. It is very difficult for Westerners to really understand what life was like under Communism. We are so used to the freedom of thinking, saying, and doing more or less what we like, that trying to grasp what it was like to live under a system which was essentially a vast prison camp is practically impossible. Under Communism, people learned to practise self-censorship in order to survive, in the face of a party apparatus, a vast system of repression, which was omnipresent in the old Soviet Union.

In more or less closed societies, such as Yugoslavia under Communism, the air of unreality was compounded by the difficulty of getting reliable news about the outside world, apart from what could be learned via the state-controlled media. Speaking of this system, and its effects on the individual, Agnes Horvath and Arpad Szakolczai say that it "had a severe, often devastating impact on everybody, by destroying values, social connections, [and] forms of behaviour." This was because Communism, "tried to influence and supervise all decisions, all movements, all initiatives; it dreaded anything that was new, spontaneous, uncontrolled."

They also speak of the "most lasting and dangerous" impact of Communism as being its effects on the "depth" of personality of those living in such societies, because of the way it forced people to make unsatisfactory life decisions, and then "made them identify themselves with the results of their own decisions." Thus, there was a huge pressure to conform, to go along with the system, to think with the system, and at the same time, a constant feeling of being under "their" control, of being observed, in a way that allowed no real freedom and little chance of escape.[19]

That this abnormal, indeed absurd, system should have finally collapsed was inevitable, but while it existed it was able to do enormous psychological and emotional damage to many of those imprisoned within it. The whole economic system under Communism was topsy-turvy. It was simply not set up for, or capable of meeting, the needs of ordinary individuals, and thus there were widespread shortages and inefficiencies, along with interminable queuing for basic needs. This constant struggle for economic survival was another debilitating influence of Communism. When we add to this the system of surveillance which was firmly in place, and which included a network of informers and collaborators, we have a situation where individuals could never know who they could trust—or what was in government files about them.[20]

But perhaps the most insidious effect of a "pressure-cooker" system like Communism, was the way its mentality also affected those opposed to it. That is, such was the power of the Communist system, of its propaganda, that it affected not only the external behavior of those living under it, but also their thinking, indeed their very selves. People could begin to lose their moral bearings as the corrosive effects of years of Communist misrule would gradually wear them down, and their own "collaboration" with the system would be a further negative influence.

This type of thing could also affect the way that ordinary believers would interact with their priests and bishops. It was not unknown for the latter to be "co-opted" by the regime, that is, to collaborate with it in some respects, and so people lost their sense of trust even towards Church officials. This was obviously very corrosive of basic Christian charity, and undoubtedly created a great deal of mistrust and suspicion—which no doubt suited the Communists very well. And given the situation in Bosnia-Herzegovina, with its long running Franciscan-Secular dispute, this was bound to create special difficulties.

Putting all this together, we have, under Communism, an intrinsically corrupt and corrupting system, and it is also in the light of this that the experiences of the Medjugorje visionaries have to be assessed and understood.

Charismatic "Prophecies" about Medjugorje

Shortly before the visions began, an important Charismatic conference was held in Rome, in May 1981. We are told that, "Fr Tomislav Vlasic ... had gone to Rome for an international meeting of leaders of the Charismatic Renewal. During the conference, he asked some of the leaders to pray with him for the healing of the Church in Yugoslavia. One of those praying, Sr Briege McKenna, had a mental picture of Fr Vlasic seated and surrounded by a great crowd; from the seat flowed streams of water. Another, Emile Tardiff [sic] OP, said in prophecy: 'Do not fear, I am sending you my mother.' A few weeks later Our Lady began appearing in Medjugorje."[21] Fr Ivo Sivric, in his important book on Medjugorje tells us that, "according to Marija Pavlovic, in front of certain visionaries that ... [Fr Vlasic] knew, one month in advance, ...[he] mentioned that the Gospa would begin appearing in Yugoslavia." At this time, he was the chaplain at Capljina, located about nine miles south of Medjugorje.[22] It is worth noting that in no other approved apparitions do we find anyone coming forward in advance of them, to say that they are going to begin in a month's time.

What is even more revealing, though, is that, according to Wayne Weible, the Protestant convert and Medjugorje advocate, Briege McKenna's "vision" actually contained further details, and that she had seen Fr Vlasic "in *a twin-towered church* sitting in a chair and surrounded by a great crowd." As Weible notes, this is an important point because the only church with twin towers which Fr Vlasic knew of was St James's parish church at Medjugorje.[23]

There was a continuing Charismatic interest at Medjugorje, too, even after the visions had begun. This is apparent from the fact that an important Charismatic service was held there from 23–25 August 1983. It seems that all the visionaries, as well as some priests and nuns connected with the parish, received the "baptism of the spirit." The organizers of this meeting were Dr Philippe Madre of the Charismatic "Lion of Judah" community, (later renamed the "Beatitudes" community), Fr Tardif, the priest mentioned previously who had spoken in "prophetic" terms to Fr Vlasic in Rome, and Fr Pierre Rancourt. Fr Tardif apparently "taught the faithful to prophesy, [and] to speak in tongues." Because of government opposition, however, the three visitors were arrested by the police, interrogated, searched, and finally given the choice of prison or leaving the country immediately. Not surprisingly, they chose the latter.[24]

Fr Laurentin and the Charismatic Movement

Fr René Laurentin, the French mariologist, claims that the influence of the Charismatic Renewal was not at work in the early days of Medjugorje, but his arguments do not seem credible in the light of the above evidence. It is certainly worth noting that he refers to "certain fears" that were expressed, "especially at Rome in September, 1983," of mixing Charismatic elements with the activities of the visionaries. He raises the question as to whether such a combination might "produce excesses," but reassures his readers as follows: "No doubt precautions must be taken against such a thing happening if the apparitions go on for a long time, but it is more likely that they will soon cease."[25] Elsewhere, he tells us he believed this because at that point, the duration of the visions had been constantly diminishing from about twenty minutes in 1983, to about a minute in early 1984, while his other reason was that nearly all the alleged secrets had been revealed. This belief has clearly turned out to be quite mistaken, and indeed how empty that reassurance now seems more than twenty years later.

The modern Charismatic Movement, in the sense of *glossolalia*, or speaking in tongues, began in the American Midwest from the 1870s onwards, and it received further impetus in the early twentieth century at Topeka, Kansas, and later at Los Angeles. This led to a massive growth in Pentecostal churches throughout the United States, such that now they number their adherents in the millions. There were also revivals in European countries, which were characterized by episodes of, "weeping, moaning and shaking."[26]

The Charismatic Movement bases itself on the descriptions found in passages from St Paul's Epistles, such as 1 Cor 12:8–10. Those who are said to have received this "baptism of the Spirit," are said to show signs such as speaking in tongues; interpreting the *glossolalia* of others; demonstrating healing and prophetic powers, and displaying the ability to discern spirits.

The Charismatic Movement and the Church

The Charismatic Movement, as it has become established within the Catholic Church, however, is essentially a post Vatican II phenomenon. Pope John XXIII had called for a spiritual renewal within the Church, and one of the results of this was the formation of a group of students and staff at Duquesne University in Pittsburgh, in the Sixties, to explore new forms of spirituality. Some individual priests and lay people had taken part in Pentecostal "Full Gospel Fellowship" meetings as early as 1962, but it was in 1966–67 that Catholic participation really blossomed at Duquesne. Those involved began to pray in the Charismatic manner, experiencing glossolalia, and thus began the movement within Catholicism, which later spread, with great rapidity, to other centers, such as the University of Notre Dame in South Bend, Indiana. It was also taken up at Ann Arbor, Michigan, ultimately becoming a worldwide movement of Charismatic groups and communities.[27]

The worrying thing about the origin of this movement within the Catholic Church, then, is that it was not a spontaneous "Catholic" experience, but rather was derived from Protestant Pentecostalism.[28] It also seems that the "healing ministry" within the Charismatic movement, with all its claims for the "miraculous," was also strongly influenced by Protestant sources, remotely, in the nineteenth century, by groups such as the Christian Science movement of Mary Baker Eddy, and more recently by Episcopalian and Presbyterian "healers."[29]

The movement was characterized by days of renewal and yearly conferences, such as those held at Notre Dame, and it attracted influential sponsors such as Cardinal Suenens of Belgium, who was given responsibility for the Charismatic Renewal within the Church by Pope Paul VI. It is certainly the case that the Charismatic Movement has had a very large impact on the Church, and many clergy and religious have testified that it has "saved their vocation." However, one sympathetic observer, Morton Kelsey, had this general comment to make about glossolalia: "Tongue speaking is a powerful invasion of the unconscious. It can be dangerous for the weak ego and should never be forced on anyone."[30]

Similarly, regarding the particular messages "given" to individuals via this approach, Kelsey notes that a number of religious leaders have come to regard such practices as divisive, and also points out that it can lead to a certain spiritual pride, as some Charismatics begin to feel that they are better than "ordinary" Christians. In particular, he makes the following rather illuminating remark: "Some persons who speak in tongues suddenly find themselves getting God by the tail and receiving messages that 'God told me this about you ...' or 'God wants you to do this ...' and these are usually the very people who receive messages for everyone but themselves."

Kelsey also notes the adverse psychological effect glossolalia may have for some people, since it can be, "a liberating experience, freeing the unconscious to flood out into the individual." Such a "liberation" may clearly be extremely dangerous for certain unbalanced individuals,[31] and so the problems involved in some Charismatic practices are clear.

Fr Laurentin wrote a book on the Charismatic Movement entitled *Catholic Pentecostalism,* which was published in 1977, in which he tells us that he "became interested in Catholic Pentecostalism as early as 1967, the very year of its birth." The very fact that such a title could be used—with its emphasis on the word *Pentecostalism*—clearly indicates the actual origins of this movement within Catholicism. He goes on to say that he spoke with Fr Edward O'Connor, one of the "founders of the movement," who assured him that the future of the Church was bound up with this movement, a feeling Fr Laurentin apparently eventually came to share. Certainly, he took more than a passing interest in the work of the Charismatics, since he informs us that during the seventies he attended a number of their conferences, gathering information about the movement.[32] It is probably worth noting that Fr O'Connor later wrote a largely uncritical work entitled *Marian Apparitions Today: Why so Many?*

Reading Fr Laurentin's book, published only four years before Medjugorje began, it is clear that by then he was completely committed to the Charismatic Renewal, and thus he cannot really be said to have approached the visions and the visionaries in a detached and objective manner. The work even has a chapter entitled "Mary, Model of the Charismatic." Rather, he was predisposed to see the actions of the Holy Spirit behind all their activities, and this bias has clearly colored his later writings on the subject. He admits as much himself, in speaking of the "harmony ... established between the apparitions and the charismatic renewal."[33]

It should be reiterated that this chapter has not been meant as a general criticism of the Charismatic Movement, since clearly, given the right conditions, good leadership, and proper discernment, such activities may well have a part to play in the life of the Church. But regrettably, it is precisely in the area of discernment, and particularly the discernment of Medjugorje as an overall phenomenon, that the modern Charismatic Movement has been found wanting. It is impossible to get around the fact that right from the beginning there has been an intimate link between the Charismatic Movement and the growth of Medjugorje. This link goes so far as to include the initial Charismatic "prophecies" about the visions themselves, as well as the subsequent publicity campaign conducted pre-eminently by Fr Laurentin. More than anyone else, he has been responsible for the worldwide fame of Medjugorje.

3

The Medjugorje Tapes
and the Visionaries

Questions about the Visionaries

If we look at the visionaries as individuals, and likewise at their general backgrounds, we can better understand the *milieu* in which the visions arose. It certainly seems fair to describe their family life as less than ideal: for example, Vicka Ivankovic's father was an overseas worker, while her mother suffered from depression; in addition, Ivanka Ivankovic's mother had just died, and according to Fr Sivric, another, Mirjana Dragicevic, may well have had psychological problems.[34]

This general point is backed up in an interview, which took place on 27 February 1983, between Marinko Ivankovic, a "father figure" to the visionaries, and Fr Svetozar Kraljevic, the author of *The Apparitions of Our Lady at Medjugorje*. Marinko, the next-door neighbor of both Marija and Vicka in Bijakovici, was asked by the priest why he had involved himself with them, given that he was nearly forty, and a grown man with a family of his own. He responded to this by saying "the children have sometimes found themselves in difficult circumstances, especially Ivanka. She was the first in the group who saw the light and the Madonna. Her mother was dead and her father was in Germany. Practically, too, Jakov does not have a father; he lives in Bosnia but rarely visits here. Then Mirjana's family lives in Sarajevo. *In one way or another, the children did not have parental advice or the protection of parents.*"[35] Mary Craig described them as follows: "They were very different in temperament, social background and mental capacity—their intelligence ranging from slightly above to way below average."[36]

These are indications that the visionaries were to a greater or lesser extent emotionally vulnerable in some way, and therefore susceptible to the risk of things going wrong in any encounter with the preternatural.

The French anthropologist Élisabeth Claverie points out another possible source of the visionaries' experiences, that is, the prevalent societal interest in parapsychology, which she describes as being very widespread in Yugoslavia during Tito's time.[37] Parapsychology is the belief in, and investigation of, allegedly extrasensory phenomena such as telepathy, clairvoyance, ghosts, or poltergeists, and apparitions of the dead. It could be argued that this type of mentality might have predisposed the visionaries to "see" something on Podbrdo.

As noted above, it is also the case that the visionaries were apparently not part of Fr Zovko's Charismatic prayer group, that is they were not particularly "religious," and thus to some extent were outsiders.[38] Contrast the above deficiencies with the beautiful picture of family life which emerges from Sr Lucia's second volume of her autobiography, *Fatima in Lucia's own words II.*[39] This gives us the background to the apparitions, and shows how the three seers of Fatima, Francisco, Jacinta and Lucia, were very privileged in that they were brought up in a wonderful Catholic atmosphere, both in terms of their home life and the surrounding culture. Although they were relatively poor in physical terms, they were very rich in the blessings of the Faith, and in particular they did not come from families which were to some extent or other troubled.

The Medjugorje Tapes

Many of the standard accounts of the Medjugorje are based on interviews made by Frs Tomislav Vlasic and Svetozar Kraljevic about a year and a half after the original visions began in June 1981, or on the interviews with Vicka conducted by Fr Janko Bubalo. These were published later on, in 1985, as part of *A Thousand Encounters with the Blessed Virgin Mary in Medjugorje*—the title being a reference to Vicka's alleged claims of daily visions since 1981. Obviously, eighteen months or more is a long time during which to retain detailed memories of the crowded first days of the alleged visits of the Blessed Virgin, and so it is legitimate to raise questions as to just how reliable those interviews really were. Fortunately, much earlier material is available: namely, the original seventeen interviews with the visionaries which were taped at Medjugorje by Fr Zovko, and Fr Cuvalo, the parochial vicar, from 27–30 June 1981.

The great value of these tapes lies in their spontaneity, in the fact that they are true-to-life dialogues between the two priests and the visionaries, in which all the essential details about what happened during the first week or so become apparent. They are a "warts and all" depiction of what really took place, and as such they are innately superior to the better-known but much later Medjugorje accounts. It is true that sections of the tapes are indistinct, but overall there is certainly enough clear information on them to justify regarding the tapes as the primary source material on Medjugorje; in any case, the quality of the tapes is understandable given the circumstances under which they were made. Clearly, these contemporary interviews are far more likely to give an accurate record of what actually took place during those crucial first days, than any interviews conducted later on, but they have been almost completely ignored by the principal Medjugorje chroniclers such as Fr Laurentin.

Mary Craig details a conversation between Fr Zovko and his housekeeper immediately on his return to Medjugorje, during the first week of the visions, in which he asked her if Fr Cuvalo had spoken to the visionaries. She responded: "Yes, and he's recorded the conversations." Craig then tells us that Fr Zovko found the cassette and listened to it, and that he "began tape-recording all his conversations with the children." Further on, she even mentions the 30 June interview between Fr Zovko and visionaries, saying "the tape of this interview still exists."

Similarly, Fr Michael O'Carroll, another pro-Medjugorje author, in speaking of the fifth day of the visions, Sunday 28 June, mentions that after Mass that morning "the children went through a wearying interrogation by the parish priest, Fr Jozo."[40] Likewise, as we will see, Fr Janko Bubalo was certainly aware of these tapes, and challenged Vicka about elements from them during his interviews with her. But apart from Daria Klanac, pro-Medjugorje writers do not give us any extended details of them, and thus in their accounts we are asked to rely largely on recollections which were recorded much later.

Regarding these original tape-recorded interviews, then, although the methodology used by the priests was far from perfect, they do give essential source material about the visions. It was believed that the Communist authorities had confiscated these tapes when Fr Zovko was arrested, but Fr Sivric relates that his friend, Grgo Kozina, had managed to copy them beforehand, and was then able to pass on duplicates to him. From the evidence provided by sources such as Fr Bubalo, it is clear that other copies of these tapes must also have been in circulation. Fr Sivric then painstakingly transcribed their contents and published them in full in the lengthy appendices to his book on Medjugorje.[41] Daria Klanac, a Canadian citizen of Croatian origin, and a Medjugorje supporter—who by 2001 had organized more than sixty pilgrimages to the town, involving thousands of pilgrims—has also published transcripts of the original tapes in her book *Aux Sources de Medjugorje*. She tells us that she likewise obtained her tapes from Grgo Kozina.[42]

Given this, it is perhaps not surprising that when these two versions of the transcripts are compared—one by a pro-Medjugorje writer, and the other by a critic—they are found to be substantially the same. However, it is rather curious that Klanac completely omits the first three tapes recorded by Fr Cuvalo, before the return of Fr Zovko. In any event, of the remaining tape transcripts, as regards the essential points, they are in agreement.

Reasons for Differences

Such variations as there are mainly involve differences in word order, which are understandable given that the transcriptions in Fr Sivric's *French* edition of his book were translated from the original language into English, and then into French, whereas Daria Klanac did her translation directly into French. Also, naturally enough, in the process of translation, since words can have more than one meaning, a particular word in the original language can be translated in more than one way—and this clearly also affects phrases and indeed whole sentences.

The remaining differences between the transcriptions can be categorized in a number of ways. These include short sections which Fr Sivric was presumably unable to satisfactorily translate, perhaps because of the poorer quality of the tapes he had to work with, or because he was older and thus his hearing was less acute than that of Daria Klanac—always bearing in mind, of course, that at times the material on the tapes was very confused, with interruptions or voices being mixed up indiscriminately. This also led Fr Sivric to occasionally mistake one speaker for another. But equally, Klanac acknowledges the difficulties involved in transcribing the tapes, and admits that some words and phrases escaped her.[43] Another category of differences involves sections of the tapes which Klanac includes, but which are missing in Fr Sivric's text— although, in one instance, involving the tape made of the interview between Fr Zovko and Ivan, on the evening of 28 June, Fr Sivric has more material than her.[44]

The essential point to note is that the "missing" material is not crucial to the arguments presented in this book. This mainly comes from two of the interviews with Jakov, the youngest of the visionaries. In the interview carried out on the morning of 27 June 1981, Klanac has approximately 40% more material than Fr Sivric,[45] while in the interview on 28 June, there is a more serious discrepancy, since Klanac's has approximately 80% more material.[46] But as noted above, this material is not of crucial importance, and essentially involves Jakov elaborating on his experiences, including such aspects as reporting some of the purported words of the Gospa, indicating how the visionaries prayed on the hillside, and giving the reaction of his mother. Regarding the material on the tape of the interview with Mirjana on the morning of 28 June, Klanac has just under 50% more material, but again it is essentially a question of her describing her experiences in more detail, under questioning from Fr Zovko.[47] There are also a few other instances of this type amongst the other transcripts.

It is not clear why this material was missing on Fr Sivric's tapes, but it may well be that during the process of copying it was not thought worth preserving, or perhaps practical considerations such as fitting the interviews onto tapes of differing lengths were involved. Or the person doing the copying, Grgo Kozina, may have mistakenly failed to copy some of the interviews in their entirety. Certainly, it does not seem that any sinister motive can be imputed for these particular differences because the material involved is really quite innocuous.

The last category of differences would appear to be easier to explain, as it involves statements which might well have proved embarrassing if not dangerous for those involved, had they been widely circulated during the early eighties, when Communism was still in place. An example of this is found in the interview with Mirjana of 27 June, in which Fr Zovko asked her if she had been persecuted at school in Sarajevo because she went to church, to which she replied in the affirmative.[48] There are further examples in the transcript of the last tape, which involved five of the visionaries. One section, which mentions the Communist militia, is missing in Fr Sivric's version, while another, which mentioned that one of the young women present with the visionaries that day, Ljubica Vasilj-Gluvic, worked for the local Communist "executive committee," is also missing. There is also a missing section which speaks of the mother of Vicka—arguably the "principal" visionary—as being depressed, and which also gives personal details about her family. There is mention, too, of cassettes with Croatian hymns which were decorated with forbidden nationalist symbols. A section which refers to the chief of the militia, a certain Zdravko, has also been removed, as have two further references to the executive committee, including the name of a certain Marinko Sego, who is described as its president.[49]

It is important to realize, however, that the majority of the tapes, as transcribed by the two authors, are virtually the same, once allowance is made for differences in word order, and the points noted above. This also includes other minor considerations, such as short unintelligible sections which Fr Sivric conscientiously noted. The material on seven of the twelve tapes dealt with by Daria Klanac is virtually the same as that found in Fr Sivric's transcripts, and overall, if we exclude the three tapes indicated above, those involving Jakov and Mirjana, then approximately 92% of the material is common to both authors. If we include those tapes, then approximately 85% of the material is substantially the same.

The Tape Transcripts are Reliable

Clearly, these tapes are of primary importance in understanding Medjugorje, and that is why a study of their contents forms one of the central aspects of this book. The reality is that they are a severe embarrassment to the official position held by supporters of Medjugorje. The most important sections of the tapes are fully dealt with in the chapters which follow, and it is undoubtedly providential that they survived. No one of any credibility has challenged the fact of their existence and importance, but there have been attempts to question the validity of Fr Sivric's transcriptions by Fr Ljudevit Rupcic, a zealous Medjugorje supporter. He argued that because the transcriptions in Fr Sivric's *French* edition of his book have been translated from the original language into English, and then into French, that this somehow calls into question their content. But this is clearly not the case since all that matters is whether or not these translations have been accurate.[50]

Anthropologist Élisabeth Claverie, who is the research director at the French organization, CNRS, spent a great deal of time in Medjugorje during the early nineties, and could be described as being "neutral" with regard to the reality or otherwise of the visions. In the section of her book detailing the sources she had used, she agrees with the position taken above in indicating that the differences between Fr Sivric's transcriptions of the tapes, and those of Daria Klanac, are minimal. But after discussing both transcriptions with various parishioners in numerous discussions, her preference was to base her own book on the work of Fr Sivric rather than that of Daria Klanac. Furthermore, Claverie writes that following her own research and crosschecking, she came to the conclusion that the tapes used by Fr Sivric were reliable copies of the original recordings.[51]

Prelude to the Visions

Fr Laurentin claims that Fr Jozo Zovko only arrived at St James's parish in Medjugorje shortly before the first vision, but this is incorrect. In fact, Fr Zovko had been appointed pastor nine months before, in October 1980, but he was not present when the visions began, and only learned of them on 27 June, when he returned from a retreat he had been giving at a convent in northern Croatia. Just before the first vision, Medjugorje was struck by a particularly violent thunderstorm, which raged during the early hours of the morning of Wednesday 24 June. The post office was struck by lightning, caught fire, and was half burnt down. The lightning strike put the phones out of order and thus Fr Zovko was not fully aware of what was going on in Medjugorje; on his return he was confronted by a huge crowd outside his church.

To put all this in the context of the ongoing situation in Eastern Europe and further afield, the assassination attempt on Pope John Paul II had taken place only the previous month, on 13 May 1981, and there was rising tension between the Solidarity movement in Poland and the Communist leadership. Thus, the visions began at a critical moment.[52]

First Day – Wednesday 24 June 1981

The first vision allegedly took place later that afternoon as Ivanka Ivankovic and Mirjana Dragicevic were walking along the road near Bijakovici. Ivanka claimed that she could see the "Gospa," although Mirjana was apparently uncertain. Later on, having left a message for Vicka Ivankovic, the pair climbed up to Podbrdo—to collect the sheep according to Ivan Dragicevic's testimony—and saw a vision. Ivan was close to them, having been picking apples nearby with another Ivan, Ivan Ivankovic, a twenty-year-old local man who later dissociated himself from the visionaries because he disapproved of their behavior.

In his taped interview with Fr Cuvalo, which took place on the afternoon of 27 June, Ivan Dragicevic says that he heard somebody saying: "The light is appearing up there." Then Vicka and Ivanka called to him inviting him to go up, since they said that something, "like the Gospa" had appeared to them. He then said that they went up and had a similar experience. Fr Cuvalo asked Ivan what he saw once he had reached the girls and looked up, to which he replied: "I saw the light." However, he was not very articulate, and could hardly find the words to describe what he had seen, but it appears that he saw a vision of a "feminine" figure bathed in light, wearing a veil, and a crown which "shone like silver," hovering on a cloud above the stony ground.[53]

The Blessed Virgin – or Something Diabolical?

One of the strangest aspects of Ivan Dragicevic's testimony on this occasion is that he tells us that the hands of the Vision were "trembling." This is clearly out of character with regard to the Blessed Virgin, who is obviously by nature calm and serene. So this raises the question as to whether it might indicate a diabolical involvement. This point is emphasized by Msgr Farges, author of the celebrated study entitled *Mystical Phenomena:*

> The signs of diabolical intervention are well known. The devil's deeds always carry with them at least some ridiculous, unseemly, or coarse details; or even something opposed to faith and morals. If his vices were too obvious his influence would soon be unmasked; they are therefore always disguised under more or less inoffensive appearances, even under deceitful traits of virtue and sanctity. He transforms himself at will into an angel of light. God occasionally allows him to assume the most majestic forms, such as those of our Lord, the Blessed Virgin, or the saints. Nevertheless—for God could not otherwise permit it— the disguise, no matter how bold, is never complete, and he always betrays himself in some particular which cannot escape an attentive and prudent observer. Furthermore, the work of the devil becomes very soon unmasked by evil results, for an evil tree cannot bring forth good fruit.[54]

According to Vicka's *Diary,* as translated by Fr Sivric, which he tells us was actually written for her by one of her sisters, Ana, she returned to the apparition site at around 6:30 p.m., with Mirjana and Ivanka, and it was the latter who then first saw the Gospa, at which point the others also saw her. Vicka claims that the Vision was holding a baby-like object, while waving at them to come closer, but that she got frightened and ran back to the village. The visionaries told everyone that they had seen the Gospa, and some apparently responded that since that day was the feast of St John the Baptist, perhaps they could expect something miraculous. During the vision, Mirjana had apparently asked for a sign so that everyone would believe them, and, according to Vicka, the hour hand on a wristwatch turned right around, which she took as a sign.

However, Bishop Zanic later took this particular watch to a watch-maker who confirmed that it was broken, and because of this, the dial could rotate and thus, at the least touch, modify the position of the numbers. Vicka reports that: "We kept touching her and kissing her, and she kept laughing."[55]

The Smoking Visionaries

It seems that Fr Cuvalo had suspicions that Podbrdo was a place which some young people visited to smoke—this certainly seems to be the drift of some of the questions he put to Vicka, Ivanka and Marija during the first interview he tape recorded. Regarding the people who were with them during the first vision, he asked if they had smoked.[56] They denied this, but it would be a strange question to put unless he had suspicions on the matter. Certainly, according to René Laurentin and René Lejeune, the girls *had* been smoking—they describe Mirjana's embarrassment at Ivanka saying she was seeing the Gospa, because "they had been out smoking secretly."[57]

Fr Laurentin later made the position even clearer when he wrote: "The first two visionaries, Ivanka and Mirjana, held back for some time the fact that they were not only going to listen to some tapes that day, but were actually planning to go and smoke some of the tobacco which they threaded all day long with their families." He then says that "personal details" like this should remain private,[58] but this is ridiculous: the beginning of the visions is such a crucial moment that we are entitled to know as much about it as possible.

  The evidence indicates, then, that the two visionaries did indeed smoke once they arrived at Podbrdo. In other words, just prior to their supposed meeting with the Blessed Virgin, the Mother of God, the Queen of Heaven, the two visionaries had been smoking. This certainly puts the initial stages of the Medjugorje event in a new light, and makes it very difficult to accept that this was a genuine supernatural visitation.

Wayne Weible gives us even more of these "personal details," telling us that on the first evening, "Ivanka and Mirjana, having finished evening chores, had slipped off to a secluded spot to listen to rock music while smoking cigarettes pilfered from their fathers."

Sadly then, not only had the visionaries been smoking and listening to music, but they had also stolen the very cigarettes that they smoked. It would be interesting to know exactly what music they had been listening to, given the way that some types of rock music clearly have evil, not to say diabolical, connotations. Weible argues that: "To millions who would later journey to Medjugorje on pilgrimage, this venial act of experimentation would serve as an example that God chooses ordinary people for extraordinary missions."[59]

Or alternatively, and more accurately, one could argue that these further details make it even more unlikely that the visionaries did actually see the Blessed Virgin. There is a curious parallel here to what took place at Garabandal in Spain, in the 1960s. There, the four young visionaries involved had been stealing apples immediately prior to the first vision they saw, allegedly of an angel, on 18 June 1961.[60] Like Medjugorje, Garabandal has never received any official Church approval.

When Mirjana was interviewed by Fr Zovko on 28 June, she described what had happened at the local hospital at Citluk, where she had been offered a cigarette by one of the doctors, and had refused saying: "I don't smoke." He had responded by saying: "You don't smoke this kind?"—undoubtedly a reference to the possibility in his mind that she may have been smoking drugs—to which she even more emphatically responded: "No cigarettes at all!"[61] Clearly, on this occasion she had not told the truth, which certainly calls her general credibility into question.

In fact, rumors that at least some of the girls were smoking drugs were circulating in the village within the first few days. Mary Craig reports what Fr Cuvalo said to Fr Zovko on his return: "One of the girls, Mirjana Dragicevic, comes from a grammar school in Sarajevo and they're saying she brought drugs with her, maybe in cigarettes. She's started giving drugs to the children, and now they're claiming to see visions." Following intervention by the increasingly concerned authorities, on the afternoon of Saturday 27 June the visionaries had been taken to a nearby town, Citluk, for medical tests. Fr Cuvalo, though, expressed his displeasure that no blood or urine tests for drugs had been taken: "Look, we've heard that the girl from Sarajevo brought in drugs. And another thing, they say that one of the children is an epileptic and a hysteric."[62]

All of this indicates that the accounts of the first day's visions were unclear. Moreover, as we will see, these accounts are totally unlike those found in cases of authentic apparitions of Mary.

The Gospa and the Light

As regards the actual appearance of the Gospa, the tapes give us the basic details. The visionaries described her as being aged between nineteen and twenty, with a white veil and gray dress. Her veil covered her black hair, her eyes were blue, and her head was crowned with stars. She was said to float above the ground. Of particular note is the fact that the visionaries saw her gradually emerge from a "light"—the importance of this point will become apparent as we proceed—and that the Vision was prone to appear and disappear.[63] That the Vision had a "gray" dress has given rise to unfavorable comment, gray not being a color normally associated with the Blessed Virgin.

Jakov's remarks certainly seem to indicate that he really did see something. This is apparent in his taped interview with Fr Zovko, which took place on the afternoon of 27 June. In response to the priest's question as to the appearance of the Gospa, when she manifested herself, he said: "It lighted up three times when I saw her. Three times, it lighted up and all of a sudden, the Gospa appeared up there."[64] So once again, the theme of "light" is present, but the indications that the visionaries were able to touch and kiss the Vision, and that she was laughing, seem rather strange, and indicate that the Vision was not the Blessed Virgin. The last point in particular, that the Vision was laughing, is quite disturbing, and completely out of character with the deportment of Our Lady during her approved apparitions—she has been known to smile on occasion, but there is obviously a big difference between this and outright laughter.

More Questionable Evidence

Mirjana's testimony, available to us in an interview taped by Fr Zovko on the afternoon of 27 June, substantially supports what was said by the other visionaries. Her response to the Vision, however, did not follow the traditional pattern. She describes how she became excited at seeing the Gospa, saying how the experience was "delightful" for her, and that she wasn't afraid.[65]

Msgr Farges, however, has this to say on the difference between divine and diabolical visions:

> The divine vision produces at first a feeling of fear and astonishment in the soul that is conscious of its unworthiness, but it ends by bringing peacefulness and heavenly joy. The diabolical vision, on the contrary, begins by bringing joy, a sense of safety and sweetness, and ends in anxiety, sadness, fear, and disgust. The first develops the virtues, especially humility, in the soul of the seer, who will seek to hide such great favours in silence and secrecy. The second, on the contrary, develops feelings of vanity, vainglory, and a wish to parade the visions. The public effects should also be noticed. Divine visions never produce scandal, disorder, or trouble in the Church, while the others inevitably engender these evils.[66]

Regarding Mirjana's experiences, it is clear, in the light of the above evidence from Msgr Farges, that what she was describing does not seem to bear the characteristic of the divine. Ideally, Fr Zovko should have asked her about how she had felt later on, but he neglected to do this, and so all that can be said with certainty is that her initial reaction followed the negative pattern outlined above by Msgr Farges.

Regarding his second point, on the way the vision ends, that is with feelings of "anxiety, sadness, fear, and disgust," the following testimony from Marija, as taped on 27 June, is very interesting. She told Fr Cuvalo that on returning home on the second evening, she had to repeatedly explain to her parents what had happened. They then prepared supper for her and placed it before her on the table, but she reacted as follows: "I was scared, I wasn't able to eat, my hands were completely white; when I saw her for the first time my hands were cold like ice."[67]

In the interview with three of the visionaries taped by Fr Cuvalo on 27 June 1981, it emerges that the visionaries saw the Gospa holding something on the first evening. Ivanka testified that: "We saw something like a baby ... then she covered it up ..." They were apparently not close enough during this first vision to see any more, and it does not seem as though the Vision said anything on this occasion, although she did nod her head when Vicka asked if she was going to come the next day.[68]

It is hard to imagine why the Vision would have wanted to cover up the Baby Jesus, if it really was the Blessed Virgin, and this event contrasts strongly with the incident in 1925, when Lucia of Fatima, who was by then eighteen, had become a postulant with the Sisters of St Dorothy at Pontevedra in Spain. On Thursday 10 December 1925, the Blessed Virgin, accompanied by the Child Jesus on a little cloud, appeared to her in her cell. Lucia recounted that Mary rested one hand on her shoulder, while showing her a heart encircled by thorns in her other hand. Far from being covered up, the Child Jesus actually then spoke to her, saying: "Have pity on the Heart of your Most Holy Mother. It is covered with the thorns with which ungrateful men pierce it at every moment, and there is no one to remove them with an act of reparation."[69]

Second Day - Thursday 25 June 1981

Ivan Dragicevic was absent on this occasion, having decided to spend the evening picking tobacco. According to the interview taped by Fr Cuvalo on 27 June, Vicka said that other people could see something on the hill, and she tells us that a woman told them to go up since they were being invited. It is apparent, too, that the visionaries were receiving directions from onlookers, and that when they reached Podbrdo, they "spotted her," and that "the light" was all around them.[70]

The mention of other people seeing "something" is very interesting, and certainly goes a long way towards explaining why the visionaries' stories were taken seriously by some villagers right from the beginning—although it seems that by the end of the first week the general mood had grown less supportive. Certainly, Vicka's testimony here seems convincing, since, given that she was speaking only a few days after the event, it would have been very easy for Fr Cuvalo to have checked up on this point regarding other witnesses. It is hard to believe that he would not have already spoken to local people, and thus have instantly contradicted Vicka if he had thought she was not telling the truth. Ivanka also made similar claims of other people seeing "the light" on Podbrdo, including her sister, and some other women.

We also have this testimony from Marinko Ivankovic, who claimed that about three weeks into the visions, at about 11 p.m., he was on Podbrdo with a group of people, including the visionaries. He looked up and could see a very bright light coming towards them. Marinko was the local man, who, as has been noted above, initially acted as the unofficial "protector" of the visionaries.

Generally speaking, then, the information on their contact with the Gospa given in the taped interviews by the visionaries certainly does have the ring of truth about it. They speak of coming very close to her, and even touching her, although Vicka makes the quite extraordinary comment that, "when you touch her … the fingers bounce off as if they were of steel." Once again, though, the Gospa said nothing on this, the second day.[71]

In assessing these visions of the first couple of days, then, what surely strikes the impartial observer is firstly, the absence of factors that are normally observed in apparitions which have been subsequently accepted by the Church, and secondly the presence of other factors which raise serious doubts as to their authenticity. Whether it is the fact that some of the visionaries had a possible involvement with drugs, or that the Vision's hands were trembling, or that at one moment the Vision was laughing—while in general she said nothing—all of this is very strange. None of this accords with the serene, calm presence of the Blessed Virgin, speaking words of reassurance to those who have been favored with her presence that one finds in her recent recognized apparitions. But conversely, it does seem that some people did see strange lights, and so we do not seem to be dealing with hallucinations. It appeared that something was happening up there on Podbrdo, but the exact nature of that "something" still had to be determined. However, the initial signs were hardly encouraging.

4

True and False
Visions of Light

Third day - Friday 26 June 1981

The information from Fr Cuvalo's first taped interview of 27 June has Marija testifying that she saw the Gospa on the third evening, but the impression we get from her words is that the Vision only gradually appeared: "At first, I saw a little cloud below, then her [*the Gospa*], her body and head."[72] Ivanka then testified that they asked her why she had come there, to which the reply was given: "Because there were a lot of faithful, that we must be together." Ivanka also asked about her recently deceased mother, and was told that she was with the Gospa, and that she should obey her grandmother. Mirjana asked about her grandfather, and was apparently reassured in a similar manner. They also asked if she was going to come again, to which the reply came: "Tomorrow at the same place," although no reply was made to their request for a sign.

The Gospa Sprinkled with Holy Water

Vicka tells us that she took along blessed salt and water, as a way of testing the Vision to see if it really was the Gospa, on the assumption that the devil would be driven away by such sacramentals. After invoking the Trinity, she sprinkled the Vision while saying: "If you are the Gospa, remain with us. If you are not, get lost." There is some confusion in the ordering of events on the tape, but according to Jakov's interview with Fr Zovko, on the afternoon of 27 June, the sprinkling of the Gospa coincided with the moment when, according to Ivanka, she herself, Marija, and Mirjana, lost consciousness, at least to a degree.[73]

According to Fr Bubalo's interview with Vicka of December 1983, this "holy water" consisted of blessed salt and ordinary water, and had been made up by her mother, who merely mixed the two together.[74] This certainly calls into question whether this really was holy water, although the blessed salt on its own would have provoked some sort of reaction.

Ivan Dragicevic was also present on this occasion, and says in his interview with Fr Cuvalo that he, too, once again saw and heard the Gospa, substantially confirming what the girls had told the priest in their interview with him. He was quite insistent that he was not lying when pressed by Fr Cuvalo. He said that on this occasion, he didn't see the Gospa straight away, rather Vicka saw her first; he didn't hear her say anything. When asked how his family had reacted to this news of visions, he remarked that they had said that they believed that the visions were true because so many other people had seen something.[75]

Fourth day – Saturday 27 June 1981

Fr Cuvalo interviewed Marija on the evening of 28 June in the Rectory at St James's Parish Church. He began by saying that the previous evening he had been with the crowd which had gathered, and had seen her looking upwards and heard her exclaim: "There she is!" She confirmed this, and then he asked her exactly what she had seen. She responded: "The light". From the conversation which follows it is unclear whether Marija actually said, "there *she* is," or "there *it* is," but from her later responses it seems that she just saw a light initially, rather than a figure, since further on she says that the first things that she saw were the "light and the stars." Fr Cuvalo then asked her what kind of light she saw, and where it was situated, on the ground or in the sky. Marija said that it was in the sky, and that she saw "the Gospa, her body", and that she wanted to see how close to the ground she would lower herself.

Fr Cuvalo then established exactly where the other visionaries were positioned in relation to Marija, and got her to confirm that she had indeed seen the light first before seeing any figure. It is noteworthy that she did not see a rosary on the hand of the Gospa, and that in particular the Vision made no attempt to initiate a conversation.[76] According to Marija, the Vision disappeared and reappeared, ascending and descending, while Vicka "loudly asked her questions."[77]

Mirjana's taped interview with Fr Zovko, gives us more information about exactly how the Gospa disappeared. She told him that: "She goes slowly. She is disappearing slowly. She is climbing up there and then, the sky lights up. ... She goes straight and disappears, little by little. There is more and more mist. ... Mist appears all around her and she goes towards the sky."[78]

At this stage, on the fourth day, Fr Zovko was clearly concerned that the Gospa was not saying anything of particular importance to the visionaries, and he insistently questioned Mirjana about this, and about what they were all expected to do.[79]

Fifth and Sixth days of the Visions

By the fifth day, June 28, it appears that the initial light phenomena, which were certainly seen by some of those on the hillside, were no longer present.[80] But Mirjana was still speaking about the "light" that the visionaries could see as the Gospa appeared to them, since in an interview on that same evening she testified that: "I first spotted the light. Then I poked the others: 'Do you see the light?' They responded that they did. Then I saw how she is gradually descending and it is becoming clearer and clearer as she descends lower and the little stars all around her. It is so beautiful." A little further on Mirjana clarified this point: "As soon as I spot her, it becomes clearer and clearer. When she descends down, then it becomes completely clear that I see her."[81]

Mirjana, at least according to the taped interviews we have, was the first one to mention that the visionaries asked the Gospa, on the fifth evening, to appear in the church, "so that everybody can see her." It may well be, though, that they were prompted to ask this question by someone else. Certainly, a little later in this interview, Fr Zovko made his concerns plain, asking why there was no message, and why the Gospa wasn't appearing in the church. Apparently, Mirjana had absolutely nothing to say to any of these questions.[82] Contrast this with Fatima where, amongst other things, Lucia asked that she and Jacinta and Francisco should be taken to heaven, but not that Our Lady should appear here or there, according to her own desires.

Fr Zovko is Skeptical ... and Concerned

Fr Zovko's interview with Ivanka, made that same evening, also brought out the point that there was no definite message emerging from the visions, and his unease at this: "Why did she appear to you when there is no message? ... That looks like clowning to me. She came in vain and she doesn't have anything to say." In his interview with Ivan, too, it is clear that Fr Zovko was concerned about this lack of a message, pressing him on this point. By this stage, Fr Zovko was getting worried about the size of the crowds gathering on the hillside, and the lack of any sign to show that the visionaries were telling the truth.[83]

Fr Sivric describes the atmosphere at the time as being explosive, since with each day the crowds thronging Podbrdo were growing ever larger. This ultimately led the Communist authorities to block all access roads.[84]

After raising the possibility with Mirjana that she could be seeing Satan, an idea which she rejected, Fr Zovko went on to ask her what else she saw in her vision apart from the Gospa. She responded: "When I look at her, the images come to me from the birth of Jesus when the angel approached her while saying to her: "Hail Mary," that she was going to conceive the Lord and become his mother. All that turns and comes into my head. Then, I saw it, how she was poor ... I see all that in front of my eyes as in a film. ... I look at her and all that appears in my head."

This mention of images turning over in her head certainly sounds much more like an hallucination than a genuine divine apparition. And surely, the fact that Fr Zovko could ask Mirjana if she wasn't afraid that Satan could pretend and say he was the Blessed Virgin Mary during this interview, is a clear indication of the way his thoughts were running, at this stage of the visions.[85]

The Move from Podbrdo to the Church

By the time Fr Zovko came to interview Ivanka, that same evening, 28 June, it is apparent that he wanted to try and arrange for the visions to take place in the parish church from that point onwards.

He queried if they had asked the Gospa about that—but she could not remember.[86]

The only comment to be made about this idea, is that in none of the authentic apparitions of the Blessed Virgin has there been any suggestion that their location is in any way subject to human considerations or desires.

On Monday 29 June, the feast of St Peter and St Paul, Fr Zovko wrote out a declaration on the visions which was read out after Mass. In this, as reported by Mary Craig, he stated that he had talked to the children and recorded the conversations, but, having "listened again to the cassettes, I must insist that there is no public revelation here. If anything is being revealed, it is of a private nature, for the children's benefit alone. Whether this will change I do not know. So far, Our Lady has said nothing that is meant for anyone else."

So, on the sixth day of the visions, Fr Zovko was openly acknowledging that there was no substantial public message being given to the visionaries.

That same evening, according to Mary Craig, the people of Bijakovici were summoned to an emergency meeting of the local Socialist Alliance, and were given explicit instructions by the local Communist leaders that the gatherings on Podbrdo were to be obstructed by all necessary means, and were also informed that: "If you must do these things, do them in church." The same message was given to Fr Zovko the next day, when both he and Fr Cuvalo were summoned by the Communist authorities to a further meeting at the regional centre of Citluk, and informed that it was necessary that the crowds be moved into the church where the situation could be controlled. This helps to explain why Fr Zovko became so insistent on the tapes that the visionaries should move into the church and away from Podbrdo.[87]

The Light and the Mist

Fr René Laurentin comments on the "light" associated with the Gospa, and its influence on the visionaries, as follows: "The Gospa … attracted them by her sweet tonic and therapeutic light. Just like at Lourdes, this light preceded her. She came in this light, which illuminated like an interior sun."[88]

However, there are important differences between the "light" surrounding the Gospa, and the light which preceded the Blessed Virgin at Lourdes. One of the early chroniclers of the apparitions there was J. B. Estrade, and he recorded Bernadette's recollections on this point as follows. She told him that there "came out of the interior of the grotto a golden-colored cloud, and soon after a Lady, young and beautiful, exceedingly beautiful, ... came and placed herself at the entrance of the opening above the rose bush."[89] In this instance, we get the impression that rather than the Vision coalescing from the light which preceded her, as appears to have happened at Medjugorje, for Bernadette rather, the apparition of the Lady was *distinct* from the golden-colored cloud, and was not a part of it. This is an extremely important characteristic, as is clear from these other examples.

At Rue du Bac, Catherine Labouré initially heard a sound like the rustling of a silk dress, before seeing the Blessed Virgin descend the altar steps of the convent chapel, and seat herself on the director's chair. Catherine then threw herself at Mary's feet, put her hands on her lap and looked up into her eyes, later describing that moment as the sweetest of her life.[90] Here, once again, there is no suggestion of the apparition of Mary gradually appearing, rather she was fully formed from the first moment that Catherine was aware of her presence, to the extent that she heard the noise of her dress, and could even physically touch her.

The same is true of the apparition seen by the children at La Salette. Mélanie was the first to see a dazzling globe of light at the top of the mountain, and called to Maximin. Both children shaded their eyes from the glare of the globe as it grew bigger and began to open, revealing a seated woman with her head in her hands. She then stood up and spoke to them: "Come, my children. Do not be afraid. I am here to tell you great news."[91] Thus, although the children saw the Blessed Virgin emerge from the globe of light, she was not part of that light, but quite distinct from it.

The situation was similar at Fatima, where we read that while the three little children were at the Cova da Iria with their flocks, on 13 May 1917, suddenly there was a bright flash of something like lightning. They looked up, thinking a thunderstorm was coming: but to their surprise the sky was clear and there was no wind. They had just agreed to go home in case it was a storm when there was another flash, and they looked up to their right to see, in Lucia's words, "a lady, clothed in white, brighter than the sun, radiating a light more clear and intense than a crystal cup filled with sparkling water, lit by burning sunlight."[92]

Here, too, it is clear that the children saw the apparition immediately and distinctly, and so we can see that there is a definite pattern to the way that Mary has been seen by the seers of her recognized apparitions. Although an aura of light usually accompanied her, it was distinct from her person. There was no question of her gradually appearing out of this light in an indistinct way, as at Medjugorje, but rather the apparition was fully formed and recognizable right from the beginning.

The Angel of Portugal

Incidentally, this is also the case with the apparition of the Angel of Portugal seen by the Fatima shepherds on three occasions in 1916. In her *Second Memoir*, Lucia tells us that previously, in 1915, along with some other young companions, she had seen a mysterious being which she described as follows: "we saw a figure poised in the air above the trees; it looked like a statue made of snow, rendered almost transparent by the rays of the sun." The indications are that because of its brilliance she couldn't discern its features. Then, in the spring of the following year, while she was with Francisco and Jacinta looking after the sheep, following their lunch and the rosary, they began to play a game, but they were interrupted by a strong wind which shook the trees.

She continues: "Then we saw coming towards us, above the olive trees, the figure I have already spoken about. Jacinta and Francisco had never seen it before, nor had I ever mentioned it to them. As it drew closer, we were able to distinguish its features. It was a young man, about fourteen or fifteen years old, whiter than snow, transparent as crystal when the sun shines through it, and of great beauty."[93]

Here, too, it isn't the case that the figure gradually emerged out of a light; rather it was as if made of light and the very intensity of this light made it difficult to distinguish its features.

Msgr Farges has some very interesting observations about the process of a false vision gradually appearing. He is speaking particularly about hallucinations, but from what he says, it is clear that in certain cases such phenomena may be diabolically induced. He describes the way certain visions only become "gradually visible, with increasing clearness", beginning as a "vague light." As an example, he speaks of crystal-gazing as related to fortune-telling: "The visionary who gazes into the mysterious crystal begins by seeing nothing at all, then he sees there vague clouds, then in these clouds personages are traced; finally these become clearly defined, move, and often they speak."[94] While this analysis can be applied to subjects who are hallucinating, it is also a classic description of the activities of fortune tellers, some of whose powers, historically, can undoubtedly be related to diabolical activities.

Some Examples of False Visions

Certainly, this idea of Mary gradually appearing out of a cloud or mist, or being obscured in some way, is present in false or suspect visions. For example, this is what happened during some of the false visions which followed Lourdes. The first great chronicler of the apparitions, Fr Cros, interviewed some of these false visionaries as adults in 1878, including one Laurent Lacaze, who said that he remembered going "to the Grotto with other children: [and] that I saw a *kind of shadow,* but I have no idea whether *it* had any outline, or whether it was a man or a woman." Another, Jean-Pierre Pomiès, went into more detail: "I used to go often to the Grotto, attracted by all the stories of what was going on there. During these visits I twice had a vision, the first time I saw a dazzling light in the hollow of the rock, and in the middle of it, *a rather thick shadow.* The light was neither red nor white, and stood about three feet high. I could not distinguish any face. This lasted about a quarter of an hour."[95]

Another suspect series of visions were those claimed at a Carmelite convent at Lipa in the Philippines, in September 1948. These began when a young nun, Sr Teresita, claimed to have heard a voice while in the convent garden, and turning, saw a "small, white cloud" from which emanated rays of light. The voice, which spoke out of the cloud, said: "Fear not my child, kiss the ground. Whatever I shall tell you to do you must do. For fifteen consecutive days come to visit me here in this spot. Eat some grass."

These visions were ultimately judged negatively by the local bishop, and it seems clear that the "message" is nothing more than a reworking of what happened at Lourdes.[96]

Another example comes from the experiences of Mary Ann Van Hoof, the visionary associated with Necedah, who described how the Blessed Virgin emerged from a "blue mist" in her backyard on 28 May 1950. On another occasion, she described how she went out into the yard about midday, to the "Sacred Spot" where she "did not see Our Lady, only a sort of haze." She did however feel her "Heavenly Presence."[97]

A more recent example comes from Falmouth, Kentucky, where a woman called Sandy claimed visions and locutions during the 1990s. She described one of these events as follows: "I heard a sound. I've heard this before. It's like a musical, heralding-type sound from off in space. Then I looked up, and I saw a brightness ... and she [Mary] started to appear through this brightness."[98] It should be pointed out that there is no reason to believe that any of her experiences have been supernatural.

This idea of visions of Mary gradually appearing out of cloud or mist, or in an indistinct form, then, certainly raises suspicions as to authenticity. We do not find this type of manifestation in the approved Marian apparitions, but it is one of the main characteristics of false or suspect visions. Thus, the fact that this is precisely how the Gospa appeared to the visionaries at Medjugorje is regrettably not a good sign, and in fact points to the questionable origin of these visions.

5

The Visions Continue

Did the Visionaries really see Something?

The transcripts of the tapes certainly give a very strong impression that the visionaries did actually see something during those first crucial days on Podbrdo, and that on this point they were telling the truth. For example, in response to the question from Fr Zovko, on how she felt about the fact that people didn't believe her, Ivanka was adamant that she had seen the Gospa, whether or not other people believed her, and that a sign would be left.

It is hard to imagine that only five days into the visions she would be making such a vehement statement unless she really was seeing something.

This was certainly also the feeling expressed by Bishop Zanic in his 6 August 1981 press release, wherein he said of events at that stage: "*Everything indicates that the children are not lying.* However, the most difficult question remains: Did the children have subjective, supernatural experiences?"

The first part of the above statement has been extensively quoted by supporters of the visions—who have tended to ignore the qualification which followed—but it has to be borne in mind that this was just his first impression, gained only a matter of weeks into the visions, when the excitement over the whole affair was still very palpable. The Bishop was certainly open to the possibility that the visions were authentic at this stage, and only gradually came to view them as false. It seems, too, that Bishop Zanic was being advised by the Holy See "to proceed slowly and not to make a hasty official judgement," and if we also remember the critical political situation, both within the country and with regard to Communism in Eastern Europe generally, we can see that he was under pressure from all sides.[99]

Bishop Zanic's Difficult Situation

Fr Robert Faricy, who went to visit Bishop Zanic in the autumn of 1983, acknowledged that the situation had been vastly complicated by the "strong opposition of the Communist government." This opposition meant that Bishop Zanic was being "closely supervised," and, according to Fr Faricy, if the Bishop had approved the visions at that time, the government would certainly have taken "severe repressive action" against him, and also presumably against the local Church. That these were no idle threats is clear from the fact that in the autumn of 1981, following Fr Zovko's imprisonment, two other Franciscans were given jail sentences of eight and five-and-a half years respectively for publishing articles favorable to Medjugorje. At this time, Bishop Zanic assured Fr Faricy that he had appointed an "investigating commission" to look into the visions, but the Vicar General also pointed out that there was no hurry. Fr Faricy accepted this saying "given the opposition of the government and other local governing authorities and the police," he understood the need for great caution.[100]

Fr Faricy once again visited Msgr Zanic, in May 1986, but this time he was more critical of his role despite having earlier acknowledged the constraints hampering the Bishop. Fr Faricy mentions the document issued in February 1978 by the Congregation for the Doctrine of the Faith, under its then head, Cardinal Seper, which gave guidance to bishops on how they should deal with reports of alleged apparitions. In 1986, this document was still secret, that is, it was not to be publicly disclosed, but since then that restriction has been relaxed and it is now more generally available. Given that the instructions in the document were general guidelines, it seems fair to say that Bishop Zanic probably did as much as he could in the circumstances to carry them out.[101]

It is certainly the case that on 11 January 1982, Bishop Zanic did institute a commission of inquiry comprising four members, and that he studied the events at Medjugorje carefully, while also keeping the Vatican informed of developments. This led to the submission, on 2 June 1982, of a report to the Congregation for the Doctrine of the Faith. The commission of inquiry was enlarged in 1984 to fifteen persons, made up of clerics from different dioceses and faculties of theology in the country, as well as some doctors. On 30 October 1984, Bishop Zanic published his *Position* document and in April 1986, he sent his definitive negative conclusions on Medjugorje to Cardinal Ratzinger—now Pope Benedict XVI.[102] By the mid-eighties, then, Bishop Zanic's stance on the visions was quite clear: he had definitely decided that they were not genuine.

Criticism of Bishop Zanic

Bishop Zanic was later criticized by Fr Ljudevit Rupcic, a Croatian Franciscan, on the grounds that he had not sufficiently involved himself personally in events at Medjugorje. He argued that: "Nothing can substitute for 'on the spot' verification and personal insight. But the bishop has deliberately kept some distance from the facts."[103]

Actually, during the major approved apparitions of the 19th and early 20th centuries, this has been precisely the policy of those bishops charged with investigating such incidents. They have almost invariably adopted such a policy because it was the only way to avoid being unduly influenced in their decisions.

Fr Laurentin thinks that the relevant part of the 1978 CDF document on apparition discernment, which states that, "the competent ecclesiastical Authority has the serious obligation to inform itself without delay and to carry out a diligent investigation," implies that the bishop involved should not stand back, "as many did," but "should quickly discern the facts."[104] This is true as far as it goes, but it certainly does not indicate that any bishop has to personally investigate such reports. It is sufficient, surely, that he oversees the investigation.

Criticism of Ratko Peric

Fr Rupcic in collaboration with Fr Viktor Nuic, also criticized Ratko Peric, who visited Medjugorje in the first half of August 1981, while he was still resident in Rome, over a decade before his appointment as Bishop Zanic's successor. They describe how Bishop Peric interviewed some young girls who had been present at a number of late night visions on the hillside, during which he was told that "an unnamed visionary said in a raised voice: 'Turn off your batteries [torches], Our Lady will not appear if you do not turn off all the lights!' " Something similar happened the next night, as someone cried out: "Put out your cigarettes! If you do not put out your cigarettes, Our Lady will not appear."

Bishop Peric's response to this was to say to his companion, "we could leave now. There is nothing authentic here! Our Lady is not as sensitive as we that she would be bothered by—a cigarette!" Although, his companion was more open to the possibility that something genuine was going on, surely Bishop Peric was right to come to this conclusion.[105]

As we will see further on, this idea that the visionaries or their supporters could somehow "stage manage" particular visions, is completely unsustainable. If Our Lady really is appearing somewhere, then such an appearance is *not* dependent on the moment-by-moment behavior of particular individuals in the crowd, nor on essentially trivial points such as whether or not people had turned off their torches. We can be quite certain that when she appeared on 13 October 1917 at Fatima, to an estimated crowd of 70,000 people, that a good number of these were openly skeptical and scoffing of the whole idea, and no doubt acting in a far from reverential way—and yet this did not prevent her from appearing.

Pressure on the Visionaries

Returning now to the taped interviews, concerning the one conducted with Ivanka, on 30 June 1981, it emerges that Fr Zovko was worried at the way things were turning out regarding the visions. He asked her what they were planning, and what the people should be told. To this Ivanka responded that they would discourage the people from coming to Podbrdo.

It was apparent, too, that Ivanka and the other visionaries were also under pressure, including pressure from their friend Marinko, since further on in the tape she tells us that he had told them to say that there would be no more visions. Up to this point Marinko had been providing questions for the visionaries to put to the Vision. Farther on, Ivanka said that she was going to ask the Gospa if they were allowed to tell the people that the visions would soon be ending.

But at times, the contradictory nature of what the visionaries were saying is clear from the further questions that, prompted by Marinko, they asked the Gospa. The first of these, put by Ivanka, concerned their ability to endure their new situation, to which the Gospa apparently replied: "You will be able to, my dear angels!" The second, of far greater importance, concerned "how long she was going to remain with us." Ivanka told Fr Zovko that she had replied: "As long as you want, as long as you wish!"[106]

Once again, it is totally inconsistent with authentic manifestations of the supernatural, that Our Lady's appearances should in any way depend on human desires.

Thus, on the one hand, the visionaries were apparently looking to find a way out of their predicament as public figures, while on the other hand, the claim was being made that the Gospa was prepared to appear to them almost indefinitely. It may well be that by this, the seventh day, 30 June, Ivanka, and perhaps some of the other visionaries, were beginning to lose the ability to discern the reality of what they maintained was happening. This is perhaps not surprising when one considers all the pressures they were facing from their families, the local community, the Franciscans, and the Communist authorities.

Ivanka and the "Unbelieving Judases"

Then, as the tape continued, there is the incident concerning the lady doctor present during the vision, who asked if she could touch the unseen Gospa. Ivanka recounted how the Vision had apparently responded: "There are always unbelieving Judases. Let her come near!" Fr Zovko immediately seized on this remark: "But Judas was not without faith," to which Ivanka responded: "Without faith! But he was a traitor!" Vicka also used the word "Judases" in recounting this incident to Fr Janko Bubalo. Fr Zovko was puzzled by this phrase, as he couldn't understand why the Gospa had mentioned Judas since he had had faith like the other apostles.[107]

On this evidence, we are obliged to ask why in his reputedly authoritative *Chronological Corpus of the Messages*, Fr Laurentin should have changed the Gospa's response to: *"There have always been doubting Thomases. Let her come.*"[108] Why should he have been willing, in this instance, to change the wording of a message in order to present it in a better light? Whatever the explanation might be, it seems beyond doubt that the Blessed Virgin could never have used such an expression.

Fr Zovko Takes Control

At this point, it seems that Fr Zovko came to a decision to try to put a stop to the visions, or at least bring them under control, endeavoring to get the visionaries to say that the Gospa had said that she wouldn't be coming any more, and thus the people should stay at home. He also put the accusation that Marinko not only wrote the questions put to the Gospa but also her answers, an accusation which Ivanka strongly denied.[109]

Fr Zovko then asked why the Gospa didn't appear in the church, before asking Ivanka to explain what was really happening. Her reply was revealing, in the sense that it seems to indicate that she sincerely believed she was seeing *something:* "I believe in it, I see her. What can I do? If people would see her and I wouldn't, I wouldn't believe it either."

It hardly needs to be pointed out that it is quite unthinkable to ask the Blessed Mother to do what we want in the manner here being suggested by Fr Zovko.[110] Farther on, Fr Zovko asked about the sign the Gospa would leave, to which Ivanka replied hesitantly that people were "talking about water," presumably in the hope that some sort of miraculous spring would appear. The most natural interpretation for this is that a connection with Lourdes was being made, and this is a point which will be discussed in more detail further on.

Fr Zovko's suspicions are equally evident in the following state-ment: "Can't you see that satan [sic] is present there and not the Gospa?" He said this because of the amount of cursing that was still going on amongst the local people, before coming back insistently to his point that the visions would have to stop: "Listen, Ivica [*Ivanka*] are you going to obey me? Go and tell the people!"[111]

After once again discussing Marinko's role in formulating the questions put to the Gospa, Fr Zovko then began to insist to Ivanka that he should be the one to compose what they would say to the people. But she was not happy with that and said that she wanted to ask the Gospa. In response, he strongly insisted that the people should come to the church and pray there, and she agreed to this, but only if that was what the Gospa wanted. He pressed on, however, despite her objections and told her she should come into the church and pray the rosary before the congregation.[112]

Mirjana and "Two or Three More Days"

Fr Zovko also taped his interview with Mirjana that same morning, 30 June, and she told him that some other Franciscans had said that the visionaries should now come down to the church to have their visions, rather than go to Podbrdo. She also said: "Today, I want also to ask her how many days she is going to remain with us. Let her tell us exactly how many days she can remain with us, because this evening, it is already the seventh evening!"

Fr Zovko expressed his exasperation at the whole business, and asked her how she would "get out of this?" She responded: "What can I do, if I see her and they don't see her?" He then came back to the important point of how much longer the visions were to last: "What do you think about it? How many more days will you be seeing her?" Mirjana replied: "Something tells me, two or three more days."[113]

Mirjana also told him that when "Vida [*Vicka*] sleeps, she keeps saying in her sleep: 'Leave a sign!' " This information came from her cousin who slept in the same room, and is a further indication that Vicka really was seeing something.

As in his interview with Ivanka, Fr Zovko was preoccupied with the question of how the affair was going to be resolved: "Oh, what are we going to do with the people? That's my difficulty. Give me a solution!" Mirjana told him that she needed to ask the Gospa, but he expressed his concern that they were not seeing the Gospa, that the behavior of the onlookers, and particularly the cursing, just did not fit in with that. He went on to point to the severe punishments meted out by God to those in the Bible, or the early Church, who propagated "wrong messages," saying that he was "terribly afraid."

It seems that at this point Fr Zovko may have come to the conclusion that the visionaries were hallucinating or seeing something non-supernatural, since he then said: "If those messages are only in your mind, not for the people: that's the problem. Listen, you can have [*visions*], but she isn't giving any message to the people. You shouldn't have spread it around."[114]

As in the case of Ivanka, he tried to persuade Mirjana to move the visions from Podbrdo to the parish church: "You invite people this evening to come to church, agreed?" She was still noncommittal, though, and so he tried to convince her to ask the Gospa to appear in the church, but she remained unsure. She pointed out that people began to go up to Podbrdo from the early afternoon, so how could she convince them to go to the church? But Fr Zovko continued to press his point, agreeing with her that the Communist militia were less likely to harass the visionaries if they were inside the church, rather than on the hillside. Eventually she agreed to do what he asked, and go to the hillside at 6 p.m. and tell the people to go to the church, but then she brought up the question of what Marinko might think of all this, and so this particular dialogue ended on an uncertain note.[115]

Vicka and Fr Vlasic

Fr Zovko similarly taped an interview with Vicka on the same morning, 30 June, and she told him that they were going to ask the Gospa some questions—including a request for a sign—in addition to asking how many more days she would be appearing to them. He then went on to point out to her that the Gospa had not answered any of the questions on the previous evening, saying: "Well! that means that you didn't see her, my Vicka!"

The visionary had asked what the Gospa wanted to happen in that place, but there had been no response. At this, Fr Zovko said: "Who is this Gospa that doesn't know? Then she is less than a child?"

Next, he asked her what she was going to tell the people that evening, to which she responded: "I am going to tell the people not to come at all." As with the other visionaries, he then tried to persuade her to invite the people inside the church, but she too was uncertain. Fr Zovko then put a straight question: "When are the apparitions going to end?" Vicka responded by saying that she thought they would end after the Gospa gave a sign.

There was also an interesting exchange concerning Fr Tomislav Vlasic. Fr Zovko commented on how popular the visionaries had become and Vicka responded by telling him that a Franciscan from Capljina had asked her to go there. It emerged that this Franciscan was Fr Vlasic,[116] and this certainly seems to indicate that he was expressing a keen interest in the visions and the visionaries during the first week, and that he had already visited Medjugorje. According to his own testimony, as recorded in Fr Kraljevic's book, Fr Vlasic met five of the visionaries at the house of Marinko Ivankovic, on "St Peter's Day"—presumably a reference to 29 June, the solemnity of Saints Peter and Paul.[117]

This was quite possibly the occasion, on which, as already indicated above, Fr Vlasic told the visionaries that he had already predicted, one month in advance, that the Gospa would begin appearing in Yugoslavia—this would certainly explain why he was so anxious to meet them once news of the visions reached him.[118]

Thus, the evidence from the tapes continues to present a strange paradox: it seems evident that the visionaries really were seeing something, but at the same time it is pushing the boundaries of credibility too far to believe that what they were seeing really was the Blessed Virgin.

6

Three More Days of Visions

Fr Zovko Interviews Five of the Visionaries

One of the most important interviews took place at about 6:30 p.m. on the evening of 30 June. This involved Fr Zovko and five of the six visionaries, as well as two other young women, social workers, who had driven them, via a roundabout route stopping at various points, to a place called Cerno, near Medjugorje, where their visions took place that day. The idea has grown up that the visionaries were in some way "abducted" by these social workers, as part of a Communist plot to discredit them. But it seems that the visionaries knew them and agreed to go. Indeed, the evidence from the tape clearly indicates that the visionaries themselves wanted to go to a different place, in order, presumably, to see if the Gospa would also appear to them there. Ivan Dragicevic was not present on this occasion, nor had he been with the others in the afternoon.

After some preliminaries, Fr Zovko asked Mirjana if she had said anything to the Gospa. She responded that she had, asking her "how many days she is going to remain with us. Exactly how many days she will remain with us. She said: "Three days.' ... that means until Friday."

Fr Zovko made no particular comment about this response from the Gospa, and Mirjana continued: "Then we asked her if she would be annoyed to see us going to the church rather than to the hill. However, she seemed indecisive when we asked this question, as if she did not like it. Nevertheless she said that she wouldn't be annoyed."

At this point, it must be emphasized that it is quite ridiculous to imagine that the Blessed Virgin could possibly have acted in such a hesitant and uncertain manner.

One of the other visionaries then said that the Vision would appear at the same time as usual, before Mirjana related that the Gospa had asked about Ivan, saying: "Where is the other boy?" This is rather strange, since when asked by Fr Bubalo if the Gospa knew their names, Vicka responded: "Ah! Does she know our names! Why she called us by our names the very first day."

This event certainly does not fit in with the principle that Mary is our universal spiritual mother, who has a personal care and concern for each and every human being, which includes knowing their names and using them, rather than impersonal terms such as "the other boy." Fr Zovko returned to this point later on, pointing out that if they were really seeing the Gospa she ought to have known his location and what his name was.[119]

Three More Days of Visions

Meanwhile, he realized that the visions would now be taking place in the church, in the evening, and that the Gospa had agreed to this. But as Mirjana once more pointed out, this would only be until Friday, "that means Wednesday, Thursday, Friday."

A heated debate then followed in which they discussed the best way of informing the people of these new developments, and it is clear that although some of the visionaries were still unhappy about the proposed move from the hillside to the church, they were prepared to accept this.[120]

Then Fr Zovko realized that the two young women who had been with the visionaries that afternoon, Mica Ivankovic, and Ljubica Vasilj-Gluvic, were outside, and so they were called into the room. It emerged that they had initially taken the visionaries on a sightseeing tour, and both testified that they had watched them while they were having their visions, hearing the questions put to the Gospa, and noting the responses of the visionaries. To the question of how many more times the Gospa would be appearing, Mica Ivankovic said that she heard them say together: "Three times," repeating the response of the Vision.

This point was taken up further on in the tape when Mica, and one of the visionaries, again related that "[t]hree more times" were specifically mentioned by the Gospa, and that everything would end on Friday.[121]

Thus, we have independent confirmation that at this stage, 30 June 1981, there were only supposed to be another three visions.

Indeed, Fr Bubalo brought this up in his interviews with Vicka, when, after saying that he had been playing back the cassettes made during the first week, he challenged her on this point. Her response was rather uncertain: "I really don't know that. I don't recall." She then went on to explain things as follows: "Someone said that just so that they would leave us in peace. Fra Jozo really wore us out. Here, there. Ask this, then that. And, then again. Your mind stands still!"[122]

It is clear from the further explanations she gave on this point that she was seeking to put this clear discrepancy in a positive light. But the evidence on the tapes is not amenable to such an explanation, and Vicka's account here is very unsatisfactory.

It is significant, too, that a little later, while Mica was relating the afternoon's other events, which included a confrontation with the police, Jakov, the youngest of the visionaries, burst into the conversation and claimed that one of them had pulled out a gun and threatened to kill them. But he was quickly rebuked for making this up.[123]

To sum up, by the end of the first week, the clear expectation amongst the visionaries was that the visions were only supposed to go on for another three days.

Fr Rupcic's Criticism of Fr Sivric

Frs Ljudevit Rupcic and Viktor Nuic, however, take issue with Fr Sivric's approach. They claim that because, on the morning of 30 June 1981, Fr Zovko questioned the three visionaries Ivanka, Mirjana and Vicka separately, and asked them different questions about how much longer the visions would go on for, and received different answers, then it is inadmissible to only choose Mirjana's reply. This, as the reader will recall, was: "Something tells me, two or three more days." Ivanka had reported the Gospa as saying: "As long as you want, as long as you wish!" while Vicka thought that a sign would be left before the visions ended.

However, it has to be borne in mind that Fr Zovko was not conducting a methodical series of interviews with the visionaries, in which exactly the same set of questions was put to each of them. Moreover, they would naturally have focused on what concerned them and what they could remember, as well as the general tenor of the questions. Their testimony on other points is not in exact agreement, so why should we expect that to be the case in this instance?[124]

Frs Rupcic and Nuic then go on to discuss the recording of the meeting between Fr Zovko and five of the visionaries on the evening of 30 June, immediately after their experience at Cerno, which was just dealt with above. On that occasion, as we have seen, Mirjana said that she had asked the Gospa "how many days she is going to remain with us. Exactly how many days she will remain with us. She said: 'Three days.' ... that means until Friday."

Likewise, we have also seen how Mica Ivankovic, one of the young women who had driven the visionaries to Cerno, stated that in response to the question, how many more times was the Gospa going to appear to them, she heard them say together: "Three times".

Three Days or Three Times?

Regarding these statements, Frs Rupcic and Nuic advance the rather strained argument that because Mirjana used the word "days," and Mica the different word "times," to describe the remaining visits of the Gospa, then somehow this invalidates the fact that all the evidence does indeed indicate that there were only supposed to be a three further visitations. They accuse Fr Sivric of "manipulation" but surely no sensible person will read any great significance into the fact that these different words were used—and all Fr Sivric was actually doing was accurately transcribing the words on the tapes. Given that the visions had been taking place daily, then whether it is said they were going to go on for another three days or another three times, surely it is unreasonable hairsplitting—and a sign of some desperation—to argue that there is any real problem here.[125]

However, despite the above argumentation, Frs Rupcic and Nuic acknowledge that there is a discrepancy between Ivanka stating that the Gospa would remain with the visionaries as long as they wished, and Mirjana stating that she would only be remaining with them for three days.[126] They attempt to explain this by attributing this difference to the pressure which the visionaries were under from the Communist authorities, but this does seem to be a case of grasping at straws. Rather it seems that the Vision uttered these contradictory statements, which once again indicates that we are not dealing with a genuinely supernatural event—the real Blessed Virgin would not speak in such a confusing way.

Some Untenable Arguments

Frs Rupcic and Nuic then go on to advance an even more precarious argument, namely, that the "three days" should not be understood chronologically but *theologically.* They put forward the idea that the "third day" in biblical use signifies a moment of salvation, as in Christ's resurrection from the dead taking place on the third day, saying: "If the expression 'three days' is taken this way in the Biblical revelation, then why cannot it be taken in the same way in Mirjana's prophetical statement?" Daria Klanac also seems to take a similar line, in stating that the three days could be symbolic.[127]

It should be clear, though, that there is nothing "prophetical" or theological about what Mirjana said, rather she precisely delineated the end of the three days by saying "until Friday."

Fr Laurentin, in commenting in a footnote in his own volume *Medjugorje Testament,* on Bishop Peric's book *Prijestolje Mudrosti (The Seat of Wisdom),* attempts to argue that the three days can be understood in a different way: "I've noted here the contradictions or lies with which the visionaries were trapped. Vicka would have said on June 30, 1981 that the apparitions would end in 3 days. During these troubled times, under the threat of the police, she meant the end of apparitions on the hill, an error of perspective, as can occur, even in the Bible."[128]

Daria Klanac also apparently puts forward the view that the three days could be understood in this way.[129] But in both cases, a plain reading of the text does not allow such an interpretation. The question asked was not, "how many more days was the Gospa going to stay with them on the hillside before moving to the church," but, quite simply, "how many more days was she going to stay with them," to which the reply was "until Friday."

Sadly, these type of arguments only illustrate the lengths to which some Medjugorje proponents will go to in an attempt to justify their position. They also indicate that there is an ambiguity in Klanac's thinking on this question of the three days. She seems to be saying that they may be symbolic—but also that they are real as regards moving from Podbrdo to the church. It is difficult to see how both of these interpretations can be valid, and it is strange that Daria Klanac cannot see this, since her own transcription of the interview on 30 June makes this clear:

> Fr Zovko: "Well! This interests me. Three more times. So, when do these visions finish?"
>
> Mica: "They said: 'Immediately.' Later, they said: 'It finishes on Friday.' "
>
> Fr Zovko: "But where is it going to finish on Friday?"
>
> Jakov: "In the church."
>
> Mirjana: "If Gospa doesn't tell us, perhaps for the last day, she wishes that it may be on the hill!"[130]

Personal Criticism of Fr Sivric

It is also necessary to assess Fr Rupcic's personal criticisms of Fr Sivric. Fr Rupcic claimed that because some of Fr Sivric's relatives in Medjugorje were opposed to the visions, then this affected his own objectivity[131], but this is a rather insecure argument. As we will see, Fr Sivric was absent from Medjugorje from the early 1940s, and had in fact emigrated to the United States, where he taught for many years. Thus his links to his relatives were remote, to say the least, and far from his criticisms of Medjugorje being to his advantage, they were a cause of hostility from some of his fellow Franciscans—including Fr Rupcic.

On the other hand, if we examine Fr Rupcic's own attitude to Medjugorje, it is clear that he was not a disinterested and neutral observer. His writings reveal a fanaticism towards Medjugorje which will not countenance any possibility that the visions are not genuine. He made it his business to champion Medjugorje at a very early stage, and was, according to Fr Michael O'Carroll, the first to "write substantially on Medjugorje." Indeed, Fr O'Carroll was content to include criticism of Bishop Zanic, from the pen of Fr Rupcic, comprising over thirty pages, in his own book on Medjugorje.[132] Fr Rupcic was also the author of an intemperate book entitled *The Truth about Medjugorje,* which again was highly critical of Bishop Zanic. He followed this up with further books attacking those who questioned Medjugorje, including Fr Sivric. We also need to bear in mind that Fr Rupcic was a Franciscan and thus associated with the Herzegovina Franciscans who have been in dispute with both the local bishops and Rome for many years.

Who then is more likely to be biased? Fr Sivric, who opposed Medjugorje at some personal cost, or Fr Rupcic, who demonstrated an obsessive attachment to the visions and the visionaries, to the extent that he was prepared to defend Medjugorje with far-fetched arguments, such as those discussed above?

Fr Rupcic and the Medjugorje Tapes

We have seen that Élisabeth Claverie, following extensive research and crosschecking, gave preference to Fr Sivric's transcripts of the original tapes, rather than the version produced by Daria Klanac, but Fr Rupcic was not slow to criticize Fr Sivric on this point also. He claims that the tapes are incomplete and unreliable, but as is clear from the appendices to his book, Fr Sivric was very careful to indicate when sections of the tape were incomprehensible, or where there was an interruption in recording. Louis Bélanger, the Canadian researcher who collaborated with Fr Sivric in the production of *The Hidden Side of Medjugorje,* tells us that: "It was important to me that the taped documents he had be carefully translated, tapes that were apparently identical to those given to me by the Bishop of Mostar. At my request, Father Sivric began to make a Croatian transcript and then dictated an English translation ... in July, 1986 we exchanged tapes and verified that our sources were complementary."[133]

Fr Rupcic makes a further criticism of Fr Sivric, regarding those parts of the tapes which are unclear: "Since all the participants in these taped conversations are still living, it boggles the mind that the author does not attempt to fill in or clarify those missing parts. The participants to the conversations were all available to him at the time of his sojourn in Medjugorje."[134]

The Visionaries as Reliable Witnesses?

Surely, though, it would be asking too much to expect the visionaries to remember later exactly what they had said while they were being recorded. What guarantee do we have that their recollections after such a period of time would do anything to clarify what was on the tapes? And that is assuming that those recollections would have been reliable, whereas there is evidence that some of their later accounts contradict what is on the tapes, as in the case of the discrepancy between the reason given by the visionaries for going with the two social workers on 30 June, and the later accounts of this incident that were circulated. This is what Vicka said to Fr Bubalo about this outing: "Two girls came for us about two in the afternoon. And, they offered to take us about a bit in their car. Not suspecting anything, we got ready and left." However, on the 30 June tape, when asked by Fr Zovko if someone else had told them to try "another hill," Vicka explicitly says, "we chose the place and the rest and we didn't need anyone to tell us what to do," while Jakov adds: "We marked the place."

Fr Bubalo challenged Vicka about this discrepancy saying: "It's uncomfortable for me, but I must. Lately I replayed some of the cassettes including that conversation with Fra Jozo. And, I came across one of your assertions that does not agree with what you just told me. ... you told me here, and you always maintained it, that the girls tricked you into that outing."[135]

Vicka attempted to explain all this away, but the fact is that her later account does not tally with what is on the tapes.

Fr Rupcic also says: "The true sources still today are the living people, the partakers of those events: in the first place, the Seers, their families, and the Pastors and Assistants. The author, nonetheless, relies on a few taped conversations involving some of the direct witnesses."[136]

This betrays a fundamental misunderstanding of what constitutes reliable evidence as opposed to the unreliable variety. It must be apparent that tape recordings of the events done within a matter of days, even allowing for certain sections which are unclear, are a far superior source of evidence than recollections gathered months or even years later.

The Silent Gospa

The conversation of the Gospa—or rather the lack of it in the early days—is an extremely important point to note. There was apparently no message for mankind during these days, a point which disturbed Fr Zovko. In speaking to Mirjana on the evening of 28 June, he got a negative response to the question: "And she does not say anything?" He then continued: "She never says anything first if you do not ask her a question." To this Mirjana replied: "Nothing. First of all, we ask her something." This prompted Fr Zovko to say: "So there is no message. Good, Mirjana!"[137]

Similarly, in his interview with Ivanka on 30 June, Fr Zovko was still worried about the lack of any message from the Gospa, and particularly about the lack of any specific prayer for the visionaries. He questioned Ivanka on this point, but her reply was negative. He responded by saying that in previous apparitions, such as Fatima, there had been a message to pray the rosary. Ivanka's retort was extremely revealing: "Nothing like that! She answers all that we ask her but nothing else." One can sense the frustration in Fr Zovko's answer: "But how is it that she doesn't say anything new to you, but always answers the same thing?" Ivanka responded weakly: "What do I know?"[138]

This failure to take the initiative on the part of the Gospa is, of course, completely out of line with authentic Marian apparitions, where the Blessed Virgin has always known exactly what she was doing. Later on, in the messages produced over the last quarter century, the Gospa would find her voice, and produce a veritable torrent of words—but much of this, as will be seen, is completely out of character with what we know of the utterances of the Blessed Virgin during her approved apparitions.

During his long interview of 30 June, Fr Zovko also remarked on the Gospa's request that the visionaries, "[r]econcile the people," questioning them as to whether this referred to everyone or just to local parishioners. They responded that it referred to the neighbors.

On this point, Fr Sivric observed that there was a definite need for reconciliation in the locality.[139]

Fr Zovko Commits himself to the Visions

Fr Zovko's general impressions of the first days of the visions, and of the visionaries, as reported by Mary Craig, are worth noting. He complained that their answers were "terribly vague," and that he found them "ignorant and shallow," to the extent that he was "terribly afraid" that the whole thing was "just a joke with them." His concluding thoughts were particularly disturbing: "How can these children possibly have seen the Blessed Virgin? It was unthinkable that anyone could have seen her and not be radically changed by the experience. There was tension among them too. They argued a lot and disagreed among themselves about what had happened. Vicka and Mirjana seemed to be jostling for position as leader."[140]

But as time went on, it became clear that the parish priest had radically changed his position. Fr Svetozar Kraljevic spoke to Fr Zovko on 11 August 1983, and during this interview the latter related "the first sign from God which led him to believe in the apparitions." He was apparently speaking of the events which took place on 1 July 1981, when the authorities were looking for the visionaries while he was in the church. He claimed that despite the fact that the building was empty he heard a "voice" saying: "Come out and protect the children."[141]

Thus, two years after the visions began, Fr Zovko was claiming his own locution, although he had been highly critical of the visionaries up to 30 June 1981. Was this the reason why he changed his mind about the visions?

According to E. Michael Jones, Thursday, 2 July 1981, the day when the visionaries alleged that the Virgin had appeared to them in the afternoon, in the parish church, with Fr Zovko and a large crowd present, was the "the crucial turning point in the history of the so-called apparitions." The priest had preached a revivalist sermon which whipped up the emotions of those present to fever pitch. It was really from this point on, when the visions were henceforth said to take place in the church, that the community as a whole took them on board and accepted them as real in their own minds, and in the sight of the world.[142]

Henceforth, Fr Zovko became one of the prime movers behind the visions, and it was his premature acceptance of them as genuine, at least as far as informing his parishioners was concerned, which was a crucial catalyst in the formation of the whole Medjugorje edifice. We will perhaps never know the ultimate reason why, instead of adopting an attitude of "wait and see," he suddenly changed his mind about the visions and rushed to judgment. It was certainly a strange about turn—perhaps his account of hearing something in the church was genuine? But whatever the reason it was a decision which would have far-reaching consequences.

The Last Vision

Regrettably, there is no tape of the events which took place on Friday, 3 July, the day on which the visionaries had said they would experience their final encounter with the Gospa. But Fr Sivric was able to interview one of the witnesses present at the Rectory at St James's church, Fr Tadija Pavlovic, who, as a neighboring parish priest, was in Medjugorje helping with confessions. He heard the visionaries state quite clearly that this was indeed the last vision. Additional witnesses at this meeting included local priests Frs Umberto Loncar and Stojan Zrno, as well as Mijo Gabric, a reporter for the paper *Glas Koncila,* and Ivo Magzan. Next day, Saturday, 4 July, however, Fr Pavlovic was surprised to hear from his own parishioners that the Gospa had apparently once again appeared, and the same thing was reported to him the following day, Sunday, 5 July.

Fr Sivric notes that after this he refused to return to Medjugorje to say Mass or to hear confessions. Fr Pavlovic was also somewhat scandalized, when, on returning to Medjugorje on 25 July, to visit his mother, he was present at the feast day Mass at St James's church, and was struck by the lack of devotion displayed towards the Eucharist by the visionaries, and the way they talked, and walked around the church.[143]

According to Frs Rupcic and Nuic, Fr Zovko "categorically denies that after the apparition the visionaries stated that Our Lady told them that this was the final apparition." They go on to say that

Fr Umberto Loncar recorded in his diary that the visionaries "did not say anything about the vision but immediately left the church." However, we then learn that Jakov and Vicka spoke to those gathered outside, via loudspeakers, and that although Jakov did not say anything about a last vision, amongst other things Vicka stated that: "Tonight she appeared for the last time ..."

The rather incredible response of Frs Rupcic and Nuic to this is to say that: "Vicka said that and not Our Lady. At least Vicka does not say that Our Lady told them this!"[144]

The fact is that Fr Rupcic, in a separate earlier account, contradicted himself when, in one of his polemics against Bishop Zanic, he said: "Nor was he right in saying that there were some priests present during the last apparition on 3 July because Fr Jozo was actually the only one present at that apparition."[145]

Given this discrepancy, there are certainly legitimate question marks about the accuracy of Fr Rupcic's recollections.

Even though the visions did not end on 3 July, it is clear that the expectation that they would not go on indefinitely was present during the early years. As an example of this, we have the testimony of Fr John Bertolucci, who was interviewed by Fr Vlasic. Although no date is given, this interview must have taken place sometime between 1981 and 1983. After expressing some reservations about exactly what was taking place in spiritual terms while the visionaries were experiencing their visions, he went on to say that: "The children themselves ... say the apparitions will end."

Fr Laurentin made the same point when writing in January 1984. He commented on the fact that one of the visionaries—Mirjana—was no longer seeing any visions, and that this was "a harbinger of their impending end."[146]

Medjugorje and Lourdes

The fact that the visionaries testified that the visions were due to end within "three more days,"—in other words, less than two weeks after they had begun on 24 June 1981—has proved a grave embarrassment to some promoters of Medjugorje. They have downplayed this fact and tried to explain it away in the face of the thousands of further visions subsequently alleged to have taken place. An example of this is found in the interview between Fr Zovko and Fr

Svetozar Kraljevic, which took place on 11 August 1983. In this interview, Fr Zovko claimed that he had given the visionaries a book on Lourdes and that from the number of apparitions which Bernadette experienced—nineteen—they too thought that they should expect a further three visions, since they claimed to have experienced sixteen visions up to that point.

It does seem, from the taped conversation of 27 June 1981, that Mirjana, at least, had read a book on Lourdes the day after the first vision. But the above idea, that there would only be a total of nineteen visions, as an explanation for the "three more days" assertion, is completely unacceptable in the overall context of what was said both on this day and on 30 June. There was simply no mention of the figure nineteen, rather, as we will see, the visionaries were only aware of the *eighteen* main apparitions at Lourdes.

Apart from that, at least one other visionary, Jakov, was also aware of the basic story of Lourdes, as is clear from the tape of the interview he had with Fr Zovko, also on 27 June.[147]

The first taped interview, with only three of the visionaries, Ivanka, Vicka, and Marija, was undertaken by Fr Zrinko Cuvalo, the parochial vicar at Medjugorje, on the morning of 27 June. In this interview, four days into the course of the visions, Fr Cuvalo asked them why they had returned to Podbrdo after the initial vision on 24 June, the feast of the birth of St John the Baptist. To this, Ivanka explained how they had been repeatedly told how the Blessed Virgin had appeared at Lourdes eighteen times.[148]

This is an interesting admission, and indicates that already the visionaries were under some external pressure to carry on going to Podbrdo. It also indicates that the story of Lourdes was well known in the village, to the extent that at least some villagers were aware that there were eighteen main apparitions at the grotto—which is certainly not something the average Catholic would know. But we should note, too, that there is a discrepancy between the eighteen apparitions mentioned by Ivanka, and the figure nineteen used by Fr Zovko to explain the problem of the "three more days." The last apparition to Bernadette took place some time later, on 16 July, and is not considered to be part of the main sequence of Lourdes apparitions.

The point, however, as regards Fr Zovko's assertion, is that if anything, the visionaries ought to have said, "*two* more days," given that they were aware of the number eighteen, rather than nineteen. So the whole idea that the "three more days" was somehow tied in with the young people's knowledge of Lourdes is untenable, and breaks down completely under investigation.[149]

Fr Laurentin's explanation for all this is extremely feeble: "On that day [30 June] Mirjana thought that she understood that the Gospa would return for three more days, until Friday. But it was only her interpretation."[150] It is not clear exactly what he based this statement on, but it simply cannot be reconciled with the original tapes.

The Visionaries and Lourdes

Apart from all this, there are points of contact between the accounts of the visionaries and the apparitions at Lourdes, which certainly indicate that they were aware of what had happened there. For example, as already indicated, on the third day, Vicka took along some "blessed salt and water" and sprinkled the Gospa with it. We find Bernadette also sprinkling holy water on the apparition she saw. The particular significance of this is that, as we have seen, on this occasion Vicka said: "If you are the Gospa, remain with us. If you are not, get lost," while Bernadette asked her beautiful lady "to stay if she came from God, to go away if not."[151]

Similarly, when Ivanka was speaking with Fr Zovko about a "sign," she said that while the best sign of all would be that the Gospa should appear to everyone, failing that, "she would cause 'water' to spring up," which equates with the appearance of the miraculous spring at Lourdes.[152]

The evidence suggests, then, that the visionaries were aware of what had taken place at Lourdes, and this surely illustrates an important point which has not been sufficiently grasped. Because accounts of the recognized apparitions of Mary have been freely available now for decades, it is quite possible for individuals to be influenced by these accounts. This is not to say that the visionaries consciously set out to fabricate the entire manifestation right from the beginning—the evidence from the tapes clearly indicates that they did see something during the first week. Rather, once they came down to the church from Podbrdo, there was enormous pressure on them to maintain the stance that they really were seeing the Blessed Virgin.

The tragedy of this whole affair is that the visionaries have been as much the victims of what has taken place at Medjugorje as its originators. As we have seen, there were a number of factors at work in and around Podbrdo which led them to believe they were seeing visions of the Blessed Mother, and thus, it would be too simplistic to say that Medjugorje was fabricated according to a predetermined plan. Rather, it arose haphazardly, and there were a number of ingredients which contributed to it, among which accounts of the events at Lourdes were one factor. But in the end, its initial success can probably be attributed mainly to Fr Zovko, who after expressing clear disbelief during the early days of the visions, was led to change his mind and become a fervent supporter of Medjugorje.

7

Medjugorje:
God or the Devil?

Medjugorje: A Diabolical Origin?

In the light of the evidence cited above it is legitimate then to ask whether or not the original visions, of the first week of so, were not in fact diabolical in origin, as Fr Zovko himself suggested on more than one occasion. If we look at the whole phenomenon from the perspective of the devil then some very interesting points emerge. He has a great deal of experience in this area. He knows all about human weakness, foolishness, and sinfulness—and how to exploit these to the maximum.

If it is the case, then, that the devil—or some sort of diabolic vision—was in fact appearing during the first week at Medjugorje, it can be said that his main concern, initially, would be to avoid frightening the visionaries away by acting in a precipitate way. Therefore, he would, of necessity, adopt a non-threatening attitude towards them. The devil does not know the future with precision—the fact of human free will and the power of God's grace make that too difficult—and therefore each case like this has to be treated on its own merits.

So on the first day, the Vision said nothing, but just allowed the visionaries to get used to their new experience. Similarly, the Vision did not say anything on the second day, but did allow the visionaries to touch its form, presumably as a way of gaining their trust. Fr Cuvalo questioned them on this point, asking if the Vision said anything as they were doing this. Marija replied: "Nothing at all, she kept looking ... She told us, she laughed, what else ..."[153]

Thus, if the Vision was in fact diabolical, that would explain why Satan first of all ingratiated himself with them, by allowing them to touch the visionary form he had assumed, and also by laughing, thus putting them more at ease.

Garabandal and Medjugorje

This parallels what happened at Garabandal, a Spanish village, where in the early 1960s, four young girls claimed to have had visions of the Blessed Virgin, although not one of the successive Bishops of Santander has accepted these visions as authentic. On Sunday, 2 July 1961, they alleged that she had appeared to them as Our Lady of Mount Carmel, and that they spoke to her for a long time. One of them, Conchita, later recorded in her diary that they told her mundane details about the village hay-making, and that "Mary's" response was to laugh at the things they told her.[154]

It is hard to believe that the real Blessed Virgin would have engaged in such trivial chit-chat with the girls. But as a diabolical method of drawing the children more closely into visions which were not supernatural, as also seems to have happened during the first week at Medjugorje, it makes perfect sense.

On 3 August 1961, the Garabandal visionaries made the first of their "ecstatic walks," which involved their walking either forward or backwards, without apparently looking where they were going. These walks were often conducted at tremendous speed, to the astonishment of onlookers who could barely keep up.[155] There are interesting parallels here to some of the accounts of the Medjugorje visionaries during the first week, including those recorded on the tapes transcribed by Fr Sivric. For example, Marija spoke of following people down the hill, and moving to another location after one of the visions, and of feeling "as if somebody got hold of me and kept dragging me. ... Something kept attracting me."

In Fr Sivric's translation of her *Diary,* Vicka makes a similar claim, speaking of how on the second day, 25 June 1981, she ran up the hill with the other visionaries who were present, because the Gospa was calling them: "We felt as if some force were drawing us up there." Speaking of this occasion, Mirjana related that they had quickly climbed up the hill, "but ... did not become tired," despite the fact that it was a long way up.[156] Vicka also had this to say about that day's events:

> The Madonna called to us to go up on the hill, and we went. When you look up there from the bottom of the hill, it looks close, but it is not. We ran quickly up the hill. It was not like walking on the ground. Nor did we look for the path. We simply ran toward her. In five minutes we were on the hill—as if something had pulled us through the air. I was afraid. I also was barefoot, but no thorns had scratched me. When we were about two meters away from the Madonna, we felt as if we were thrown to our knees. Jakov was thrown kneeling into a thorny bush, and I thought he would be injured. But he came out of it without a scratch.

The interesting thing is that these experiences were not just the subjective feelings of the visionaries, but were also witnessed by onlookers, as Fr Kraljevic indicates: "Those who watched the children run up the hill testify to the truthfulness of Vicka's words. They were amazed by the speed with which the children ran, and were not able to follow them to the top of the hill."[157]

We do not find anything like this "ecstatic" running in the approved apparitions of the Blessed Virgin, whereas it is disturbing to note this clear parallel with the activities of the Garabandal visionaries.

There is No Message

As we have seen, on the third day, Ivanka asked the Vision why she had come there, and was told: "Because there were a lot of faithful, that we must be together." She asked, too, about her recently deceased mother and was told that she was with the Gospa. Mirjana, too, was reassured about her grandfather. The visionaries then asked if she was going to come again, and were told: "Tomorrow at the same place": but their request for a sign was ignored.[158]

Here, too, we can see how this "small talk" was conducive to this process of ingratiation with the visionaries, while the "message" itself—"that we must be together"—is completely trite and unnecessary.

In the light of what has happened during genuine apparitions, it is astonishing to note that up to this point, the Vision had made no serious attempt to initiate any conversation, or pass on any message of substance, and in this regard, it was exactly the same on the fourth day. Rather, the Vision allowed the visionaries to take the initiative, and become used to its presence. Indeed, as already indicated, by this stage, Fr Zovko was becoming somewhat exasperated at the lack of any clear message from the Vision, and he pressed Mirjana on this point.[159]

His perplexity continued following the events of the fifth day, when he was not able to get a straight answer on this point of a lack of a specific message, neither from Mirjana, nor Ivanka, nor Ivan. Finally, as already noted, on the sixth day, Fr Zovko publicly acknowledged that no official message was being given and that, "Our Lady has said nothing that is meant for anyone else."[160]

This virtual non-communication to the visionaries from the Gospa, during the crucial first week or so of visions, contrasts very strongly with the way that the approved apparitions of the Blessed Virgin have developed. In most such cases, a week has been quite sufficient for her to say everything she wanted to say, but at Medjugorje during this period the Gospa did not pass on anything of significance.

This does not mean, though, that everything about Medjugorje is necessarily diabolically inspired. As we have seen, Medjugorje arose in part because of the weakness of fallen human nature, especially on the part of the visionaries and their immediate associates. These elements facilitate the work of the devil, but as this work is invisible, it is therefore difficult to identify. Satan achieves his objectives by a kind of counterfeit grace in the heart and mind, by which people are drawn into believing in false visions almost without being aware of what is happening. For, clearly, the vast majority of those who have been to Medjugorje have gone there in good faith.

The Pattern of the Approved Apparitions

Whether it is the Blessed Virgin speaking to Juan Diego at Guadalupe, in 1531, when she imparted a series of messages to him, or Rue du Bac, where Mary spoke in detail about the mission she was giving Catherine Labouré, or Fatima, where the message contained a specific request to the Pope, the pattern of the approved apparitions of the past has been consistent: the Blessed Virgin has something definite and of vital supernatural importance to say regarding mankind's salvation, and she wastes no time in conveying her message.

This is also true of her apparitions at Lourdes, La Salette, Beauraing, and Banneux. She always leads the conversation, and is the one who initiates important elements. This does not mean, however, that she unthinkingly brushes aside unimportant questions; rather, as a true mother, she shows that she understands the mentality of her children, and where their questions can be answered, she does so. But her intention is very definitely to convey a specific spiritual message in a relatively short space of time. In most cases, she did this with very few words, and this aspect seems to coincide with her reticence in the Gospels, where likewise, she said very little. In addition, her words are concerned with her mission as the spiritual mother of mankind, and not with generalities or matters not related to salvation: she says nothing unseemly or contrary to the Faith.[161]

Indeed, it is fair to say that if *all* the reported words of Mary, in the period of over four hundred years between Guadalupe and Banneux, were put together, they would not amount to much more than a document of ten or eleven sheets. How many people realize how little she actually said during her recognized apparitions? At Knock and Pontmain, she said absolutely nothing—although a few words did appear on a banner at her feet during the latter apparition—and, for example, the following words at Banneux were so few, that they could easily be written on the back of a postcard:

"This stream is reserved for me, Good evening."
"Push your hands into the water."
"I am the Virgin of the poor."
"This spring is reserved for all the nations—to relieve the sick."
"I shall pray for you. Au Revoir."
"I come to relieve suffering."
"Believe in me, I will believe in you. Pray much. Au Revoir."
"My dear child, pray much. Au Revoir."
"I am the Mother of the Savior, Mother of God, Pray much. Adieu."[162]

Our Lady's words at Fatima

The same principle can also be illustrated by looking at the following dialogue with Lucia which took place during the first apparition at Fatima, and which began with Mary smiling and reassuring the children:

"Do not be afraid, I will do you no harm."

"Where are you from?"

"I am from heaven."

"What do want of me?"

"I have come to ask you to come here for six months in succession on the 13th day, at this same hour. Later on, I will tell who I am and what I want. Afterwards, I will return here yet a seventh time."

"Shall I go to heaven too?"

"Yes, you will."

"And Jacinta?"

"She will go also."

"And Francisco?"

"He will go there too, but he must say many rosaries."

Lucia then asked about two young women who had died recently, and was told that one was in heaven, and that the other would be in purgatory "until the end of the world."

"Are you willing to offer yourselves to God and bear all the sufferings He wills to send you, as an act of reparation for the conversion of sinners?"

"Yes, we are willing."

"Then you are going to have much to suffer, but the grace of God will be your comfort."

Lucia recounted that, at that moment the Lady opened her hands, "communicating to us a light so intense that, as it streamed from her hands, its rays penetrated our hearts and the innermost depths of our souls, making us see ourselves in God, Who was that light, more clearly than we see ourselves in the best of mirrors. Then, moved by an interior impulse that was also communicated to us, we fell on our knees, repeating in our hearts: 'O most Holy Trinity, I adore You! My God, my God, I love You in the most Blessed Sacrament!' "

After a few moments, before she disappeared, the Lady left them with a request: "Pray the Rosary every day, in order to obtain peace for the world and the end of the war."[163]

We can see here that Our Lady initially reassured the children that she is indeed from heaven, and that they will go there too, before answering the questions which naturally come to Lucia's mind. Then she moves straight on to the important spiritual substance of her message, namely, asking them to offer themselves to God, to accept suffering in reparation for sin, and to pray the rosary. The contrast with the lack of any substantial spiritual message from God on the part of the Medjugorje Vision during the first few days could hardly be greater.

To sum up what we have been considering so far, the primary evidence provided by the taped interviews recorded at the time of the visions clearly demonstrates that the first week's visions at Medjugorje present us with major difficulties. They bear no resemblance to the way the approved Marian apparitions developed during a similar, or an even shorter period, sometimes amounting to as little as a single apparition, as in the case of La Salette.

The Vision is Reluctant to go to Church

What really seems to clinch the argument that the Vision was not the Blessed Virgin, is the following very important admission, which, as we have already noted, was made by Mirjana during Fr Zovko's interview with the visionaries on 30 June: "[W]e asked her if she would be annoyed to see us going to the church rather than to the hill. However, she seemed indecisive when we asked this question, as if she did not like it. Nevertheless she said that she wouldn't be annoyed."[164]

The whole idea that the Blessed Virgin defers to purely subjective human whims, as to where she is to appear, is absolutely out of the question, and by itself, raises very serious doubts as to the nature of the Medjugorje Vision. However, if, for the sake of argument, we assume that it was Mary, how can one then explain that she was "indecisive" and at first looked "as if she did not like it" when the visionaries asked if they could go to the church in future, rather than return to the hillside? To think that Mary could not have been pleased that they wanted to go into the church, where her divine

Son is really present in the tabernacle, is frankly quite unbelievable. However, if the Vision was not in fact Mary, but in some sense diabolical, then its reluctance to appear before the Blessed Sacrament in the church becomes understandable.

Regarding this question of a diabolical deception, on Tuesday 30 June, while Fr Zovko was interviewing some of the visionaries individually, two other Franciscans, Frs Pervan and Dugandzic, arrived at his office. Fr Zovko refused to allow them to participate in the interviews, but when he emerged later on, he found Fr Pervan proclaiming that the children were possessed by the devil. He suggested exorcism but Fr Zovko, in the words of Mary Craig, "dismissed [this] as too alarming for all concerned and unlikely to bring them any nearer to the truth."[165] It is certainly significant that Fr Pervan should have thought of diabolical possession as an explanation for the visionaries' activities, and this indicates that at this stage he felt there was something unwholesome about the whole business.

A Visionary Pattern Established

Once the visionaries had moved from Podbrdo to the church, a pattern was established, which remained practically unchanged until 1985. Every evening, after saying the rosary in the church, they would assemble in a room opposite the sacristy, which became known as "the chapel of the apparitions." This had a crucifix on the wall above a movable altar, and a statue of Our Lady of Lourdes to one side. This mention of the statue is an interesting point in itself, since it adds to the evidence that the apparitions at Lourdes formed an accepted part of parish life. During their visions, they would stare at a precise spot on the south wall of this room, having fallen to their knees as a group. Within a month, this pattern, according to Vicka's *Diary,* involved the Gospa appearing to the visionaries at half past six, greeting them with the words, "Praised be Jesus," and then engaging them in conversation. The themes at this stage apparently centered on the need for conversion and penance, and it seems that her customary saying as she departed was: "Go in God's peace!" Exactly a month after the visions began, on 24 July 1981, Vicka was still describing the arrival of the Vision in similar terms to those used right at the beginning, that is of a light slowly descending.[166]

The "Sign" Promised

From the second day onwards, 25 June 1981, the visionaries were very concerned that the Gospa should provide a "sign" in order to indicate that they were telling the truth, and thus satisfy the understandable expectations of the crowd.[167] It certainly seems that the visionaries thought that this sign would appear "very soon," and the common opinion amongst both them and the Franciscans at this time was that this sign would be given during 1981. According to Fr Sivric, Fr Zovko had announced in a sermon that a sign would be given roughly about the time of the feast of the Assumption—that is around 15 August 1981.[168]

Frs Rupcic and Nuic dispute that the Gospa explicitly promised the visionaries a "sign," but there is no question that according to the testimony of the latter they certainly expected something to happen. As we have seen, when questioned concerning a sign by Fr Zovko, Ivanka had replied: "She certainly is going to leave it," while Vicka maintained that she thought the visions would end after the Gospa had given a sign. This point is even clearer in Vicka's *Diary,* as translated by Fr Sivric, where in the entry for 27 August 1981, she tells us that in response to their further questions about a sign, the Gospa responded: "It is going to be soon since I have promised you."

Once again, Frs Rupcic and Nuic attempt a "theological" explanation, this time for the use of word "soon," arguing that because in the Bible "thousands of years can mean one day," therefore "Vicka's statement should not be any more suspicious than the statements by Biblical prophets."[169] The danger with this type of approach, of course, is that it can be used to twist the plain meaning of a word into whatever we want it to mean.

However, it might be further argued by Medjugorje supporters that this use of the word "soon" by the Vision parallels the way that Our Lady at Fatima told Lucia that unlike Jacinta and Francisco, who would *soon* go to heaven, she would have to stay on earth, "some time longer," whereas in fact, Lucia lived on into her nineties. But clearly, it would have been heartbreaking for her to have been told this as a young child, and we can see in the words "some time longer" Mary's motherly concern to spare her unnecessary anguish. And indeed, in saying that she would take Jacinta and Francisco to heaven "soon" she was saying nothing other than the truth, since both of them died shortly after—here "soon" was used very literally.[170] The other point to make is that when Our Lady spoke of the miracle that was to come at Fatima, she did not use a vague word like "soon," but specified the very month—October—and indeed the very day—the thirteenth.

The Garabandal "Great Miracle"

In any event, something similar to what was claimed for Medjugorje, a future "great miracle," was also prophesied at Garabandal, and this was supposed to occur in such a manner that it would be seen by all in the vicinity of Garabandal on a particular day, with an advance notice of eight days. According to Sanchez-Ventura y Pascual's book *The Apparitions of Garabandal,* originally published in English in 1966, it was also foretold that, "the Pope and Padre Pio will see it from wherever they happen to be; that the sick who are present will be cured, that sinners will be converted, that the miracle will last some fifteen minutes; that the Bishop will raise his prohibition beforehand, so that priests may be there; and that a permanent sign will be left as a proof of the miracle ..." According to one of the visionaries, the miracle was to be, "as great and spectacular as the world needs," and she also claimed to know its date.[171]

Needless to say, there has been no great miracle at Garabandal, and the chances of there being one in the future would appear to be remote. Padre Pio died in 1968, and this talk of a sign seems to have been nothing less than a device to keep up some sort of interest in Garabandal, by attempting to force the Church not to come to any definite decision about the alleged visions until they had been "proved" by this expected miracle. There have been attempts to circumvent the inconvenient fact of Padre Pio's death by claiming that he had a private vision of the miracle beforehand, but this goes against the plain sense of the above "prophecy."[172]

Indeed, the only genuine Marian "great sign" of recent times has been the one to which Our Lady referred in July 1917, when as part of the Fatima secret she foretold the strange illuminations in the night sky which would be seen in many parts of the world, and which took place in 1938. "When you see a night illumined by an unknown light, know that this is the *great sign* given you by God that he is about to punish the world for its crimes, by means of war, famine, and persecutions of the Church and of the Holy Father." Of course, the miracle of the sun itself at Fatima was also an extremely important sign, given so that all might believe.

Garabandal not as Popular as Medjugorje

Garabandal was very popular at the time, and still has a sizeable following to this day, but it never managed to attract anything like the support garnered by Medjugorje. There are probably a number of reasons for this, including the fact that despite the problems emerging at the time of the Second Vatican Council, the Church was still in an essentially healthy condition at that time. But a case can certainly be made that Garabandal, and other claimed apparitions, including Amsterdam, prepared the minds of many Catholics for the possibility of a lengthy series of visions. In addition, such alleged visions, which often involved opposition to the wishes of the local bishop, also prepared the way for the sort of confrontation with the episcopacy which has developed at Medjugorje.

But what was missing at Garabandal was a worldwide support network of the sort provided by the Charismatic Movement, and also very crucially, a group of religious and priests, the Franciscans of Bosnia-Herzegovina, prepared to back Medjugorje. In addition, the early eighties were one of the low points of the Church's fortunes in recent years. Pope John Paul II had only been in power for a brief period, and it would be some time before his policies and personality would begin to impact on the Church. All of these factors combined to provide a suitable atmosphere in which Medjugorje could flourish.

With the passage of time, though, it must be obvious to any unbiased observer that Garabandal and Medjugorje have much more in common with each other than either of them have with any of the approved Marian apparitions. In both cases, the Church, in the persons of successive local bishops, has spoken out quite clearly to either actually, or effectively, condemn the alleged visions, despite concerted promotional campaigns in their favor. Surely the message of all this is that sensible Catholics must align themselves with the mind of the Church in these matters? To adopt an attitude which puts one's own private judgment before that of the Church is to do nothing less than to court spiritual disaster.

Fr Zovko is Arrested and Imprisoned

On 11 July 1981, Fr Zovko preached a fiery sermon, taking as his subject the Israelites wandering in the wilderness for forty years. The authorities regarded this sermon as having veiled political and nationalistic implications in connection with the years of Communist rule in Yugoslavia. *Novosti* (*The News*), a daily newspaper, accused him of wanting to revive the Ustasha nationalist movement, "in the very place of the crime." Fr Laurentin links this to the killing of some local Marxists, and the atrocities carried out by Tito's partisans, but fails to mention the brutal massacre of the Serbs at Surmanci, which is surely the crime to which the paper was referring.[173]

Meanwhile, Bishop Zanic had visited Medjugorje on 25 July, and it seems that at this very early stage he was open to the possibility that the visionaries might be telling the truth. He was also aware of the hostility of the government, and, on 6 August, he issued a press release in defense of the priests and the visionaries, who were being attacked in Communist newspapers. Indeed subsequently, on 12 August, Podbrdo was put off-limits by the civil authorities.

We can gauge the impact the Medjugorje phenomenon was having locally by noting that on the Feast of the Assumption, Fr Zovko was able to announce to a huge crowd of 25,000 that a sign would be given by the Gospa on 17 August 1981. Meanwhile, another indication of how feverish things had become during the early days came from the variously timed announcements by Marinko that a large church would suddenly appear on Podbrdo, or that a local hill would simply disappear. These statements were reported to Fr Sivric by his various informants in the village.

There was a sign on 17 August, but it wasn't quite the one Fr Zovko had expected; rather it was the arrival of the police to arrest him because of his earlier "political" sermon, which led to a summary trial for the priest. His place was taken by Fr Tomislav Vlasic who was to remain the pivotal influence over the visionaries, as their spiritual director, until September 1984, being later followed in this role by Fr Slavko Barbaric. In 1988, Fr Vlasic would begin a mixed religious community in Italy, one involving young people, including the visionary Marija Pavlovic, and a German woman named Agnes Heupel who had supposedly been cured of a partial paralysis at Medjugorje.[174]

Fr Zovko was put on trial in Mostar on 21 October 1981, and convicted the following day, receiving a prison sentence which would only see his release in February 1983.[175] This crackdown by the authorities illustrates another of the factors which helped to fuel support for Medjugorje in the early days, namely, the opposition of the Communists, which led many people to conclude that the claimed visions must be genuine. They had suffered for so long under a Communist regime which was maintained by lies, that it almost seemed natural to believe the opposite of what they said, regardless of whether or not it might be true.[176]

8

Problems with
the Medjugorje Messages

Some Unbelievable Messages

At this stage, early in the life of Medjugorje, some of the visionaries were prone to making rather extreme statements. For example, Fr Sivric reports that in late August or early September 1981, Vicka announced, in front of a certain Jure Ivankovic and a priest, that "Germany and the United States will be destroyed, ... that the Pope will be exiled in Turkey, [and] ... that Bisce, the plain south of Mostar, will be covered in knee-deep blood." Fr Sivric notes that this supposed prophecy did not originate with Vicka, because as a child he could remember similar prophecies being repeated. This illustrates the effect of the popular culture on her, and her difficulty in differentiating between fantasy and reality. But the fact that she should have said such a thing at all is clearly disturbing.

Similarly, Fr Sivric tells us that on 4 September 1981, Vicka wrote in her *Diary* about the infamous "bloody handkerchief" incident, which concerned a meeting between a "driver" and a man covered in blood—Christ according to the visionary—who ordered that a handkerchief soaked in blood should be thrown in a river. This driver then met Mary who asked for the handkerchief, although he was apparently reluctant to hand it over. Then the Blessed Virgin reportedly said, "If you had not given it to me, that would have been the end of the world." Vicka stated categorically that: "The Gospa said that was the truth."

However, by the time Vicka was speaking with Fr Bubalo, in 1983, she was putting forward a different version of this story, saying: "I'm surprised that people continue to associate me with that hankie, when it really isn't my affair." She goes on to attempt to distance herself from this bizarre account, but it is all very unconvincing. She does not deny, however, that the Gospa *had* corroborated the story, when she said that she later asked her about it.

Perhaps not surprisingly, Fr Laurentin did not include this incident in his "Chronological Corpus of the Messages,"[177] and attempted to justify himself regarding it as follows: "I will not go back on this story which has been badly attested. I had suggested to Father Bubalo to eliminate this confusing and insignificant event from his book."[178]

The Medjugorje Culture and Folklore

It is important to put the visions and the visionaries in the context of the local culture of which they are part. Fr Sivric speaks of a very specific culture and folklore in the area, one which is quite credulous in believing tales of miraculous events, and thus very open to the possibility of visions. Farther on he speaks of a "tendency to dramatize" in the culture. It is worth noting, too, that the local villages had their own "prophets" and "prophetesses," whose predictions were remembered and passed on orally within the community. During the summer of 1986, Fr Sivric heard of a local prophetess, who had apparently often said: "Woe to the people of Medjugorje when they have bad priests!" Thus, when the accounts of the visions began to circulate, they found a ready local audience happy to absorb them and then pass them on to others. This attitude also influenced individuals who claimed that they too were seeing visions.[179]

The question of alleged cures at Medjugorje will be dealt with in a subsequent chapter, but there is also apparently a cultural factor to take into account in assessing these claims. Paolo Apolito, an Italian researcher, makes the following comment on this point, arguing that the visions at Medjugorje became mixed up with elements of local medicinal folklore: "At Medjugorje … an entire pre-existing tradition of popular medicine connected to poultices of plants and flowers mixed with earth was revived and found new efficacy through the phenomena of the apparitions." He then cites instances where pilgrims seem to have relied as much for relief from illness on infusions of soil and grass found on Podbrdo, as on prayers to the Gospa.[180]

Questionable Content of the Messages

It can certainly be argued that the content of the Medjugorje messages leaves a lot to be desired. Some Medjugorje supporters have claimed that they have a cohesiveness and spirituality which could only have come from heaven, but it is a mystery how anyone who has looked at them in any detail can seriously maintain that argument. The fact is that there is nothing inherently unlikely about the proposition that the majority of the messages do not have a supernatural origin. Regarding their intrinsic nature, it is certainly true to say that they have a quality of "sameness" about them, which of itself is highly suspect, to say nothing of the questionable theology some of them contain.

There is an element of flattery in the following message, from 1 March 1984, the idea that the parish had been "specially chosen", an approach which is completely foreign to the genuine messages of Our Lady: "Dear children! *I have chosen this parish in a special way and I wish to lead it.* I am keeping it in love and I want everyone to be mine. Thank you for your response this evening. I wish that you will always be in greater numbers with me and my Son. Every Thursday I will speak a special message for you."

This idea is repeated in the following message, from 15 November 1984: "Dear children! *You are a chosen people and God has given you great graces.* You are not aware of the importance of every message I am giving you. Now I only wish to say: Pray, pray, pray! I do not know what else to tell you because I love you and wish that in prayer you come to know my love and the love of God. Thank you for your response to my call."[181]

The idea that the Blessed Virgin would continually thank people for responding to her call, is, of course, completely untenable. It suggests that people are thereby conferring a favor on her, and as such, it is without precedent in any of the approved apparitions.

The following message, from 21 February 1985, seems to disclose a rather petulant Gospa, who will go away and sulk in the corner if her demands are not met: "Dear children! From day to day I have been appealing to you for renewal and prayer in the parish. But you are not responding. Today I am appealing to you for the last time. This is the season of Lent, and you, as a parish in Lent, should be moved to love by my appeal. *If you are not, I do not wish to give you any more messages.* Thank you for your response to my call."[182]

Theologically Suspect Messages

Some of the messages are also theologically suspect, or at least ambiguous. For example, the message dated 24 July 1982 is as follows: "The body, drawn from the earth, decomposes after death. *It never comes back to life again.* Man receives a transfigured body."[183]

While it is true to say that our bodies will be transfigured at the resurrection, it is clearly not true that they will never come back to life again, since this would imply that the same bodies that we have on earth are not part of the resurrection of the body. That this is not the case is clear from scripture, (Cf. Rom 8:11; Phil 3:21), and was also proclaimed at the Fourth Lateran Council as follows: "They will arise with their bodies which they have now."[184]

Similarly, this message, dated 31 August 1982, calls into question Mary's mediatory role: "*I do not dispose all graces.* I receive from God what I obtain through prayer. God has placed His complete trust in me."[185]

This first sentence is clearly contrary to the generally accepted Church teaching regarding Our Lady, that she is indeed the Mediatrix of all graces.[186] In contrast, this is what St Louis de Montfort, the great Marian saint, had to say on this point: "God has entrusted Mary with the keeping, the administration and distribution of all His graces, so that all His graces and gifts pass through her hands."[187] This part of the message is also at odds with the experience of St Catherine Labouré at Rue du Bac, during the apparition on 27 November 1830, when she saw Mary standing on a globe with rings on her fingers flashing with light rays, which she was explicitly told represented graces.

Surely, this "message," of itself, disqualifies Medjugorje from being seriously regarded as a supernatural event?

There is also an unhealthy preoccupation with the devil in many of the messages, a preoccupation which is absent in the approved Marian apparitions. Satan is mentioned in over sixty of the messages listed between 1984 and 2004.[188] This appears to be more an indication of the dualistic tendency already noted in Croatian popular religion, than evidence of truly supernatural messages.

A particular point to note is that the Wisdom literature in the Bible has a number of passages which are critical of excessive talk, a quality which certainly seems to characterize the messages from the Gospa. For example, Proverbs 17:27 tells us that: "He who restrains his words has knowledge, " while Ecclesiastes 5:2 is even more explicit: "Be not rash with your mouth, nor let your heart be hasty to utter a word before God, ... therefore let your words be few." Mary's words in both the Gospels and in her approved apparitions have generally been few but to the point.

Sometimes, too, the encounters with the Gospa could descend to the level of farce. Mrs Patricia Waters, an ex-promoter of Medjugorje, describes how she was present at one of these in the early eighties, during which Jakov asked the Gospa about a football match, and how his favorite team had done. This caused the other visionaries to burst out laughing. Wayne Weible confirms that this bizarre incident did in fact take place.[189]

Fr Jordan Aumann OP, in his Spiritual Theology, makes the following general comment on the above points: "Revelations concerning merely curious or useless matters should be rejected as not divine. The same is to be said of those that are detailed, lengthy, and filled with a superfluity of proofs and reasons. Divine revelations are generally brief, clear, and precise." [190]

Themes of the Messages

It is possible to discern, from a very early stage, a predominance of Franciscan themes in the messages. For example, the emphasis on Franciscan prayer formulas, such as the seven Our Fathers, Hail Marys, and Glorias, an old Franciscan devotion, is evident, as is the stress on fasting on bread and water.[191] An important part of the worldwide message being propagated in the name of Medjugorje has been one of "prayer, conversion, and fasting." Undoubtedly, this focus on such traditional Catholic practices was a great help, in the early days, in convincing many that Medjugorje might well be genuine. But as we have seen, these elements were conspicuous by their absence from the messages of the first week or so—in fact, the message of the first week was that there was no message!

And specifically regarding fasting, Fr Laurentin is quite clear that this did not come about as a result of a request of the Gospa. He tells us that it "began as an initiative of the parish priest: there was not as yet a message from the Virgin. How did he get this idea? Perhaps it was inspiration but above all he was basing himself on an ancient tradition of Bosnia-Hercegovina."

Apparently, following his experience on 2 July, when Fr Zovko claimed he had heard a voice telling him to "protect the children" and had subsequently preached to his parishioners, he had challenged them thus: "Are you ready to pray and fast (for three days)?" Their response had been strongly affirmative.[192]

The Duration of the Approved Apparitions

There is also the problem of the sheer volume of messages, as well as the length of time the visions have apparently been continuing. Most recognized apparitions have begun and ended in a relatively short time. As we have seen, all the words of the approved modern apparitions come to no more than about a dozen pages of text at most. Why after being so sparing of words in the past, to the point of taciturnity, why should Mary suddenly become so expansive and talkative? It just doesn't make sense.

At Guadalupe, Mary appeared only four times to Juan Diego, while at Rue du Bac, Catherine Labouré was privileged with only three major apparitions. At La Salette, Mary appeared only once to the two children, while at Lourdes she appeared eighteen times to Bernadette. Both Pontmain and Knock involved only a single apparition, while at Fatima, Mary appeared on six occasions. The number of apparitions at Beauraing was something over thirty, and at Banneux, eight. Thus, the average number of apparitions was only just over eight, and their longest duration was less than six months, in the case of Fatima. Although it is true that Mary appeared to Sr Lucia on a number of occasions in later years, it is clear that these apparitions were of a different order and thus were not a part of the original series of apparitions, although they were organically linked to them, and represent important developments of the message of Fatima.

Thus, the norm for approved apparitions is one which has, for each particular place, a number for apparitions usually in single figures, and a duration of weeks, or possibly months, but not years.

The Medjugorje Visions and False Prophets

Contrast this with Medjugorje, where it is claimed that the Blessed Virgin has been appearing daily to at least some of the visionaries for nearly twenty-five years—that is, over eight thousand times. What this means in practice, if these events are genuine, is that for some reason Mary has abandoned the approach she has previously taken, of appearing only a relatively small number of times and over a short period, and instead has been appearing virtually "on demand." As detailed above, the average number of appearances for genuine Marian apparitions has been in single figures—but if Medjugorje is authentic, then suddenly this average has been boosted by a factor of a thousand! And there seems to be no end in sight to all this activity.

Does this seem probable? Would God change, in such a dramatic fashion, a method of approaching humanity which has been in place for hundreds of years? Is it not rather evidence, as was the case with the large numbers of false prophets who contended with the genuine prophets sent by God in the Old Testament, that these messages are not supernatural?

This is evident, for example, from the fact that Elijah had to face the false prophets of Baal in his struggle against the paganism encouraged by the wicked king of Israel, Ahab, and his wife Jezebel. It is significant that there were four hundred prophets of Baal ranged against the solitary Elijah (1 Kings 18). Likewise, the prophet Micaiah had to face a further four hundred false prophets who foretold victory for Ahab and Jehoshaphat, the king of Judah, if they attacked Ramoth in Gilead. But Micaiah said that it had been revealed to him that a deceptive spirit had been put into the mouths of the false prophets, in order that Ahab should be led to his death, as subsequently happened (1 Kings 22:5–38).

Later on, the prophet Jeremiah complained about the false prophets he had to face (Jer 14:13–15), and similar condemnations are found in Ezekiel against both male and female false prophets (Ezek 13:2–16). Thus, there is nothing new about false prophecies or false messages being propagated. In addition, as the prophet Isaiah indicated (59:1), God's hand is not shortened, that is, he does not have to struggle or shout to get his message across: he is omnipotent. This point is emphatically made in another passage from Isaiah: "For as the rain and the snow come down from heaven, and return not thither but water the earth, making it bring forth and sprout, giving seed to the sower and bread to the eater, so shall my word be that goes out from my mouth; it shall not return to me empty, but it shall accomplish that which I purpose, and prosper in the thing for which I sent it." (Isa 55:10–11)

God's "word," in the form of the approved Marian apparitions, has been extraordinarily fruitful, and with a minimum of words and appearances. Mary appears once, and for a few hours, at Pontmain and Knock—and probably for no more than half an hour at La Salette—and three great pilgrimage sites spring up: she allegedly appears thousands of times at Medjugorje, and even after more than twenty years, the official spokesmen of the local Church, the successive bishops of Mostar, are still not convinced that the visions are truly of divine origin.

Why so many Messages?

Why are there all these messages then, if they don't tell us anything new? The simplest reason would appear to be that, if these alleged visions do not come from God, then unless there was this element of repetition they would quickly have been forgotten.

Vicka spoke about this point in one of her conversations with Fr Bubalo. He asked her why she thought the Gospa was appearing to the visionaries for so long a time, and she responded by saying that the Virgin had said that "this was her last appearance on earth," and that she couldn't "accomplish what she wants so fast either." Fr Bubalo then asked her to clarify what she meant by that, to which Vicka replied: "Why, think about it: how would all this seem if the

Virgin had appeared only ten or twenty times, and then disappeared. Why, in the hustle and bustle it would have been forgotten by now. Who would believe that she was here?"[193]

Indeed, we have to question whether people would still be going to Medjugorje if the visions had stopped very quickly. As we have seen—according to clear taped testimony—this is what was supposed to have happened, but instead, contrary to the negative verdict of the successive local bishops, people continue to go there in large numbers, primarily because it is alleged that Mary continues to appear to some of the visionaries every day. Without these daily visions, the whole phenomenon would no doubt have dried up and been long forgotten by now—but instead it is promoted as vigorously as ever, regardless of the problems this is causing for recognized shrines which promote approved messages.

Problems with the Franciscans

The Holy See's reaction to Medjugorje at the beginning was one of extreme caution and indeed suspicion, as is evident from the following remarks of Cardinal Seper, the then head of the Congregation for the Doctrine of the Faith, which were made in 1981. He was asked to comment about Medjugorje, and, given that he was a Croat and was fully aware of the religious situation in the country, his remarks are doubly significant: "When the Franciscans obey the decrees of the Holy See then I shall consider this phenomenon, not before. For me, the sign of obedience is the sign of a genuine Catholic faith. Its absence in Medjugorje on the part of the Franciscans, its sponsors and advocates, renders the whole enterprise suspect."[194]

Indeed, as Joachim Bouflet points out, obedience is one of the main criteria for the proper discernment of private revelations— that is, obedience to the legitimate pastors of the Church, and particularly to the local bishop of the diocese where the alleged revelations have taken place. This obedience is linked to humility, and without these two central virtues there can be no question of an authentic private revelation. Padre, now Saint, Pio is a good example of a model religious who submitted without murmur to the disciplinary measures taken against him, even when it could be said that he was treated unjustly.[195]

According to Mrs Patricia Waters, in April 1984 she was present in the sacristy with about fifty other people waiting for the visionaries to enter, when Fr Slavko Barbaric came in and said: "Unless some of you go out of this room, the apparition will not take place." This was the point at which she began to have suspicions about the whole Medjugorje edifice. How could Fr Barbaric possibly decide on the conditions for Our Lady to appear? Her own explanation for the demeanor of the visionaries at these times was that she thought that they might well have been hypnotized in some way.[196]

Dangerous Manipulation and More Problems

There is also evidence of a tendency on the part of some of the Franciscans to induce other young people to have visions. Louis Bélanger wrote to Fr Laurentin about an incident, in January 1985, when Fr Slavko Barbaric showed him a video in which Fr Ivica Vego was with some youngsters from a village near Medjugorje. He was apparently encouraging them to "see" the Gospa, insistently asking them if they could see her and giving them writing materials to note any messages they might receive. Bélanger comments that: "It was in the purest tradition of the occult. We know that those who induce automatic writing in young people can cause them more or less permanent damage in their identity formation."

It does not seem that either Fr Barbaric, a psychotherapist, or Fr Vego, were concerned about this danger.[197]

This incident is reminiscent of an experiment conducted by the writer Carlos Staehlin, as reported by Fr Karl Rahner, on six youths aged between fifteen and eighteen. They were told to imagine that a battle between medieval warriors was going on above a tree; two apparently saw or heard nothing, two saw the battle and the last two both saw and heard it, with their reports apparently agreeing.[198] Staehlin's experiment was clearly hazardous. He deliberately encouraged the youths to fantasize in what could have been a psychologically dangerous manner, to say nothing of inviting a possible diabolical intervention. Comparisons with experiments with "Ouija" boards, and all the hazards involved in such matters, come to mind.

Fr Sivric tells us how Bishop Zanic had to deal with problems caused by Fr Barbaric, who had been the acting parochial vicar in

Medjugorje for two years, before being transferred to another parish in 1985. Despite this he had continued to visit Medjugorje on a daily basis, and the Bishop had threatened to revoke his canonical jurisdiction if he did not stop these visits. Fr Barbaric then embarked on a tour of countries in Western Europe, but on his return continued to visit Medjugorje daily, in complete disregard of the Bishop's orders.[199]

Ivan's Threatening Letter

Prior to this, as Fr Sivric reports, Bishop Zanic had received what can only be described as a threatening letter from Ivan Dragicevic, dated 21 June 1983. In this, he claimed he had received a message from the Gospa, in which she demanded the Bishop's "immediate conversion on [sic] the happenings in the Medjugorje parish before it is too late," and warned him not to, "cause nor incite dissension among the clergy," nor emphasize the "negative side" of the visions. This was to be a "last warning" that he should "convert and change" otherwise the "verdict" of the Gospa and her Son would "reach him."

Does it need to be pointed out that it is completely beyond the bounds of credibility to believe that the Blessed Virgin Mary could possibly have given such a message?

Although it was established that this letter was written in Ivan Dragicevic's hand, it does not seem at all likely that he actually composed it.[200]

To conclude, the evidence examined in this chapter has brought to light many of the serious problems associated with Medjugorje, including both the content and duration of the messages as they began to develop after the initial visions of the first week, when effectively no messages of any substance were given by the Gospa. It has also become quite clear that both the visionaries, and the Franciscans who have been most involved with them, have emerged with serious question marks as to their credibility. But for the most part these negative points have not been disclosed as part of the publicity surrounding Medjugorje. Instead, it has been presented as perfectly acceptable in a religious sense, and this is the impression that most of the pilgrims to Medjugorje have received.

9

Medjugorje:
Messages and Secrets

The Origin of the Messages

As we have seen, by mid-1982 Bishop Zanic was quite clear that the visions and the messages associated with them were not genuine, and this was the conclusion he steadfastly maintained from this point onwards. In the same way, his successor, Bishop Peric, has held to a similar stance to this day. If this is the case, that the messages are not genuine, and all the evidence suggests that this is the case, then we have to ask how these communications arose.

Mart Bax, a professor of political anthropology at Vrije University in Amsterdam, outlines what he believes actually went on. Bax carried out more than a decade of research in Medjugorje from 1983 onwards, spending several weeks there each year, including during the war years in the early nineties. Although not a Catholic, he published the results of his research in *Medjugorje: Religion, Politics, and Violence in Rural Bosnia,* a book which makes compelling reading, and gives a unique non-religious perspective on local society in the area. The relevant points of his research will be dealt with in subsequent chapters.[201]

Basing himself on information received from a close relative of one of the visionaries, Bax says that in late 1982, they began to go back to Podbrdo at regular intervals, rather than have their visions in the church, thus drawing large numbers of pilgrims with them. This caused tensions between the visionaries and the Franciscans, which broke out into open confrontation in the spring of 1983. The cause of this dispute was a new message from the Gospa which appeared one day on the church notice board, urging the people to "turn completely to God and His sacraments. I want more and more of you to always come here and be with me and my son in God's house."

According to Bax, when the visionaries read these words, they "were totally taken aback. Indeed, one of them got furious, but his elder brother—a key informant of mine—persuaded him to keep calm and quiet." This "message" was a clear challenge to the religious position of the visionaries within the community, since it was focusing on the exclusive role of the clergy with regard to the sacraments. In response, for the next couple of weeks, the visionaries issued any messages from the Gospa directly from their homes, and in the evenings went to Podbrdo rather than the parish church, where "their seats remained vacant." This tussle between the visionaries and the Franciscans undoubtedly went unnoticed by the majority of pilgrims, and after a while, things returned to normal with the visionaries back in their places for evening Mass, although they now took it in turns to appear.[202]

Fr Rudo Franken tells us that in March 1985, Bishop Zanic wrote to Fr Tomislav Pervan, who at that time was the parish priest at Medjugorje, setting out a list of demands which included preventing the visionaries from appearing in public, and stopping any of the visions taking place in the parish church, or in any building adjacent to it. These demands were partly met in that the visions no longer took place in the "apparition chapel," which was actually the sacristy, and moved instead to the presbytery. This took place at the suggestion of Archbishop Franic of Split. But as Fr Franken further points out, what sort of figure does this turn the Blessed Virgin into, that she is unable to decide herself where to appear?[203] How can this possibly be consistent with how Our Lady has appeared in her approved apparitions? Does this not further indicate that Medjugorje cannot be of supernatural origin?

The Nature of the Medjugorje Messages

Despite the fact that the messages emanating from Medjugorje have been coming out now for nearly twenty-five years, and that this is, in reality, one of the major factors arguing *against* their authenticity, paradoxically, it is precisely this factor which has so greatly impressed many Medjugorje supporters. The argument is put forward that surely "these children" could not possibly have maintained this performance if the whole thing were not genuine. This ignores the fact that in the first place we are mostly not dealing with children, but rather young adults, who now—a quarter of a century later—have fully grown up.

Thus, so far, all the evidence points to the conclusion that Medjugorje is not authentically supernatural, but rather, that the whole situation was thrust on the visionaries, because within a matter of days thousands of people were thronging the hillside, as the movement quickly gathered momentum. Within the first week or so, they had to make a crucial decision. It is clear from the "three more days" statements on the original tape recordings that they expected the visions to end shortly. But by then an expectation had built up, and it seems as though all the major participants were largely swept along by events and perhaps forced to react as well as they could to the growing crowds and a hostile government.

No Turning Back

It may be that after the visionaries had come down to the church and nothing happened, they then felt obliged, with a large expectant crowd before them, to pretend that once again they had seen something. Or alternatively, those involved may have very quickly realized that unless they continued to act as though they were having visions, the whole thing would just fizzle out—or, more seriously, that some of the villagers would turn against them. The expectations of the local populace had been raised, and they would not take kindly to being fooled. In the volatile and brutal culture of that area, any reaction against them would have no doubt been violent.

Thus, as we have seen, the evidence presented so far strongly suggests that after the first week or so, the pressure was on the visionaries to carry on asserting their conviction that the Blessed Virgin really was appearing. Once they had given in to this situation, and continued to issue messages, there could be no turning back without great danger. And, of course, with time, and with the growing number of pilgrims, to admit that the whole thing was not genuine would become increasingly difficult, particularly when the community as a whole had effectively committed themselves to the visions. As the years went by, and the hotels, pizza parlors, restaurants and piety stalls established themselves in Medjugorje, the local population progressively acquired as much of a vested interest in the continuation of the visions as did the visionaries themselves. The visions had brought unprecedented prosperity to the area, and the truth is that if the visionaries or the Franciscans had admitted that the whole phenomenon was not genuine, as Michael Davies points out, they would probably have been lynched.[204]

Wayne Weible describes the situation five years after the visions began, in June 1986:

> Away from Saint James Church, new buildings dotted the landscape. Commercialism grew at a rampant pace, and taxis roamed like a swarm of bees over decrepit bridges and dirt roads that were never intended to support such traffic. The roads were filled with pilgrims, and many villagers were busy adding extensions of rooms to their dwellings to house more pilgrims. For many villagers, the changes were uncomfortable annoyances, offset only by the good fruits of the apparitions.[205]

But no doubt other villagers were quite content with this new influx of wealth into their community.

The overall situation may be even more complicated in that the visionaries may have somehow managed to convince themselves that, although the later visions and messages were not genuine, the whole enterprise was justified because of the "good fruits" which were coming from it. That is, the visionaries may have become convinced that they really did see the Gospa during the first week, and used this memory as a rationalization for what later went on.

Archbishop Franic intervenes

The Archbishop of Split, Frane Franic, visited Medjugorje early on, and after seeing the visionaries during an ecstasy, and interviewing them, became convinced "as a private Christian ... of their authenticity." It seems that he was swayed, too, by the enormous crowds at Medjugorje, and certainly, despite the fact that he had no direct jurisdiction in the Mostar-Duvno diocese, he apparently implied such authority in his public remarks.

In addition, it seems that, during a December 1984 visit to Medjugorje, he went so far as to consult the Gospa about some of his own affairs, through the visionary Marija Pavlovic. As Fr Sivric comments: "It is both irritating and deplorable to watch him treat the Virgin Mary like a fortune teller."[206] Thus, it is clear that Archbishop Franic was an early, enthusiastic, and uncritical supporter of Medjugorje, and it seems that he played a role amongst fellow ecclesiastics not unlike that played by Fr Laurentin with regard to other theologians. Before his visit to Medjugorje in December 1984, he had been to Rome, and had "discussed the whole matter with John Paul II." He also tells us that, "many are calling me from Italy and France and different journalists come to see me."[207]

More Negative Evidence

Bishop Zanic issued a declaration on Medjugorje on 25 July 1987, in which after detailing his own work, and that of the various commissions, he made this heartfelt plea:

> It was said that Our Lady started to appear at Podbrdo on Mount Crnica. When the police stopped people going there, she appeared in people's homes, on fences, in fields, in vineyards and tobacco fields. She appeared in the church, on the altar, in the sacristy, in the choir loft, on the roof, in the bell tower, on the roads, on the road to Cerno, in a car, on a bus, in schools, at several places in Mostar and Sarajevo, in monasteries in Zagreb, in Varazdin, in Switzerland, in Italy, then again at Podbrdo, in Krizevac, in the parish, on the presbytery and so on. This does not list even half the number of locations where apparitions were alleged to have taken place, so that a sober man who venerates Our Lady must ask: "My Lady, what are they making of you?"[208]

Meanwhile, Mirjana Dragicevic had made it known, on 25 December 1982, that she would no longer be receiving daily visions, and from now on would only see the Gospa once a year, on her birthday. She also claimed to have received the last secret of the ten which had been allegedly given to her by Mary. As we will see, Mirjana also said that there would be no more visions of Jesus or Mary on earth. There were also claims of secrets being received on a miraculous sheet of paper made of an indescribable material. Later, another account emerged in which the secret was now in a special code, which would only be revealed when the paper was given to a particular priest who would have the grace to understand it. In December 1982, it was stated that the first of the secrets would soon be revealed.[209]

After his release from prison in February 1983, Fr Zovko was sent to a different parish, leaving Fr Vlasic in charge of the visionaries. In December of that same year, the latter wrote to the Pope outlining events in his parish. This letter claimed that the visions at Medjugorje were the "last apparitions of the Blessed Virgin on earth," and that this was "why they are lasting so long and occurring so frequently." The visionaries also reiterated their claims that they had received numerous secrets, and spoke of the "visible" sign that would be left at Medjugorje.[210]

Summarizing the Situation

At this stage, it is probably good to summarize some of the main points discussed previously regarding the visions, so that the reader has clearly in mind the grave difficulties associated with accepting Medjugorje as genuine.

Firstly, there are the problems regarding the difficult family background of a number of the visionaries. Then there is the question of possible drug use by some of them, which obviously complicates the discernment of their experiences. We also have the inconsistent phenomena surrounding the appearances of the Gospa, such as the light which preceded her, and the way the Vision emerged from this light, as well the tendency for the Vision to appear and disappear haphazardly. This contrasts strongly with the way Our Lady appeared in her recognized apparitions at Lourdes, Rue du Bac and Fatima, and points strongly to a non-divine source. Then, there are the unthinkable things said or done by the Vision—that, for example, the visionaries saw it holding something like a baby which was then covered up, or that the Vision's hands were trembling, or that they were allowed to touch and kiss the Vision, which was laughing—or equally, the contents of Ivan's letter with their threat that Bishop Zanic should "convert and change" or face the consequences. All of these things, amongst others, raise very serious doubts about the supernatural authenticity of the alleged visions.

Similarly, the fact that the Gospa never spoke until one of the visionaries asked questions, and that there was no message of any substance during the first week, such that Fr Zovko was forced to ask why she had appeared at all if this was the case, and then remark that the whole thing looked like clowning to him: all of this is completely out of line with what has happened during the authentic apparitions of Mary. In addition, we have the concerns raised by Fr Zovko that the visionaries might well be seeing Satan, because of the amount of cursing that was still going on in the locality, even as the Vision was supposedly appearing.

There is also the problem of the Gospa being asked to do what the visionaries or Fr Zovko wanted, specifically to appear in the parish church. Or the idea that Mary would continue appearing to the visionaries for as long as they wanted. Since when have authentic visions of the Blessed Virgin ever been "arranged" like this? Then we have Fr Zovko's negative conclusion at the end of the first week, that the Gospa's message was only meant for the visionaries, followed by his swift about-turn to support them, possibly on the strength of the idea that he had heard a locution of his own.

There must also be serious reservations about the conduct of those most involved in spreading the messages of Medjugorje, as for example in the way that Fr Laurentin altered the message about the "unbelieving Judases". In fact, just how reliable are any of the messages, given the ample evidence suggesting that they do not have a heavenly origin? And of course, the admission that there were only supposed to be "three more days" of visions, that on Friday 3 July 1981 the last appearance of the Gospa should have taken place, is absolutely fatal to the idea that any of the subsequent messages are genuine.

In this chapter, then, apart from the above general considerations, we have seen how the evidence suggests that Medjugorje, after the first week, developed as a "pious deception," which could be justified because of the good fruits that the pilgrims were experiencing. But as we have also seen, since then Medjugorje has grown enormously, and taken on a life of its own, to the great detriment of genuine Marian shrines.

10

Fatima and its Effects

The Fatima Apparitions – May to August 1917

Having looked in detail, then, at the events of the first week at Medjugorje and their aftermath, we are in a better position to contrast this with the basic details about what happened at Fatima. This should be regarded as the most important Marian apparition, primarily because of its unique approval by and association with the papacy from its inception, culminating in the exceptional developments in the pontificate of John Paul II, as will be discussed in a later chapter.

Fatima occurred just as the Russian Revolution was unfolding during World War I. As the war dragged on, by 1916, Russia was in a state of crisis, and this gave the Communist revolutionaries under Lenin their chance: just as the Blessed Virgin was appearing in Fatima, between May and October 1917, they were gradually positioning themselves to take power, which they did in November 1917. During the war, Pope Benedict XV made repeated but forlorn pleas for peace, and finally, in May 1917, he made a direct appeal to Mary to intercede for peace in the world. The response was her first appearance at Fatima just over a week later.[211]

Portugal was suffering greatly during this period under an anti-clerical republican regime, which freely persecuted the Church. At this time Fatima was just a small village, situated about seventy miles north of Lisbon; the three children to whom the Blessed Virgin appeared were Lucia dos Santos, aged ten, and her cousins Francisco and Jacinta Marto, brother and sister, aged eight and seven respectively. As already noted, in the spring of 1916, the three children had their first joint encounter with a being who would later identify himself as the "Angel of Portugal." This angel appeared to them twice more with a message emphasizing the necessity of prayer and reparation. These visits prepared the children for their meetings with Mary from May to October of the following year.[212]

The first of these took place on 13 May 1917, when the three children saw the Blessed Virgin at the Cova da Iria near Fatima. She smiled and told them not to be afraid, before saying that she was from heaven. Lucia then asked her what she wanted: "I have come to ask you to come here for six months in succession on the thirteenth day of the month at this same hour. Then I will tell you who I am and what I want. And I shall return here yet a seventh time." The Blessed Virgin finished with a request: "Say the Rosary every day, to bring peace to the world and the end of the war." With that, she began to rise into the air, moving towards the east until she disappeared.

At the next apparition on June 13, the Blessed Virgin again asked Lucia to pray the rosary every day. In reply, Lucia asked her to take them to heaven, but was told that although Jacinta and Francisco would shortly go to heaven, Lucia's task was to promote devotion to her Immaculate Heart throughout the world.[213]

The Vision of Hell

On 13 July, Mary again asked Lucia to continue to pray the Rosary every day in order to obtain peace for the world and the end of the war. Lucia asked her who she was and for a miracle so everyone would believe: "Continue to come here every month. In October, I will tell you who I am and what I want, and I will perform a miracle for all to see and believe." After this, Mary opened her hands and rays of light from them seemed to penetrate the earth so that the children saw a terrifying vision of hell; this was the first part of the "secret" of Fatima, and was not revealed until much later. She then related the second part of the secret as follows:

> You have seen hell where the souls of poor sinners go. To save them, God wishes to establish in the world devotion to my Immaculate Heart. If what I say to you is done, many souls will be saved and there will be peace. The war is going to end; but if people do not cease of-

fending God, a worse one will break out during the pontificate of Pius XI. When you see a night illumined by an unknown light, know that this is the great sign given you by God that he is about to punish the world for its crimes, by means of war, famine, and persecutions of the Church and of the Holy Father.

To prevent this, I shall come to ask for the consecration of Russia to my Immaculate Heart, and the Communion of Reparation on the First Saturdays. If my requests are heeded, Russia will be converted, and there will be peace; if not, she will spread her errors throughout the world, causing wars and persecutions of the Church. The good will be martyred, the Holy Father will have much to suffer, various nations will be annihilated. In the end, my Immaculate Heart will triumph. The Holy Father will consecrate Russia to me and she will be converted, and a period of peace will be granted to the world.

The first two parts of the secret only became publicly known in 1942, while the third part was only recently divulged, in June 2000.

The children were kidnapped on the morning of 13 August by the Mayor of Vila Nova de Ourem and interrogated about the secret; but despite his threats and promises of money, they refused to divulge it. In the afternoon, they were moved to the local prison and threatened with death but determined that they would die rather than reveal the secret. The mayor admitted defeat and they were released. On August 19, Lucia, Francisco and Jacinta were together at a place called Valinhos, near Fatima, where they again saw the Blessed Virgin, who spoke to Lucia: "Go again to the Cova da Iria on the 13th and continue to say the Rosary every day." Mary also repeated her promise to perform a miracle so all would believe, and again asked for prayer and sacrifice for sinners.[214]

The September and October Apparitions, 1917

On 13 September, the Blessed Virgin once more spoke to Lucia, asking her to continue to pray the Rosary in order to obtain the end of the war, again promising a miracle in October so that all would believe. This proclamation of a public miracle naturally caused the most intense speculation throughout Portugal.

On October 13, Mary appeared before them for the last time, as Lucia asked what she wanted: "I want to tell you that a chapel is to be built here in my honor. I am the Lady of the Rosary. Continue always to pray the Rosary every day. The war is going to end, and the soldiers will soon return to their homes." She reported too that Mary grew very sad and said: "Do not offend the Lord our God any more, because He is already so much offended." Then rising into the air and opening her hands towards the sun, growing more brilliant as she did, she disappeared, to be replaced by various visions of the Holy Family seen only by the children. At the same time, the crowd of 70,000 saw a true miracle. The black clouds parted, and the sun became visible as a dull gray disc that could be looked at directly quite easily. It then began to gyrate and send out different colored rays of light, before appearing to descend towards the ground, such that many of those present thought it was the end of the world. Other people witnessed the solar miracle from a distance thus ruling out the possibility of any type of collective hallucination.[215]

Francisco and Jacinta were amongst the victims of the influenza epidemic which swept Europe in the autumn of 1918, just as the war was finishing. Francisco received his first Communion, and on the next day, 4 April 1919, he died. Jacinta had to endure much suffering as various attempts were made to treat a painful chest abscess which developed following pneumonia. She finally died on 20 February of the following year, 1920.[216]

Later Apparitions to Sr Lucia

Lucia was sent away to school, later becoming a religious sister. On 10 December 1925, while at the convent in Pontevedra, Spain, she saw a further apparition, this time of the Blessed Virgin with the Child Jesus. Mary told Sr Lucia to announce that she promised all the graces necessary for salvation to those who, on the first Saturday of five consecutive months, confessed, received Holy Communion, recited five decades of the rosary, and meditated on the rosary for fifteen minutes, all with the intention of making reparation to her Immaculate Heart.

On 13 June 1929, Sr Lucia, while at prayer in the convent chapel at Tuy, to which she had transferred, saw another apparition, this time a representation of the Holy Trinity. She also heard the Blessed Virgin speak to her, asking that the Pope, in union with all the bishops of the world, make the consecration of Russia to her

Immaculate Heart which she had spoken of during the July 1917 apparition: "The moment has come in which God asks the Holy Father, in union with all the Bishops in the world, to make the consecration of Russia to my Immaculate Heart, promising to save it by this means. There are so many souls whom the Justice of God condemns for sins committed against me, that I have come to ask reparation: sacrifice yourself for this intention and pray."[217]

The Church, meanwhile, had maintained silence about the apparitions during the years from 1917, and it wasn't until May 1922 that Bishop Correia da Silva issued a pastoral letter on the subject, indicating that he would set up a commission of enquiry. In 1930, he issued another pastoral letter on the apparitions, which, after recounting the events at Fatima, contained the following brief but very important statement.

> In virtue of considerations made known, and others which for reasons of brevity we omit; humbly invoking the Divine Spirit and placing ourselves under the protection of the most Holy Virgin, and after hearing the opinions of our Rev. Advisors in this diocese, we hereby: 1. Declare worthy of belief, the visions of the shepherd children in the Cova da Iria, parish of Fatima, in this diocese, from the 13th May to 13th October, 1917. 2. Permit officially the cult of Our Lady of Fatima.[218]

Sr Lucia and the Consecration of Russia

In September 1935, the remains of Jacinta were removed to Fatima, and, on opening the coffin, her face was found to be intact. This led the Bishop to ask Sr Lucia to write what she knew of Jacinta, and this is how she came to compose her *First Memoir,* under obedience, which recounted the basic facts about Fatima, and which was ready by Christmas 1935.

In passing, it might be remarked how this contrasts strongly with the actions of the Medjugorje visionaries and their supporters, who, purely on their own initiative, have propagated accounts of their visions and publicized themselves worldwide, without any reference to the local Ordinary.

Following the outbreak of the Spanish Civil War, apparently a fulfillment of the prophecy about Russia spreading its errors, Sr Lucia's confessor, Fr Gonzalves, wrote to her asking what should be done. She replied in May 1936, and again pointed out that it was necessary that the Holy Father make the consecration of Russia, before describing how she had asked Jesus in prayer why he would not convert Russia without it. She received the following answer as an interior locution: "Because I want My whole Church to acknowledge that consecration as a triumph of the Immaculate Heart of Mary, so that it may extend its cult later on, and put the devotion to this Immaculate Heart beside the devotion to My Sacred Heart."

To this, Sr Lucia replied: "But my God, the Holy Father probably won't believe me, unless You Yourself move him with a special inspiration." She then heard the following answer: "The Holy Father. Pray very much for the Holy Father. He will do it, but it will be very late. Nevertheless the Immaculate Heart of Mary will save Russia. It has been entrusted to her." After consulting a colleague, Fr Gonzalves wrote to Bishop Correia da Silva urging him to contact Rome on the matter of the consecration of Russia, and this the Bishop did early in 1937.[219]

The Portuguese Bishops Consecrate their Country

In 1931, the Portuguese bishops had collectively consecrated Portugal to Mary's Immaculate Heart, and in 1936, at the site of the apparitions, with the prospect of the country being afflicted with Communism because of the conflict raging in neighboring Spain, they made a vow to organize a national pilgrimage to Fatima if Portugal was delivered from this fate. Their country was indeed preserved from Communism, and as a result they were able to return in May 1938 to fulfill their vow and renew the previous consecration, being joined by half a million ordinary Portuguese. Following a spiritual retreat, under Fr Pinto, the spiritual director of Alexandrina da Costa, a Portuguese mystic beatified in 2004, the Portuguese bishops also petitioned the Pope, asking that he consecrate the whole world to the Immaculate Heart of Mary, so that it could be saved from disaster, just as Portugal had been delivered from the threat of Communism.

On 25 January 1938, a strange light filled the skies of northern, as well as, most unusually, southern Europe. It was described as a particularly brilliant display of the aurora borealis, but Sr Lucia

realized that it was the "unknown light" foretold by the Blessed
Virgin during the July apparition. Sr Lucia apparently informed the
Bishop of the importance of this sign and again referred to it in her
third memoir.[220]

Sr Lucia and the Consecration of 1942

In December 1940, Sr Lucia, under obedience, also wrote to the
new Pope, Pius XII, telling him that part of the secret that concerned the consecration of Russia and the Communions of reparation. In this she asked the Pope to extend the First Saturdays
devotion to the whole world, and revealed that Jesus had made it
known to her that he would shorten the "days of tribulation" that
mankind was then undergoing. But this was on condition that Pius
XII "consecrate the world to the Immaculate Heart of Mary, with a
special mention for Russia, and order that all the Bishops of the
world do the same ..."

The time was not ripe, then, for the particular consecration of
Russia, but God was prepared to accept a general consecration of
the world, with mention of Russia, as a means of shortening the
war. In this letter to the Pope, Sr Lucia also made the following
statement, which included a reference to the consecration of
Portugal to Mary's Immaculate Heart made in 1931, and renewed in
1938, as the situation in Europe worsened: "Most Holy Father, if in
the union of my soul with God I have not been deceived, our Lord
promises a special protection to our country in this war, due to the
consecration of the nation by the Portuguese Prelates, to the
Immaculate Heart of Mary; as proof of the graces that would have
been granted to other nations, had they also consecrated themselves to Her."

The fact that Portugal was able to keep out of the Second World
War, in contrast to its involvement in World War I, was undoubtedly a sign for the Pope and the bishops of the world of the power of
this consecration, and probably contributed to Pius XII's decision to
go ahead with the consecration of the world in 1942. In 1940, it
looked as though Hitler's forces would soon overrun the whole of
Europe, including Portugal, and so this was no empty promise on Sr
Lucia's part. The danger of Spain entering the war, and the pressure
Portugal was under from the Allies to be allowed to use its territo-

ries, meant that all through 1941 the threat of the country being forced into the war was certainly real.

On 31 October 1942, Pope Pius XII spoke to the Portuguese people in a radio message. In this, he alluded to the way that his predecessor, Pius XI, had acknowledged the miraculous intervention of the Blessed Virgin in Portugal, and how this had led to the transformation of the country. He invited them to trust in Mary's maternal protection and pray for an end to the war, before continuing with the formula of consecration of the globe, including Russia, although this was not mentioned specifically by name. Thus, in this act Pope Pius XII consecrated the whole world to Mary's Immaculate Heart, whilst also going on to recall the consecration of the world to the Sacred Heart of Jesus, made by Pope Leo XIII in 1899.

This was not the complete consecration asked for by the Blessed Virgin at Fatima, but it was sufficient for God to intervene and shorten the war. This is apparent from a letter written by Sr Lucia to Fr Gonzalves in May 1943, in which she stated that the true penance that God demanded was for everyone to fulfill their religious and civil duties, before going on to say: "He promises that the War will soon end, on account of the action that His Holiness deigned to perform. But since it was incomplete the conversion of Russia has been put off to later."

It certainly seems that Winston Churchill, the British wartime leader, thought that the turning point in the war came a few days after the date of the consecration, a reference to the Second Battle of El Alamein, in North Africa, between 23 October and 4 November, 1942, which saw the defeat of Rommel's forces.[221]

Portugal before and after Fatima

A common claim made by Medjugorje supporters is that it represents the continuation or fulfillment of Fatima. But if we compare the events which have taken place in and around Medjugorje since 1981 with what happened in Fatima and Portugal from 1917 onwards, then the contrast between the two is quite stark. To do this it is necessary to retrace our steps somewhat.

During the nineteenth century, a rising tide of anti-clericalism in Portugal culminated in the assassination of the King and his son on 1 February 1908, and the proclamation of a republic on 5

October 1910. This revolution led to a period of vicious persecution for the Church, resulting in the law of the separation of the Church and state, which was voted in on 20 April 1911. When Pope St Pius X denounced this law's enactments most of the bishops were exiled and many priests were imprisoned, including the future bishop of Leiria-Fatima, Bishop Correia da Silva. The author of this law, Afonso Costa, openly boasted that "thanks to this law of separation, in two generations Catholicism will be completely eliminated from Portugal." Such was the ferocity of the campaign against the Church, and the power of the anti-clerical movement, that there appeared to be nothing to stop the Church's enemies from achieving their objective.

So what happened after 1917 to cause the Bishops of Portugal to make the following declaration, on the occasion of the silver jubilee of the apparitions in May 1942: "If someone had shut his eyes twenty-five years ago and were to open them again today, he would no longer recognize Portugal, so profound and vast is the transformation brought about by the factor of the modest and invisible apparition of the Holy Virgin at Fatima." On the same occasion, the Patriarch of Lisbon, Cardinal Cerejeira, said there was only one word to describe what had happened in the past twenty-five years: "miracle."

A Country Transformed

This astounding transformation, peacefully and from within, was brought about by two principal factors. The immediate cause was the tireless response of the poor and simple people of Portugal, who came on pilgrimage to Fatima in their tens of thousands from all over the country, praying the rosary, singing hymns and doing penance. They rejoiced that Our Lady had come down to them from heaven, in the midst of their sufferings, with her message of consolation and salvation.

October 1922 saw the publication of the first edition of the Fatima shrine's journal for pilgrims, *Voz da Fatima*, in order to make known her message and the marvels of grace and conversion that were taking place. It began with three thousand copies. In just three years, this figure had risen to fifty thousand, and by 1937, it had a circulation of 380,000. As well as the pilgrimages, there were also miraculous cures. These were collected in a book by the first historian of Fatima, Canon Formigao, who cited some twenty-four cases between 1917 and 1922. *Voz da Fatima* described more than eight hundred cures which took place in the twenty years from 1922 to 1942.

The prodigious numbers of people coming on pilgrimage—300,000 by May 1931—and the remarkable conversions taking place, in turn won over those priests who had been indifferent or even hostile, and resulted in an explosion of vocations. When Bishop da Silva was appointed to the diocese of Leiria in 1920, the seminary was closed; by 1933, it had seventy-five seminarians. In the diocese of Portalegre, there were eighteen seminarians in 1917; by 1933, the number had risen to 201, and there was a similar steady and marked upsurge in the numbers of priests, which continued to rise until the 1960s.

The second factor in the miraculous transformation of the country was the willingness of the Portuguese bishops to accept Our Lady's message, and in particular, as has been previously noted, their action in consecrating Portugal to the Immaculate Heart of Mary in 1931. This saved the country from the Communist revolution that was engulfing Spain. Later, in 1938, this consecration was solemnly renewed in thanksgiving for Portugal's preservation from that tragic conflict.

By the time of the silver jubilee of the apparitions in 1942, it was apparent that during the preceding eleven years, Portugal had been miraculously preserved in peace and freedom from the fearful persecution suffered by the Church during that period in Spain. And it had also been preserved from entanglement in the Second World War. The transformation was so extraordinary that Cardinal Cerejeira was able to tell a French journalist in 1942, "today you would hardly be able to find a handful of enemies of religion throughout the entire country."[222]

To sum up, this was all brought about by the great fidelity of the people in responding to Our Lady's requests, particularly the daily recitation of the rosary, done, as her message of 13 May 1917 had said, "in order to obtain peace for the world and the end of the war." This was in conjunction with the bishops signifying their formal acceptance of the Blessed Virgin's message by consecrating the country to her Immaculate Heart, in 1931, in 1938, and in 1940. In short, one can say that the apparitions of the Blessed Virgin at Fatima, and her message of prayer, penance, reparation, and the rosary, brought about nothing less than the resurrection of the Church in Portugal.

Further Consecrations

Nor was Portugal the only country to benefit from a Marian consecration. The intervention of Mary to obtain the deliverance of Poland from Communism in recent years, can be traced back to the consecration of the country to the Immaculate Heart of Mary made on 8 September 1946. This was done at the Marian shrine at Jasna Gora in the presence of 700,000 Poles, and using the same form of words that Pius XII had used in his consecration of the world to Mary's Immaculate Heart in 1942. Poland was thus the first country to follow the example of Portugal in making this consecration.

In 1952, as a further sign of the importance he attached to Fatima, Pope Pius XII had specifically consecrated Russia to Mary's Immaculate Heart, on 7 July, the feast of Saints Cyril and Methodius. This, however, was not done in union with all the bishops of the world, and so it did not qualify as the full collegial consecration asked for by Mary.

Pope Paul VI recalled the 1942 consecration of Pius XII, and also referred with approval to Fatima, during the Second Vatican Council, but he chose not to make the collegial consecration asked for by the Blessed Virgin, even though he was in the presence of the world's bishops. He did, however, declare Mary "Mother of the Church" at the close of the third session of the Council, on 21 November 1964. In 1967, he went to Fatima, on 13 May, the Golden anniversary of the first apparition, and presented Sr Lucia to the assembled crowds, thus giving further papal approval to Fatima. At this stage, no reigning Pope had even been to Lourdes, let alone the shrine of any other modern Marian apparition, so this was a significant move.[223]

Just about everything, then, in the above account indicates that there are very sharp, indeed irreconcilable, differences between what happened and Fatima and the events at Medjugorje. The children of Fatima were innocent, the apparitions they experienced were few in number, the message itself was coherent and has proved to be of vital importance for the Church, while the whole series of events was confirmed by the miracle of the sun. Medjugorje, though, by contrast, has shown itself to be deficient in all these areas. Similarly, as we will see, there is no comparison between what happened in Portugal after Fatima, and what has taken place in the Balkans following Medjugorje. Regarding the former, the apparitions at Fatima led to a profound change in Portugal, while ten years after the first visions at Medjugorje, Yugoslavia became embroiled in a vicious civil war.

All of the above points, then, indicate the powerful influence that Fatima has had, not only on Portugal but also on world history. In subsequent chapters this influence will be contrasted with Medjugorje and its aftermath, in a way that will make it clear that it is completely fanciful to regard Medjugorje as any sort of continuation of Fatima.

11

The Medjugorje
Propaganda Offensive

A Rush of Books on Medjugorje

By 1984, Medjugorje was starting to become known in the wider
Catholic world, principally because of the appearance of publications promoting it, some of which were authored by well-known
theologians. Among these, Fr René Laurentin was certainly the
most prominent, and it is hard to overstate his role in the worldwide promotion of Medjugorje. It is not an exaggeration to say that
without his backing, it could not have attained such a prominent
role in the Church. He tells us that he was the first to make
Medjugorje known in France, in an article in *Figaro,* as early as 23
February 1982. He was also responsible for translating and supple-
menting a book on the alleged visions by Fr Ljudevit Rupcic, which
was eventually published in English, in 1984, under the title, *Is the
Virgin Mary Appearing at Medjugorje?* This was described by E.
Michael Jones as, "the book that launched the entire Medjugorje
phenomenon," and an indication of its popularity can be seen on
the cover of the 1988 edition, (the sixth printing), which was
emblazoned with the slogan, "90,000 sold in the U.S.A.!"[224]

To grasp Fr Laurentin's crucial role in the promotion of Medjugorje, it is necessary to realize the high reputation he had previously gained as a mariologist. He had written a number of very
influential Marian books, and in particular was regarded as an
expert on Lourdes, having authored the standard six-volume work
on the subject. He had also produced studies of the apparitions at

Rue du Bac and Pontmain, and in addition had worked as a *peritus* or expert at Vatican II.[225] Thus, when he threw his weight behind Medjugorje such support was bound to be of great significance.

But the crucial point is that there is a great difference between the type of historical/theological investigations into past apparitions which he had previously undertaken, and a "hands-on" study of an ongoing phenomenon as complex as Medjugorje. The undoubted skills which he possessed in investigating the former, were not the only ones that were required in order to discern and correctly explain a continuing series of alleged visions. With regard to Medjugorje, it would regrettably appear, as we will see further on, that Fr Laurentin found himself drawn into the whole phenomenon and became too personally involved in it, and thereby lost that very necessary sense of detachment which is essential if one is to arrive at a properly informed judgment which is both impartial and objective.

Another very early and influential book was *The Apparitions of Our Lady at Medjugorje*, by Fr Svetozar Kraljevic. This was published by the Franciscan Herald Press, also in 1984. It consists of an outline of the visions, along with various testimonies and interviews. A similarly important promoter has been Fr Robert Faricy SJ, a professor of spirituality at the Gregorian University in Rome, who coauthored, with Sr Lucy Rooney, *Mary Queen of Peace: Is the Mother of God Appearing in Medjugorje?* This, too, was published in 1984, by Alba House. The book by leading mariologist Fr Michael O'Carroll CSSp, *Medjugorje: Facts, Documents, Theology,* was published in 1986, while Mary Craig's *Spark from Heaven: The Mystery of the Madonna of Medjugorje,* was published in 1988. Like the other works mentioned above, this last volume presented Medjugorje in a largely favorable light.

Thus, even before the end of the eighties, a whole series of publications promoting Medjugorje were in wide circulation amongst Catholics in the West, and were having a marked effect. At this time, the only substantial titles to appear in English criticizing the Medjugorje phenomenon were E. Michael Jones's, *Medjugorje: the Untold Story,* (Fidelity Press, South Bend, 1988), and Fr Sivric's, *The Hidden Side of Medjugorje,* (Psilog, Québec, 1989). But their impact was limited in the face of the flood of books and media publicity in favor of Medjugorje.

Indeed, following extensive research, Paolo Apolito did not hesitate to state that: "With Medjugorje, we are dealing with one of the most powerful publicity campaigns ever conducted around a religious phenomenon, as was noted from the very beginning, and from the interior of the ecclesiastic world, when *La Civiltà Cattolica* remarked, diplomatically, on the 'impression' that there might be 'a publicity campaign, very well organized on a grass-roots basis'." He likewise talks of a "veritable flood of books, articles, videocassettes, film clips, radio and television programs, ...[which] poured first into the European countries that are traditionally most open to these phenomena, such as Italy, France, Germany, Spain, and Ireland, and then on to the rest of the world." He particularly points to Italy, and the Medjugorje periodical *Eco di Maria,* which currently has a print run of 800,000 copies, and is published in 15 different languages.[226]

The main point to note about the above publications favorable to Medjugorje, is that they all base themselves on testimonies from the visionaries recorded some time after the visions, rather than the transcripts of their talks with the parish clergy during the first week, as detailed in the books by Fr Sivric and Daria Klanac. For instance, the interviews conducted by Fr Kraljevic date from early 1983, that is, some eighteen months or more after the original visions. As we have seen previously, the contemporary taped accounts are far more likely to be accurate than anything documented so much later. But that is just the problem: the whole Medjugorje movement has been largely built on these later testimonies, which do not reveal the whole truth about what happened in the critical first week. In addition, the general level of compilation of the messages produced at Medjugorje has been less than perfect, as Fr Laurentin acknowledges: "There are a great number of words, and they have not been kept methodically. The first register of the parish, where the events had been written, has been confiscated [by the authorities]. Many of the words have been repeated without anyone making an attempt to write them down."[227]

This is what Fr Michael O'Carroll has to say in his book about Fr Laurentin and his participation in Medjugorje: because of "his unique qualification and of his entire involvement, *he is part of the event.*" Farther on he says: "He became more and more deeply involved, *entangled is a better word,* in the subsequent development. He was, before long, entirely convinced of the authenticity and felt it his duty to answer criticism, to defend the visionaries."[228]

Here we come to the heart of Fr Laurentin's difficulty with regard to Medjugorje, namely that he allowed himself to become *entangled* in it. That is, instead of maintaining a proper attitude of reserve, as is fitting for a theologian investigating alleged mystical phenomena—and as the Church herself always does, when officially investigating such phenomena—he allowed himself to become too closely involved with proceedings, and ended up uncritically accepting Medjugorje.

Fr Laurentin's Pro-Medjugorje arguments

If we look at some of Fr Laurentin's arguments in favor of Medjugorje in detail, we can see that they are essentially subjective. One of his major points is that although Beauraing and Banneux in Belgium, in the 1930s, are regarded as the last Marian apparitions to be accepted by the Church, many of the more than two hundred visions which are alleged to have taken place since then were, in his view, actually authentic. He questions whether we should consider that they are all illusory, before continuing: "Is it not rather that they took place in a cultural and ecclesial environment in which they could never have been recognized?" He also maintains that: "Real discernment such as that made by Bishop Laurence at Lourdes, in a manner exemplary for his day, does not seem possible any longer."[229]

He makes similar points in a later work: "Will the Church recognize the apparitions at Medjugorje? The presuppositions which are predominant today in theology (like exegesies [sic] and universal culture) are contrary to all recognition of apparitions. If none of those which occurred in the past 50 years received official recognition, Medjugorje has very little chance of escaping the common rule."[230]

It is difficult to see how these statements can be justified, since they imply that the various Episcopal commissions which investigated those alleged visions, and either refused to accept them or pronounced negatively, were in error. If we believe that the Holy Spirit is guiding the Church—and that includes the bishops who have to deal with visions and visionaries—then, assuming that they have carried out their job properly, and invoked the assistance of the Holy Spirit, Catholics loyal to the Church should give proper weight to their decisions.

The real reason, it would seem, why Fr Laurentin is apparently so keen to accept many of the visions alleged to have taken place since the 1930s, is because they support his own position on Medjugorje, rather than because they have any intrinsic merit of their own. What he describes as a "hypercritical mentality" is actually just the normal functioning of the Church's hierarchy in this area, which always acts with great caution and prudence because of the ever-present danger of false visionaries disrupting the unity and peace of the Church.

This is evident from the work of researchers such as Bernard Billet, who details 210 alleged visions which took place between 1928 and 1971. Although in most of these cases no decision was taken by the relevant ecclesiastical authority, as regards nearly thirty of these alleged visions a negative decision was returned. According to another researcher, Yves Chiron, the period between 1971 and 1981, when Medjugorje began, tells a similar story, except that of nearly thirty alleged visions nine were subject to a negative decision.[231] This is a much higher percentage than was the case with the earlier period. In other words, the trend, if anything, prior to Medjugorje, was towards a greater likelihood of condemnation on the part of local bishops when dealing with such phenomena. More recent research, carried out by Paolo Apolito, claims that in the United States, between 1945 and 1979, a period of nearly 35 years, there were only 21 reports of visions, while in the 20 years following 1980, there have been more than 150 such reports.[232]

The Prolonging of the Visions

Another major argument advanced by Fr Laurentin involves his attempts to justify the very large number of visions. For example, he says that: "The prolonging of the apparitions to an apparently excessive degree is justified by the spiritual formation that the young people and those of the town are receiving to an ever-greater degree. This is a major aspect of Medjugorje."[233]

At first glance, this seems plausible enough, but on examination, it proves to be a rather insubstantial argument. If the Medjugorje visionaries needed such an extensive "spiritual formation," extending, at the time, to three years of daily visions, how does one explain the fact that the illiterate Bernadette of Lourdes was privileged with fewer than twenty apparitions; or that the children of Fatima only saw Our Lady half a dozen times at the Cova da Iria and Valinhos? Note that this supposed paucity of apparitions was not a barrier to the sanctification of Bernadette, nor of Jacinta and Francisco.

Indeed, to argue that daily apparitions are necessary to "spiritual formation" suggests that at Medjugorje there was a real deficiency in the power of the Vision, who needed to prolong the apparitions over a period of years in order to bring about what the Blessed Virgin was easily able to achieve at Lourdes and Fatima in a matter of months. In short, how could extending such a "spiritual formation," to include daily visions for over twenty years now, possibly be justified?

The Visionaries Compared with the Saints

It has been argued that these daily visions for the Medjugorje visionaries follow the type of pattern that we find in the lives of some of the saints, and that this is thus an argument in their favor. It is certainly true that we can read of such events in the lives of modern saints and holy people such as Gemma Galgani, Padre Pio and Alexandrina da Costa, who were certainly quite often privileged with apparitions or visions of Jesus or Mary. But there was usually a price to pay for this privilege, and that price was suffering—often extreme suffering. As we will see, this is in marked contrast to the affluent lifestyles of a number of the Medjugorje visionaries, with their large houses, expensive cars, and frequent foreign trips.

Another characteristic of the holy persons mentioned above, and of many others like them, apart from the fact that they suffered, was their extreme humility, which made them shrink from any self-advertisement or self-promotion. Again, as we will see, this contrasts very sharply with the Medjugorje visionaries who have been very much a part of the whole process of promoting Medjugorje worldwide. In particular, we find that the saints were very reluctant to reveal that they had been recipients of divine favors such as visions or apparitions.

The problem, then, for acceptance of the claims of the Medjugorje visionaries is that their activities fall between two stools, so to speak. On the one hand, it is clear that they are definitely not in the same category as saintly individuals such as those indicated above, who were privileged with visions or apparitions, while on the other hand, their lives and experiences do not follow the pattern of the seers of genuine Marian apparitions, such as the children of Fatima. They lack the sanctity of the former and the innocence and youth of the latter.

Writing in 1986, regarding the possibility that the Congregation for the Doctrine of the Faith might form a new international commission to judge the visions, Fr Faricy noted that: "It seems to be quite unlikely that Cardinal Ratzinger will appoint a new commission before the apparitions have ceased to occur daily."[234]

That was twenty years ago, and the visions are still said to be continuing up to this moment in one form or another. However, there have been visions which have been condemned as false by the local Ordinary, even while they were going on, including those at Palmar de Troya, in Spain in 1968, and at Bayside in the United States, in 1970. The Holy See, too, has found it necessary to intervene in the past, as in the case of the false visions at Heroldsbach in Germany, in July 1951, even though these were said to have continued until October 1952.[235] So it would appear that there is no intrinsic reason why the visions at Medjugorje could not be condemned by the Church, even while they are alleged to be continuing.

The Verbose and Repetitive Nature of the Messages

Fr Laurentin also says that the verbose nature of the messages is justified because they were being given out in a country which at that time was under Communist rule: "Speech that is more frequent and more prolonged may be quite opportune for the church of silence." In reality, however, when an apparition is truly of divine origin, regardless of whether it takes place in a free or a totalitarian society, God only needs a few words and a short interval of time to get his message across.[236]

Fr Laurentin also says, in connection with the Old Testament era, during which, as he acknowledges, there were periods when there was little or no prophecy in Israel, that: "Perhaps the seriousness of the period in which we live and the inertia of the world despite the voices from heaven explain this large number of apparitions at Medjugorje."[237] These points, though, in themselves do not justify the excessive number of visions claimed to be taking place at Medjugorje, and rather imply that God is losing his touch and has to adopt the modern "advertising" mentality which insists on incessantly repeating a message.

Fr Laurentin further says: "We are in a repetitive world. There is television every day. What is not repeated is submerged. This renders the prolonged repetition of the message quite useful."[238] This is a purely materialistic, utilitarian argument, which fails to refer to the alleged divine truth of their origin, and only gives further cause for suspicion as to the ultimate cause of the visions.

With regard to the devil, Fr Laurentin maintains that: "Satan seems to be excluded because these apparitions lead to Christ, to prayer, conversion, confession, and the Eucharist. If Satan were to work that way against himself we would have to say that he has had a conversion!"[239]

However, as demonstrated by Fr William Most, the devil is quite willing to encourage a certain growth in religious practices within the context of a series of false visions:

> The dangers of diabolical interference …are very grave. Many cases are on record in which the devil appeared in the guise of Our Lord, and even gave true prophecies and urged people on to virtue. The devil is willing to tolerate some real good, so long as he has hope of accomplishing greater evil out of the affair in the long run. To distinguish a vision of divine origin from one that is diabolic is extremely difficult. Even skilled theologians may err in this matter. A large number of cases of alleged visions are probably diabolic.[240]

Medjugorje and the Post-Conciliar Period

Another of Fr Laurentin's arguments is expressed as follows: "The Apparitions at Medjugorje do not give the impression of a step backward. Though they have points in common and are in harmony with the apparitions of the last century, they do not share the cultural peculiarities of these latter. They fit in with the pastoral life of the post-conciliar Church. The Virgin encourages openness and ecumenism."[241]

However, the reality is that the Medjugorje visions have essentially *nothing* in common with the approved Marian apparitions of either the nineteenth or twentieth centuries, nor does Fr Laurentin explain exactly what he means by "cultural peculiarities."

The dividing line between "ecumenism" and indifferentism in the reported remarks of the Gospa seems distinctly thin, as can be seen from this 1983 interview between Fr Vlasic and Mirjana, in which she made the following statement: "The Madonna always stresses that there is but one God, and that people have enforced unnatural separation. One cannot truly believe, be a true Christian, if he does not respect other religions as well." To this, Fr Vlasic responded: "What, then, is the role of Jesus Christ, if the Moslem religion is a good religion?" Mirjana's rather lame response was: "We did not discuss that. She merely explained, and deplored, the lack of religious unity ..."[242] Indifferentism is the principle that all religions, or the various Christian denominations, are more or less equally good and true, or that it does not matter which one you follow.

Fr Laurentin also speaks of how a "Muslim dervish from Blade (near Mostar), experienced in the mystical ways of Sufism, reacted very positively when he assisted at the apparitions ..." That an exponent of a questionable form of mysticism should react in this way, however, is surely a warning sign regarding the visionaries and their experiences, rather than anything positive in their favor.

Similarly, the fact that Pentecostals such as David DuPlessis have visited Medjugorje and given it their support, is not, as Fr Laurentin seems to believe, a positive factor, but rather a serious concern for any normal Catholic, given the subjective nature of Pentecostalism and its emphasis on the emotional. Indeed, Fr Laurentin, speaking of the praise lavished upon Medjugorje by

DuPlessis, made the following rather astonishing statement: "This is a good indication that the apparitions of Medjugorje are without any of the historical particularities of Catholicism and thus have a better quality ecumenical dimension."[243] It is unclear exactly what Fr Laurentin meant by this, but the implication seems to be that the Medjugorje visions are so lacking in the supernatural norms of approved apparitions, that they can even appeal to a Pentecostalist.

Summing up then, we can say that this chapter has indicated that one of the main reasons for the success of Medjugorje has been the massive publicity campaign waged on its behalf, principally by authors such as Fr Laurentin, whose books on the subject have sold in the tens of thousands worldwide. Similarly, a number of other prominent writers have endorsed Medjugorje, whereas there have been relatively few critical works, none of which has succeeded in reaching a mass audience. As we have seen, the really vital testimony is contained on the tapes of the interviews with the visionaries made during the first week or so—but with very few exceptions this evidence has not been reproduced in the popular works on Medjugorje, and to this day remains almost completely unknown.

We have looked, too, at Fr Laurentin's pro-Medjugorje arguments, which, amongst other things, imply that a number of the Episcopal judgments on alleged visions made during the twentieth century have been faulty. Similarly, his arguments in favor of a large number of repetitive visions surely lack any sort of credibility in the light of what happened at places like Lourdes and Fatima; the reality is that the Medjugorje messages have more in common with the methods of modern advertising than with anything likely to have come from heaven. It is also clear that Fr Laurentin has become personally "entangled" in Medjugorje, and thus he has seemingly lost the ability to discern the visions in an impartial and objective manner.

12

Medjugorje and
the Theologians

Theologians Pronounce on Medjugorje

Fr Laurentin lays great emphasis on the number of influential writers who have shown support for Medjugorje, in the belief that discernment is necessarily related to the number and reputation of those quoted. He cites the opinion of Fr Robert Faricy, in a 1983 article, to the effect that: "Medjugorje should be a place not only of national but international pilgrimage." Even before that, as early as December 1981, only six months after the visions had begun, Fr Faricy had both visited Medjugorje and spoken with Archbishop Franic. Fr Faricy also tells us that on his first visit he met Fr Vlasic, and that they were already acquainted through the Charismatic Movement. These are surely indications of connections between Medjugorje and some important Charismatics at a remarkably early stage. It is also noteworthy that following his own visit to Medjugorje that same month, Archbishop Franic wrote a positive article in which he expressed the hope that "international experts like …[Fr] Faricy will be part of the Committee responsible for verifying the authenticity of the events of Medjugorje."

A more weighty witness is Fr Hans Urs von Balthasar, who spoke about Medjugorje in Rome in the early eighties. Undoubtedly, Fr Laurentin's public support of Medjugorje was a factor in persuading the celebrated Swiss theologian to take such a stance. And as Fr Michael O'Carroll put it, "the intervention of this giant among contemporary theologians caused much surprise." In December 1984, von Balthasar wrote a very critical letter to Bishop

Zanic in response to the latter's warnings about Medjugorje, which had been widely circulated. The contents of this letter include these lines in which he accused the Bishop of denigrating "people who are renowned and innocent, deserving your respect and protection," while he also spoke of his bringing out "accusations which have been refuted a hundred times over."

As the reader will realize from the evidence presented in preceding chapters, it seems apparent from this letter that von Balthasar was not really aware of what had actually happened during the first week at Medjugorje. Rather, he seems to have been unduly influenced by the views of Medjugorje supporters. Von Balthasar expressed himself equally vigorously in an interview given in November 1985, in which he said: "Medjugorje's theology rings true. I am convinced of its truth. And everything about Medjugorje is authentic in a Catholic sense. What is happening there is so evident, so convincing."

Sadly, this quote would seem to indicate that even as influential a figure as von Balthasar was not immune from the spirit of subjectivism which has made genuine discernment regarding Medjugorje so difficult.[244] Indeed, there is no indication that he made any detailed study of Medjugorje, rather he relied on the testimony of writers like Fr Laurentin. This is perhaps as good an example as any of the modern excessive reliance on the "cult of the expert," as a means of discernment.

The Swiss theologian was also the recipient of a letter from Fr Vlasic, in 1983, which stated that: "The children have decided to enter the religious life, but they are waiting for the right moment which only they know."[245] In fact, none of the visionaries has become a priest or religious, but this was the type of information about Medjugorje which figures like von Balthasar were receiving in the early days.[246]

Finally, however, after detailing all the points he considered favorable to Medjugorje, Fr Laurentin was obliged to acknowledge the major stumbling-block faced by its supporters, a stumbling-block which has not gone away in the intervening years, despite the appointment of a new Bishop: "The most serious objection ... [is] the opposition of the Bishop to these apparitions."[247] This opposition was forthcoming and led to an unpleasant propaganda offensive against Bishop Zanic, which is dealt with below.

Criticism of Bishop Zanic

This campaign of criticism and opposition towards Bishop Zanic developed quite early on, and was certainly well in place by the time Fr Laurentin made the following remarks with regard to the expanded Episcopal commission of 1984: "Those who were chosen for the Commission were among the most critically-minded of the available experts and they were, for the most part, opposed to the authenticity of the apparitions."[248]

However, as Fr Sivric notes, Bishop Zanic's Commission was certainly "open and independent" given that its members came from a wide variety of dioceses, provinces and theological faculties. He also notes that these individuals, who were mostly professors of theology, were actually recommended by outside authorities, and so it would be wrong to suggest they were handpicked by Bishop Zanic.[249]

Fr Laurentin also described the Bishop in the following words, while at the same time managing to ingratiate himself with the Yugoslav government: "While the Bishop became adversary number one, the government recognized the peaceful order and the loyalty of this purely religious phenomenon, which was appreciated by official tourism."

He was openly critical of the Bishop's negative stance on Medjugorje, holding his judgment to be "an error," because "except for new arguments ... even the successors of the apostles are not exempt from any risks of human weakness." As we have seen, though, "new arguments"—in the form of the transcripts of the original tapes—have become available, and indeed the tapes were themselves available at the time, as the evidence from Fr Bubalo's interviews with Vicka makes clear. In addition, it is rash to go against the judgment of the local Ordinary in such instances, providing he has acted properly, as was the case with Bishop Zanic.

Fr Laurentin went on to say that: "Obedience to established authority, ... does not necessarily extinguish an *interior conviction,* nor the responsibility to prepare discreetly, a historical revision." In other words, Fr Laurentin regarded his own subjective *feelings* about Medjugorje as superior to the judgments of the Bishop. He also compared Bishop Zanic's actions to those of the Bishop, Msgr Cauchon, who was responsible for constituting the tribunal which condemned Joan of Arc to death by burning at the stake![250]

Fr Michael O'Carroll on Medjugorje

Another example of this type of criticism came from Fr Michael O'Carroll, who made the following statement about the role of Bishop Zanic: "There is no question of withdrawing the problem of authenticity of an apparition of Our Lady from the competence of a bishop. It is the bishop who really has the problem: How is he, in a case like Medjugorje, to assess the importance of worldwide opinion? It is clear … that the Bishop of Mostar has chosen to ignore this factor in his judgement of the reported visions."

Does "worldwide opinion" entitle Catholics to ignore the fact that it is for the local Ordinary to come to decisions about alleged visions in his diocese? One might ask why, if Fr O'Carroll recognized the competent authority's power to decide in this case, he was unwilling to accept his decision?

Fr O'Carroll then goes on to mention the large Catholic response to Medjugorje, plus "enlightened disinterested theological opinion," and the various scientific studies carried out on the visionaries, before concluding thus: "In view of these facts now known through the Bishop's own mode of procedure, what value, if any, would attach to any judgement he chooses to publish?"[251]

So he accepts the Bishop has the competence to pronounce on authenticity, but questions whether his judgment would have any value. We seem to be in a situation where theologians and intellectuals think they have some form of superior knowledge, which exempts them from Episcopal judgments in these matters.

Leaving aside just how enlightened and disinterested the theological opinion mentioned by Fr O'Carroll actually was, as well as just how much we can expect scientific experiments to tell us about spiritual manifestations, Fr O'Carroll's main bone of contention is that Bishop Zanic was not prepared to take note of "worldwide opinion" in coming to a decision about Medjugorje. But looking at the activities of those Episcopal commissions previously set up to investigate reports of Marian apparitions, which were almost invariably made up of locally available theologians, there does not seem to be any solid reason why the Bishop should have taken outside opinions into account. This is quite apart from practical matters such as the need to understand the local language in order to assess Medjugorje at first hand.

Regarding this idea, even Fr Laurentin could see the difficulties of supporting the views of figures such as Archbishop Franic on this point: "I did not support that opinion because the experts and native bishops have the advantage of speaking the language of the country, and are better situated for the understanding and the knowledge of the facts."

A False Analogy

Fr O'Carroll also attempts to draw an historical analogy between Cardinal Newman's essay *On Consulting the Faithful in Matters of Doctrine*—which appeared in 1859, and which explained that during the Arian crisis of the fourth century it was the laity rather than the bishops who saved the Church—and the more recent activity of the laity in supporting Medjugorje. He then comments on the fact that Pope Pius XII consulted the bishops of the world before promulgating the dogma of the Assumption in 1950, telling them that they should take account of lay devotion in this area: "Here too was recognition of the role of the laity in the area of doctrine." He then puts the question: "Has this truth ... relevance to the happenings at Medjugorje over the last five years?"[252]

What Fr O'Carroll seems to be saying is that the Arian crisis can be seen as a model for the way Medjugorje has developed, that is, just as erring bishops in the fourth century were countered by an orthodox laity, so the "erring" Bishop Zanic was being confounded by the crowds of pilgrims manifesting their "orthodoxy" by coming to Medjugorje. Regrettably, this is a false analogy, since it was Bishop Zanic who acted in an orthodox manner, in the way he responded to events, as detailed above. It is rather the theologians and pilgrims who have flocked to Medjugorje, despite all the problems associated with it, who have been misled by the complicated series of events described above, and who, in consequence, are in error in disobeying the lawful authority of the local Bishop. Further, the Arians denied a dogma of the Church. No one who disbelieves in an apparition—proven or doubtful—can ever be called a heretic just for that reason, since private revelations, even when approved, are not part of the deposit of faith.

Bishop Zanic a Communist Collaborator?

Fr Ljudevit Rupcic accused Bishop Zanic of changing his mind about Medjugorje under Communist pressure, basing himself on the testimony of Fr Zovko,[253] and this was a charge that was repeated in the film entitled *Gospa*, a Hollywood production, which starred Martin Sheen in the role of Fr Zovko, and Morgan Fairchild as a Franciscan nun. In the film, Bishop Zanic was portrayed as a Communist collaborator. Thus, it was a slur on his good name, and the Vicar General of Mostar diocese was obliged to issue an official rebuttal on 17 June 1995. His statement categorically denied this charge as follows:

> The Chancery office of the diocese of Mostar, fervently condemns as untrue all the scenes and words regarding the ecclesiastical behaviour of Msgr. Pavao Zanic, the former diocesan bishop (under the name of Petar Subic in the film) with respect to the events of Medjugorje, ... Not even a shadow of cowardliness or easing-off of the Bishop before the communist authorities was ever in question, let alone any type of collaboration with them, ...Instead, the bishop always behaved in a courageous and dignified way. [254]

The reality is that many Medjugorje supporters have chosen to disregard the negative position of the successive Bishops of Mostar on the visions. This is also to ignore the teaching of Christ, who spoke as follows of the way that obedience was due to the legitimate pastors of the Church: "He who hears you hears me, and he who rejects you rejects me, and he who rejects me rejects him who sent me" (Luke 10:16). This was also the teaching given by the Council Fathers at Vatican II, where they spoke of how "the laity should promptly accept in Christian obedience what is decided by the pastors who, as teachers and rulers of the Church, represent Christ" (*Lumen Gentium* 37).

To conclude, a major part of the pro-Medjugorje campaign has involved an over-reliance on the opinions of well-known theologians, but in reality it turns out that these have either not been in full possession of the facts, or alternatively, not particularly objective—rather, as regards some of the latter, a pre-existing Charismatic mindset has colored their views. Even apparently objective scientific analysis of the visionaries turns out to be not as decisive as has been claimed, since diabolical activity or a lack of truthfulness cannot be detected using scientific methods, as will be seen in the next chapter.

The other part of the campaign in favor of Medjugorje has involved attacks on the person of Bishop Zanic, which largely succeeded in undermining his credibility in the minds of many Catholics. Would the supporters of a genuine apparition of Mary have resorted to such methods? This was certainly not the case with previous approved apparitions. Does not this intensive propaganda onslaught rather reveal an absence of the certainty that the visions are divinely inspired, and a determination by some Medjugorje supporters to force their subjective views on the whole Catholic world, without respecting the authority of the Church to decide such matters?

In sum, all of these factors have led to a situation where Medjugorje has been overshadowing Fatima. Up until the early 1980s, the Fatima apostolate worldwide was well established, but as Medjugorje has steadily grown more popular, Fatima has been increasingly eclipsed, at least in the popular view of many Catholics. Thus, the huge amount of information put out by the worldwide network of Medjugorje centers has become a serious rival to the promotion of the message of Fatima, to the overall detriment of genuine Marian devotion.

13

Medical and
Scientific Investigations

Medical & Psychological Examinations of the Visionaries

We learn from the original tapes that on 27 June 1981, three days after the visions began, the visionaries were taken for a police interrogation and medical inspection at Citluk. They were examined by a psychiatrist, but this procedure was apparently inconclusive, and the evidence on the tape suggests that at least some of the visionaries were far from cooperative. Two days later, on 29 June, they were again taken for a medical examination, firstly to Citluk, and then to Mostar. Here they saw a Dr Dzudza, a female psychiatrist, who, according to Ivanka, apparently threatened them with incarceration in a psychiatric ward if they continued to go to Podbrdo; but she could find no definite grounds for detaining them. They were also examined by various doctors including Dr Ludvik Stopar. His conclusion was that they were not suffering from mental illness, and this seems to have been the position of those doctors who did examine them in the early years.

Having said that, though, as Fr Laurent Volken says, in his *Visions, Revelations, and the Church,* an important work on the subject, it is crucial to realize that "the examination of the psychological make-up alone can never be the basis of a judgment in favor of the divine origin of a revelation. Only by a supernatural process can we in the long run judge supernatural facts."

The initial commission set up by Bishop Zanic also did some basic work in this area, with a priest member, Fr Nicolas Bulat, applying an old-fashioned test to Vicka during one of her visions. He pricked her in the shoulder with a needle, drawing blood, but there is some dispute as to exactly how much of a reaction there was to this on her part.[255] In fact, this first commission did not apparently carry out any detailed medical examination of the visionaries, because over time they had gradually come to the conclusion that their ecstasies were not genuine—thus they did not see such examinations as a necessity.

Dr Henri Joyeux's Medical Experiments

In connection with the medical status of the visionaries, Bishop Zanic wrote to Fr Laurentin in January 1985, pointing out that: "It is not hallucinations that I wish to stress. That was the interpretation of one of my doctors. I now believe that it was something worse—simulation." In response, Fr Laurentin claimed that, "our tests ... ruled out the possibility of simulation," but there is no clear indication in the text he co-authored with Dr Henri Joyeux, *Scientific and Medical Studies on the Apparitions of Medjugorje*, that tests for simulation, that is lie detector tests, were carried out by the French medical/scientific team assembled under Dr Joyeux. In any event, as we will see, there is no guarantee that such tests are accurate.

Indeed, the French doctor was conscious of the possibility that the visionaries could have been lying, as this statement from his evaluation makes clear: "Perhaps we are dealing with collective deceit? Would not a lie detector eventually unmask such deceit? In facing up to these ... questions our team was conscious of a number of handicaps which are important to define." He then goes on to pinpoint the linguistic and logistical difficulties they faced in carrying out their tests—the team had to rely on translators, and faced difficulties in transporting their scientific equipment back and forth from France to Yugoslavia.[256]

Fr Laurentin makes much of the fact that the visionaries, during their alleged ecstasies, did not feel pinching, touching or other stimulation. But the tests carried out—on brain activity, the heart, eyes, hearing, and larynx function—were clearly not capable of eliminating the possibility that the visionaries were able to enter into self-induced trances. Just because the tests apparently ruled out factors like hallucination or mental illness, does not rule out the possibility of deception. Fr Laurentin points to the encephalogram done by Dr Joyeux's team on Ivan, on 10 June 1984, and claims that this rules out epilepsy and "pathological" hallucination. However, the crucial fact, surely, is that it does *not* exclude the possibility that Ivan was not necessarily telling the truth.[257]

It is interesting to note that another test had been planned, to verify the claim of the visionaries that they could "touch" the Vision. This would have involved photographing them from the side and noting the position of their hands. But on the same day, 10 June, Jakov claimed that he had forgotten to ask the Gospa about this, and later, in October, Ivanka and Marija said that the Vision would not agree to it.[258]

A test done on Marija and Ivanka, on 7 October 1984, illustrates the essential weakness in the approach adopted by the co-authors. During a vision on this day, Dr Jacques Phillipot placed what is described as a "screen" in front of their eyes, and we are told that neither of them "noticed the screen that was placed between them and the apparition and it did not interfere with the perception of the apparition."[259] Photographs of these incidents in the book show that this screen was actually a small piece of card, which would not have interfered with their peripheral vision. The important point to notice, however, is that the researchers, instead of adopting a critical attitude to the claims of the visionaries, assume that they really are seeing something supernatural. Thus, they did not take a truly scientific approach to their task. A much more rigorous and questioning attitude was required. How did they know that the visionaries were actually seeing anything? The only evidence they had was what they were being told by the visionaries themselves.

An Italian doctor, Dr Marco Margnelli, in an interview given in 1988, following his investigations, stated that the visionaries "pass into another state of consciousness—a condition that one can also reach through meditation techniques, such as auto-training, though not as profoundly." He went on to say that he didn't believe that they were lying because "otherwise they would react to tests of a sensory and painful kind."[260]

It is not clear how the latter points rule out the possibility of lying, since it is quite possible to envisage a person in such a trance becoming largely impervious to pain. But it is interesting that he can describe the ecstasies of the visionaries in terms of a self-induced state of alternative consciousness. Certainly if one can enter a self-induced trance, then presumably with practice this process could be refined to produce a much deeper state of mental and bodily abstraction.

This factor may well explain why during their ecstasies some of the visionaries were apparently impervious to loud sounds or very bright lights.[261]

The Visionaries' Ecstatic Experiences Analyzed

Fr Laurentin describes one of the visions videoed by the scientific team as follows: "To prepare themselves for the apparition the visionaries, standing, recite several Our Fathers, Hail Marys and Glory Bes until 'The Gospa' appears. During the early months they usually recited each prayer twice or three times before the apparition took place. Since the end of 1983, ecstasy begins before they have finished the first Our Father."[262]

The first thing to notice about this, from a critical perspective, is that by this time, the ecstasies of the visionaries were happening at a particular moment which they knew was coming, that is before they had finished the first *Our Father*. It is not as if these visions were happening completely unexpectedly.

Fr Laurentin continues: "Suddenly their gaze, already fixed on the location of the apparition, becomes more intense. There are hardly any movements of the eyelids ... They kneel down very naturally, all at the same moment. The movement is not perfectly synchronised, a fact that might be attributed to their differing reaction times, or the difference in their reflexes. But we have never noticed a signal being given."[263]

Of course, there would be no need for an obvious signal to be given because the very act of kneeling down, which he admits was not done exactly simultaneously, coming as it did during the *Our Father*, could have acted as a cue in itself. In other words, one of the visionaries could have begun to kneel down and the others followed very quickly. Remember, these were fit youngsters, who had been having these experiences since mid-1981.

Video evidence makes it clear that this act of kneeling down by the visionaries was not simultaneous on other occasions too. For example, footage from one video clearly shows Ivanka kneeling down more quickly than Vicka,[264] while another video again features Ivanka, but this time standing behind Jakov, so that she was outside his field of vision. Again, her kneeling down is noticeably quicker than his.[265]

A word or two about "reaction time" is appropriate here. A good deal of research has been carried out on this subject, and "the accepted figures for mean simple reaction times for college-age individuals have been about 190 ms (0.19 sec) for light stimuli and about 160 ms for sound stimuli." As might be expected, with practice, reaction time can be reduced, and being warned in advance also leads to a faster reaction time.[266] This means that the reaction time of a fit young person to a visual stimulus can certainly be of the order of 2/10 of a second, and even quicker for sound stimuli. Since such short reaction times are possible, it is clear that claims of apparent simultaneity for the visionaries in response to alleged supernatural stimuli are very difficult, if not impossible, to verify.

Nor is it really possible to argue that if the visions were false, then we might expect a "ripple" effect, in which one visionary would quickly follow another in kneeling down, followed by another, followed by another, each within their own reaction times, a process which would naturally take longer than a single person's reaction time. This is because they were generally very close together, and could either hear the air movements from those around them, or through their peripheral vision see movements and react very quickly to them. So it is not a question of falsity requiring a time-consuming "cascade" of movements, but rather of one visionary kneeling, and then the others very quickly following suit, with all this generally happening within the approximate duration of one person's reaction time. But having said that, as already pointed out, the video evidence indicates that at least on some occasions there was a noticeable time lag between the movements of particular visionaries.

Fr Laurentin then comments on what happened next: "Their lips can be seen moving but no voices are heard … Suddenly, all their voices become audible, and they say, in Croatian, 'who art in heaven'; 'hallowed be thy name' etc. The opening words, 'Our Father' are not pronounced."[267]

Once again, there is nothing necessarily supernatural about this, and whether a group begins to say a prayer with the first word, or, as in this case, with the third word, this does not of itself rule out a natural explanation. It would only be necessary for one of the visionaries to begin on the third word, and then, as in the case of their kneeling down, for the others to follow quickly.

What is certainly clear from these observations of the visionaries in ecstasy, is that the scientific experiments designed to test these claims were far from rigorous. Pictures in the book, and video evidence, show the visionaries wired up to various pieces of apparatus, but there is no indication that they were blindfolded, or fitted with earphones, so as to exclude visual or auditory cues from one to another. Similarly, if the experiments had been conducted with true scientific rigor, surely a far more accurate analysis would have been obtained if they had been placed in separate partitioned areas, so as to exclude cues from air disturbances caused by the person next to them kneeling down quickly.

Inaudible Voices

Ivanka's voice and larynx function were tested on 28 December 1984, by Dr Francois Rouquerol. This was to discover why the visionaries' voices became inaudible once ecstasy proper had begun. At this time, according to the evidence recorded by the instruments, there was no longer any larynx movement, only that of the lips—a process which is described as "articulation without phonation." The problem with this is that there is no way of determining whether these lip movements without sound actually corresponded with genuine language. Fr Laurentin acknowledges that they were unable to find anyone capable of lip reading in order to determine this point.

This question could possibly have been decided on Friday 8 March 1985, when Dr Luigi Frigerio, accompanied by two colleagues, attempted to test Vicka during a vision, by attaching a laryngophone to her larynx (voice box). This device can pick up very low-level sounds produced by a patient's larynx. But this vision only lasted 22 seconds, well below the usual length, and thus there was no time to properly check Vicka's larynx function during ecstasy. Her explanation for this was that the Gospa had looked at the apparatus and said: "It is not necessary."[268]

We can contrast this incident with one involving Ivan. He was videoed while in an alleged ecstasy during a Medjugorje celebration at Aylesford in Kent, England, in 1996. From the footage it seems as though Ivan's lips are moving without any words being audible, but when the sound is turned up, speech can clearly be heard coming from him. So on this occasion at least, there was no question of "articulation without phonation." What is particularly disturbing about this incident, though, is the expression on Ivan's face: it is totally bland and unenthusiastic, with a complete lack of evident joy or intimacy, let alone rapture.[269]

Dr Frigerio went on to claim that the experiences of the visionaries could only be preternatural or supernatural, and further stated that if they were preternatural then the visionaries would not be free, but, since they were apparently free, then they must be supernatural.[270] But this idea goes against the basic Catholic principle of the freedom of the human will—that is, that no outside spiritual agency can absolutely control how we act, although they can influence or tempt us. So even if someone is experiencing a preternatural experience, they still retain their essential ability to act and make free choices.

Multiple Conversations

One of the strangest aspects of the whole Medjugorje story is the way that, according to Fr Laurentin, the "Virgin may give a message to one without the others hearing and *they can hold independent conversations simultaneously.*" Dr Joyeux made a similar observation, saying, "each one of them appeared *simultaneously and successively,* to receive information from and converse with a person whom we as doctors have never seen."[271]

In other words, it is claimed that the Gospa could speak with more than one visionary at the same time. This is certainly an interesting claim in the light of what has taken place during the approved Marian apparitions. We do not find this happening at Fatima, nor at Beauraing, which in terms of the number of seers and their ages is the approved apparition which most closely corresponds with Medjugorje—although not as regards duration, since the apparitions at Beauraing only lasted between November 1932 and January 1933, a matter of a few months. At La Salette, Our Lady did speak to the two children separately, but only in order to impart separate secrets to them, which the other child could not hear. Regarding Beauraing, at various times during the apparitions, she spoke to one or another of the children, but again when she gave the three youngest personal secrets during the last apparition, this was done to each of them separately and not concurrently.[272]

In the light of all this, it does not seem at all likely that the visionaries were actually speaking in this manner to a genuinely supernatural visitor.

Fr Laurentin explicitly states that the visionaries recited the *Our Father* with the Gospa,[273] and this fact of itself raises an acute problem. Would the sinless Blessed Virgin Mary repeatedly recite this prayer which includes the phrase, *and forgive us our trespasses* [sins]?—this would not appear to be theologically possible.[274]

Fr Laurentin also comments on the fact that Dr Ludvik Stopar hypnotized Marija, and that under hypnosis she gave the same account of her experiences as when in her normal condition, except that she also revealed the alleged secrets she had received.[275] This is taken as proof that the secrets are genuinely supernatural, but, of course, that is not necessarily the case. The secrets may not have been genuine supernatural revelations, yet the visionaries may well have not told anyone outside their particular circle of their contents.

Dr Joyeux gave an interview to *Paris Match* in the summer of 1985, during which, speaking of the various experiments that had been carried out on the visionaries, he acknowledged quite plainly that: "None of them gave scientific proof that the Virgin is appearing to the visionaries and this is impossible to achieve." Even Fr Laurentin was forced to admit that, "the object [sic] who appears to the young people ... will always remain outside scientific experimentation. We will always be limited to hypotheses in that regard."[276]

Interestingly, Louis Bélanger tells us that his own researches in Canada showed that it is quite possible—using volunteers in tests done under laboratory conditions—to duplicate the states of consciousness found during the above medical tests done on the visionaries, and thus that there is nothing necessarily supernatural about them.[277]

Further Experimentation in 1986 and 1998

On 14 January 1986, a self-appointed "French-Italian scientific theological commission," which consisted of "seventeen renowned natural scientists, doctors, psychiatrists and theologians," following tests on the visionaries, issued a 12 point conclusion, which amongst other things made the following four assertions:

> 1. On the basis of the psychological tests, for all and each of the visionaries it is possible with certainty to exclude fraud and deception. 2. On the basis of the medical examinations, tests and clinical observations etc, for all and each of the visionaries it is possible to exclude pathological hallucinations. 3. On the basis of the results of previous researches for all and each of the visionaries it is possible to exclude a purely natural interpretation of these manifestations. 4. On the basis of information and observations that can be documented, for all and each of the visionaries it is possible to exclude that these manifestations are of the preternatural order i.e. under demonic influence.[278]

We can agree that the scientists were competent regarding the second point, that is regarding "pathological hallucinations" but it is obvious that they exceeded their competence with regard to matters such as excluding fraud and deception, or the demonic. Such scientific investigations of their nature cannot categorically exclude the latter, while deception is always a possibility which must be taken into account.

Apart from the fact that the Medjugorje visionaries were in some way "disconnected" from the real world during their trance-like condition, according to Dr Philippe Loron, in an interview published in 1989, there was a very close synchronization between the eye movements of the visionaries while they were "seeing" their alleged visions—to within 1/5 of a second when the ecstasy began, and when it finished.[279]

On the face of it, this seems like strong evidence to support the genuine nature of what the visionaries experienced, but we have to bear in mind what was said above about reaction time, which, for visual stimuli, is of the order of 0.19 seconds. This makes it clear that this figure of 1/5 of a second for eye movement, (0.2 seconds) is only what we would expect given a normal reaction time.

Further medical tests were done on three of the visionaries, Marija, Ivan and Vicka, in Italy, from 22–23 April 1998. As Fr Laurentin tells us, though: "Vicka was there only for some general tests because Our Lady had asked her on the 20th of April to accept being deprived of the daily apparitions until June 4th. Vicka, who could refuse Our Lady nothing, accepted. It was difficult for her, but even so she remained in perfect joy."[280]

In other words, Vicka did not subject herself to any particular tests to determine her condition during any of her alleged ecstatic states during this period.

Further research was carried out from 23–24 July 1998 at Medjugorje, this time on Mirjana, Vicka and Ivanka; while what is described as "psychodiagnostic" research involving Jakov also took place sometime between this date and 11 December 1998, when psycho-physiological research involving Marija was undertaken in Italy. This work involved a team of scientists, who carried out a wide variety of tests, and came to the conclusion that the "[r]esults of the investigation carried out demonstrate that the ecstatic phenomenology can be compared to the one from 1985 with somewhat less intensity." They went on to say that they did not believe that the visions were states of "hypnotic trance," but there does not seem to have been any particular focus on the possibility of the visionaries entering self-induced trances.

Lie Detector Tests

The statement issued by the research team mentions the "Valsecchi truth and lie detection test," so this time they were definitely tested on this point. But there is no consensus that such tests are accurate or scientific. They are subjective and rely on changes in emotional responses; it is quite possible for someone who is telling the truth to be falsely accused of lying, and conversely for a determined liar to avoid detection. For the above reasons, evidence obtained from lie detector tests is generally inadmissible in American courts, and in those of a number of other countries.[281]

Thus the conclusion regarding all the various tests to which the Medjugorje visionaries have been subject, is that none of them categorically demonstrates that their experiences are supernatural—indeed, this is in any case impossible to verify scientifically—nor have they been able to determine whether or not the visionaries have been lying. The other crucial point to make regarding these tests is that since none of them was commissioned by the proper authority, neither the respective Bishops of Mostar, nor any higher Church authority, then strictly speaking they have no relevance regarding the proper supernatural discernment of what has been happening at Medjugorje. Only the Church possesses the divine authority and competence as regards such discernment.

As we have seen, then, there is clear evidence to suggest that the initial stages of the visions at Medjugorje were diabolically inspired, but as time went on there does seem to have been far less activity of that sort there. Thus, the later ecstasies at Medjugorje seem to have had more of a human element in them, and the conclusion that they are largely self-induced trances seems very likely. Of course, if individuals claim to see visions, then, as in the case of those who desire signs and wonders, this in itself opens up the possibility, if not the certainty, of diabolical intervention. Thus, the later activities of the Medjugorje visionaries during their trances may well have also unwittingly been subject to diabolical influence.

14

Medjugorje as Cult Religion

The Visionaries as Religious Figures

Mart Bax, whom the reader will recall spent more than a decade researching into Medjugorje—which involved him spending several weeks there each year—describes how, as the number of pilgrims grew during the 1980s, the visionaries found themselves exercising a "ministry" of ever-increasing proportions:[282]

> Almost every day the seers prayed, healed people by touching them with their hands, and passed on special messages from *Gospa* to persons who had asked for them. They also had to devote a great deal of time to "blessing" crosses, rosaries, water from the well near the church and earth and stones from apparition hill. By way of these objects, ever-growing members of pilgrims wanted to partake of the 'heavenly powers' they imagined were flowing down to earth through the seers.

Bax, writing in 1990, describes a typical day in the life of a visionary in the 1980s, once the pilgrimage to Medjugorje had substantially increased. It seems he was actually describing the activities of Vicka, but the other visionaries would probably have had a similar itinerary at this time. The day would begin at about eight in the morning, when a group of pilgrims would be invited to the visionary's house, where, as they entered a large room, they would leave objects such as rosaries and crosses on a table, to be "blessed" during the vision of the Gospa for that day. The visionary would then enter and greet the pilgrims, before describing how the visions had changed her life, while members of a local prayer group dotted around the room would simultaneously translate her words.

Then the sick and those with special needs would be invited to come forward and pray with the visionary, as she knelt down and began to see the Gospa, while staring at the white wall in front of her. After five minutes or so, it was clear that the vision was over, and the visionary then "put her hands on one of the believers in front to convey the 'special grace' of the Blessed Virgin." As she left the room, she would lay her hands on those present, row by row, and bless their religious objects, receiving money from a number of them. By now, it was almost 10 o'clock, and the next group of pilgrims was waiting their turn; the same procedure was thus followed until about noon. In the late afternoon, another meeting would be held at the apparition site, Podbrdo, and large numbers of pilgrims would usually attend this. In the evening, if it was not the visionary's turn to be at the church, she might well deal with a large postal correspondence.[283]

Problems with the Activities of the Visionaries

This whole question of the visionaries' blessing objects, or people, or laying hands on them, is extremely suspect. This comes out very clearly in an incident from the life of Francisco of Fatima, as recounted in Sr Lucia's memoirs. The children had been to visit the place where they had seen the angel, as well as Valinhos, where they had seen Our Lady on 19 August 1917. On their return to the house, they found it full of people, and Lucia relates that they saw that a "poor woman was standing near the table, pretending to bless innumerable pious objects: rosary beads, medals, crucifixes and so on. Jacinta and I were soon surrounded by a crowd of people who wanted to question us. Francisco was seized upon by the would-be 'blesser', who invited him to help her. 'I could not give a blessing,' he replied very seriously, 'and neither should you! Only priests do that.' " Sr Lucia further recounts that these words "went round the crowd like lightning," and the woman was forced to beat a hasty retreat, amid a "hail of insults."[284]

E. Michael Jones describes his own experience of an encounter with Ivan Dragicevic in Medjugorje in May 1988. The visionary was with a group of international pilgrims at midday, standing by the side of the road in Bijakovici, about a hundred yards from his house. He was speaking to them with the translation being done by two tour guides. Jones describes him as looking, "a little hot and a little bored". In response to one question, as to whether or not he had seen the Blessed Mother lately, one of the guides said: "Every day he sees our Lady at twenty to seven. ... [a]t the choir loft." The conversation then turned to prayer and Ivan told the crowd that Our Lady wanted them to spend ten minutes saying the Our Father, and he further informed them that he personally needed, "two to two-and-a-half hours" to say a full rosary. The pilgrims were suitably impressed by this, but as Jones remarks it would have been hard to imagine someone like Sr Lucia of Fatima acting in a similar fashion, speaking about herself by the side of a road.[285] And in point of fact, it is obvious from her memoirs that the children of Fatima did everything they could to avoid broadcasting the details of their experiences to curiosity seekers.

With regard to activities such as these blessings, what seems to have happened is that in the wake of the Medjugorje visions, some strange and indeed superstitious practices became popular. The visionaries became a kind of "folk doctors" or "priests" of this new type of religion, whose heavenly powers could be accessed by touching them, or by a laying on of their hands. The result has been, in Bax's words, the production of a "hybrid" cult, "a mixture of 'magic' and elements of Christian rituals."[286]

Diabolical Influence in Medjugorje?

Another question to be asked is: were there possible diabolical influences at work in Medjugorje itself, that is, is there any evidence of an "evil atmosphere" in the area? Mart Bax points to such evidence, particularly as it was experienced by the women of Medjugorje. He describes one woman of his acquaintance who, at regular intervals, would hear voices, and "has the feeling that slowly but surely she is being sucked in by ... the Black Power." She claimed that a good number of women in the village felt the same way, and Bax's own investigations revealed to him a situation where many of the local women felt they were being increasingly terrorized by "devils and evil spirits".

These feelings have to be understood in the context of the rather primitive spiritual universe in which the people of Medjugorje, and specifically Bijakovici, dwelt. They had been taught for generations to think in spiritual terms of a "Middle Field," a realm between good and evil. Usually this Middle Field is in a "relative equilibrium," but "in stressful times, during wars or feuds, it is profoundly disturbed." The appearance of the Gospa in the early eighties was seen as a positive disturbance of this equilibrium, and some of the local women apparently believed that this had had a positive spiritual effect on their lives.[287]

But then, some time later, things started to go wrong, particularly after a young boy was found drowned. This accident was seen as having a religious dimension, and the local people began to ask if perhaps "*Gospa* was not strong enough after all to counter the evil powers of the Middle Field." This particularly became a concern as the village rapidly expanded to accommodate the influx of pilgrims, and other accidents occurred, so that "more and more women in the parish" gradually came to think that way, despite advice to the contrary from the Franciscans. By May 1989, over three hundred reports of "ailing" women had come to light, and there had been "approximately the same number of requests for exorcism." By any standards, such an extraordinary desire for exorcism is surely extremely significant in a parish the size of Medjugorje. Could this have arisen if the Blessed Virgin had truly been appearing on a daily basis in the vicinity?

Diabolical Obsession?

The priests, however, put all this down to hysteria—as did the men of the parish—and they refused such requests for exorcism. But it has to be remembered that, although these women may not have been physically *possessed* by the devil, and thus in definite need of exorcism, it is quite possible that they were suffering from a form of diabolical *obsession*. Fr Adolphe Tanquerey, the noted spiritual writer, tells us that obsession can be both internal and external, in the sense of the devil afflicting the emotions, imagination and memory, as well as the external senses. A strong sign of genuine obsession rather than normal temptations is when these are "at once sudden, violent, persistent and difficult to account for by natural means." The symptoms reported by these troubled women certainly seem to correspond with this description.

In any event, their condition led them to turn to some of the *Kalajdzije,* or "wise old women," of the district, whose prescriptions included "amulets and talismans worn on the body," objects whose function was to ward off the powers of the devils. Even the most trivial misfortune could be attributed to these malign beings. The village women maintained that they could discern the presence of a real devil in a particular situation because of generalized feelings of fatigue, and other symptoms, which could either be due to a little demon, or to a more powerful "heavy devil."[288]

Bax puts forward a sociological explanation for these symptoms, based on a combination of a lowered social status for many women, and the strains caused by looking after the needs of all the pilgrims. He also points to the social tensions caused by "the almost endemic conflicts and feuds between and within kin groups, which easily ended in violent vendettas." This last factor points to the completely different role played in this society by men, in which the release of male tensions by acts of violence was encouraged. No doubt there is a great deal of truth in all this, but the general female experience of an increased impression of evil might also indicate a possible diabolical connection with the origin of the visions at Medjugorje.[289]

Village Rivalries and Strange Religious Ceremonies

The villagers of Medjugorje and Bijakovici were also subject to more mundane vices. Because the pilgrimage trade was centered on Bijakovici, given that the visionaries lived there and it was at the foot of Podbrdo, it was only natural that locals made a good deal of money out of the visitation of the Gospa. This caused resentment and jealousy in Medjugorje itself, even though it was only a few kilometers away across the valley and was the site of the parish church.[290] The bad atmosphere between the two was evident even to a sympathetic writer like Mary Craig, who made the following observation: "The two villages ... have for centuries glowered at each other across the valley floor; until recently there was little love lost between them. The Croatians are a Balkan people, as fierce and unbiddable as their land. Personal feuds and vendettas lie deep in their bloodstream."[291]

Stories about "miraculous signs" on Krizevac—which was more directly in the domain of Medjugorje, and thus a suitable rival to Podbrdo—were soon in wide circulation around Medjugorje itself, although the inhabitants of Bijakovici were more skeptical on this point. In any event, Krizevac soon became a pilgrim attraction in its own right, with all the consequences that implied, including accommodation, shops and piety stalls, all of which soon sprang up at the foot of the mountain. Bax describes the uneasy state of economic "truce" between Medjugorje and Bijakovici which was in place during the eighties, in which any attempt to lower prices in one of the villages would be quickly countered by the other.[292]

As a way of overcoming the inter-clan feuding which was still a feature of life in the vicinity, it was decided, reportedly at the prompting of the Gospa, that the old sacred places associated with each clan, and the ceremonies performed there—the *slavas*, a combination of ancestor worship and the Eucharist—should be restored. This activity centered on the graveyard at Gomila, a hamlet which is part of Bijakovici, and it seems that during the late eighties such ceremonies were held nearly every Sunday.

Apparently, the messages of the Gospa, and particularly the great number of pilgrims, had encouraged the local people to behave in a more civilized manner, and indeed it does seem that from the mid-eighties until the beginning of the war there were no revenge killings, and that the crime rate as a whole dropped significantly. But this respite only lasted until a fresh round of pitiless violence broke out, once the flow of pilgrims to Medjugorje dried up in the early nineties.[293]

Strange Lights and Signs

Alleged signs and wonders in the vicinity of Medjugorje have been widely publicized in books favorable to the visions. For example, there have been many reports of lights on the hill Crnica which were taken to be supernatural; but according to Fr Sivric's investigations, these were simply fires lit on the hillside, some by shepherds as a precaution against wolves, and others by young people playing practical jokes. He also came across an account of somebody burning gasoline on Podbrdo.

Another common sign taken to have a heavenly significance concerns the massive cross on Krizevac, which some witnesses claim to have seen bathed in light, or assuming the shape of a woman, or even the Gospa. However, it turns out that such phenomena have been observable for many years, and are due to a combination of weather and atmospheric conditions. According to Fr Sivric, who made his own investigations, this effect is linked to rain and quite easy to verify. Likewise, Mark Waterinckx reports that on a number of occasions, while present in Medjugorje, he saw that when the sun was shining at about 10 o'clock in the morning, at a particular angle, the cross on Krizevac seemed to disappear.

All of this indicates that these perceptions were not supernatural but most probably optical phenomena or illusions, which witnesses nevertheless interpreted in a supernatural way.[294]

Miracles of the Sun?

However, there have been apparently trustworthy witnesses who have stated that they have seen strange phenomena associated with the sun at Medjugorje, which do seem to go beyond what can be explained in natural terms. For example, in September 1986, Mary Craig was with a BBC crew who were making a film about the visions. After interviewing a good number of individuals, they returned to the village one evening, waiting outside the church at about 6:15 p.m., for two of the visionaries to appear. She then tells us that a "sudden flash of light and tremor of excitement in the crowd made me turn and look in the direction of the sun. Almost to my horror, I witnessed what so many have called the 'dance of the sun': the sun moving back and forth as though on a yo-yo string, its central incandescent white disk surrounded by spinning circles of yellow, green and red light, for all the world like a Catherine-wheel firework."

She then heard a fellow onlooker say that he had just realized that he had been staring directly at the Mediterranean sun for fully ten minutes, and was not dazzled in the slightest. Craig was startled by this and realized that she too had been looking at the sun for the same period, as had her companion. When she questioned him, he agreed that he had also been able to look directly at the sun without ill effect. Interestingly, both of them felt that there must be a rational explanation for what they had seen, and she explicitly said that she "had no sense of the numinous, only of the passing strange."[295]

Assuming for the moment that this incident was genuinely beyond nature, we have to bear in mind that that does not necessarily mean it was supernatural. There is a genuine "middle ground," the preternatural, where Satan is able to intervene under the right conditions. Given the questionable atmosphere surrounding Medjugorje, and given particularly the great desire of many pilgrims to see something, it wouldn't have been difficult for the right conditions to arise, in order to enable the devil to produce a false miracle.

A Dangerous Desire for the Miraculous

A good example of this type of thing took place during the approved appearances of the Blessed Virgin to the five children at Beauraing in Belgium in the early 1930s. A much larger than usual crowd of about fifteen thousand persons assembled on the evening of 8 December 1932, the feast of the Immaculate Conception, for that particular day's expected apparition. The atmosphere was highly charged, primarily because of an expectation that a miracle would be performed. This was despite the fact that Our Lady had said nothing to the children to encourage this belief. Some of those present that evening, who had been standing on a nearby railway embankment, claimed they had seen "on the mountain far over toward the east a whitish light having a human form." Thus, a rumor spread through the town that others, apart from the five children, had also seen something.

When about ten of these persons were questioned the next day, they were in a frightened and emotionally upset state, and some said they had seen something like Our Lady of Lourdes, but others gave different accounts. Some "saw a blue belt, others saw blue rays emanating from the head, others saw a ball of fire." It is difficult to decide the exact cause of these visions, and although some form of multiple hallucination is possible, it seems more likely that they are evidence of a demonic intervention.[296]

There is quite a difference between these events and what happened regarding the miracle of the sun at Fatima. On 13 October

1917, a miracle had been promised and a huge crowd of 70,000 had assembled there with the expectation of seeing something, but without knowing exactly what would happen. But at Beauraing, no promise of a miracle had been given in advance, and so we can probably explain the strange visions which were seen by certain members of the crowd as resulting from an intense expectation.

This desire to see something, as St John of the Cross notes, is extremely dangerous since the devil is well able to satisfy such desires. He tells us that, "the devil rejoices greatly when a soul desires to receive revelations, and when he sees it inclined to them, for he has then a great occasion and opportunity to insinuate errors and to detract from the faith in so far as he can, for ... he renders the soul that desires them very gross, and at times even leads it into many temptations and unseemly ways."

Elsewhere he makes a similar point: "Those who now desire to question God or receive some vision or revelation are guilty not only of foolish behaviour but also of offending him by not fixing their eyes entirely on Christ and by living with the desire for some other novelty"[297]

St John of the Cross (1542–1591), is one of the greatest writers on mystical theology in the history of Catholicism, and was made a Doctor of the Church in 1926.

Regarding this idea of an intense desire for "signs and wonders," which has certainly been present among pilgrims at Medjugorje, Denis Nolan says that "it would be foolish to conclude ... that apparitions and supernatural phenomena exist merely because this thirst exists."[298]

But on this point, Nolan is completely wrong, as the teaching of St John of the Cross makes clear—apparitions and other apparently supernatural phenomena *can* very definitely occur if a sufficient desire for them is present.

Diabolical Power and Influence

We read in the book of Revelation about the Beast, that is the Antichrist, who will wage war against the Church towards the end of time. He is to be assisted by a second beast whose task will be to make all the inhabitants of the earth worship his master. To this end, he works "great signs, even making fire come down from heaven to earth in the sight of men; and by the signs which it is allowed to work in the presence of the beast, it deceives those who dwell on earth ..." (Rev 13:13–14)

This illustrates the way that during the "end times" the devil will be able to intervene in order to deceive mankind. So there is nothing inherently unlikely in his being able to exercise such powers to a lesser extent in our own days. Then, there will be an almost universal reign of evil on earth, which will give Satan great scope to act—but who will deny that the level of evil in our own days has not reached immense proportions? It is only necessary to point to the huge number of abortions worldwide, to the great prevalence of pornography in the media, to drug use, to widespread secularization, and to oppression and injustice around the globe, to realize this. Thus, with respect to Medjugorje, some sort of diabolical influence cannot be ruled out as the most likely explanation for many of the alleged solar miracles in the vicinity.

Solar Miracles and Golden Rosaries

There is also the case of the false visions at Necedah, Wisconsin, which, as we will see in a later chapter, strongly savor of the diabolic. Here, on 7 October 1950, up to 100,000 people gathered to witness a promised miracle of the sun. This is what one person, Eloise Vlasak, claimed she saw: "I looked at the crowd and everyone had golden patches on them. ...[The sun] seemed to be spinning clockwise so fast; it turned a pale gold, silver and then ... green. When it turned green it still showed a luminous disk. It was as if God held a giant spotlight and [was] changing it with color prism slides." Most people, however, including newspaper reporters, didn't see anything unusual. But the fact that some people did see a "solar miracle" indicates that under the right conditions, diabolical influences are very possible, although in this case hallucination cannot be ruled out.[299]

Claims that metal rosary links have changed color at Medjugorje, often assuming a golden hue, have been widely reported. For many people this has become the standard Medjugorje "miracle," but it cannot be emphasized strongly enough that such phenomena can likewise also have a preternatural explanation, as a result of an intense desire to experience something "miraculous."

At best, such a "miracle" can only be described as trivial and unworthy of God, and regrettably it has not been unknown for such things to have happened in association with false visionaries.

One example of this concerns the Necedah visionary, Mary Ann Van Hoof, who, like the Medjugorje visionaries, "blessed" religious items and rosaries, and similarly, there were reports of rosaries turning to gold at Necedah. When the journalist Marlene Maloney investigated Necedah in the late eighties, she was able to see one of these rosaries, confirming that the chain had indeed "changed to a gold color." But she goes on to say that this effect "certainly didn't suggest the work of God: the wooden beads had turned a dull, nauseating golden green." She took the rosary to a jeweler who explained that, on a natural level, this change could have taken place if the rosary had been dipped into a particular chemical and then warmed.[300]

Natural Explanations for the "Miraculous"

It is probable that many of the alleged miracles of the sun at Medjugorje can be explained in natural terms. Fr Sivric deals with the way it supposedly danced a little before sunset on 2 August 1981, pointing out that talk of the Gospa's visions was naturally on everybody's lips, and so there was a heightened expectation of signs and wonders in the air. Recalling that he was born and brought up in Medjugorje, he relates that as a child, during the warm summer months, he can remember seeing spectacular sunsets, which, due to particular atmospheric conditions, would give the impression of two or even three "suns" one on top of the other. It seems that most of these unusual signs took place during the early months of the visions, when excitement was at its height, in a psychologically charged atmosphere, and thus there was a predisposition to believe they were true.[301]

In addition, Paolo Apolito points to research carried out to investigate alleged solar prodigies which are supposed to have happened at Medjugorje and many other visionary sites. He particularly cites experiments by two researchers, Malanga and Pinotti, who, after studying films taken at Medjugorje and some Italian sites—films which consistently show the sun pulsating— were able to replicate the effects produced. These seemed to show the sun rotating or turning green, amongst other effects. Malanga and Pinotti thought that these effects might be due to videotaping solar light, and noted that they only occurred when the camera was set up with a particular lens aperture. At this setting, "when too much light hits the electronic circuits of the video camera, it tends automatically to close the electronic shutter which in automatic mode remains closed, but in manual mode reopens, returning to the conditions set by the operator, which produces the phenomena cyclically."[302]

So it is perfectly possible to explain, in purely natural terms, through the particular settings on a video camera, these different motions of the sun and different colors emanating from it, which thousands of people have been led to believe were of truly miraculous origin. Even Fr Laurentin accepts that the majority of these miracles can be explained in a natural way: "If one watches the sun near its setting (dazzling and not yet turned red), it ceases to dazzle at the end of a second [sic]. The center becomes dull in color, 'like a Host,' say those who are religiously struck by this sign, while the periphery stays luminate and radiant. Those phenomena do not require supernatural explanations at all."[303]

Moreover, in an interview given by Bishop Ratko Peric, and published in the diocesan newspaper *Crkva na Kamenu* (*The Church on the Rock*), he made the following interesting comment: "Medjugorje was already 'phenomenal' in the last century. Fr Petar Bakula, OFM, noted in a book he wrote in 1867 that people were even then claiming to see a very strong and pinkish light in and around Medjugorje. So the 'phenomenon of light' did not start to fascinate people for the first time in 1981, but rather goes back to the last century."[304]

This quest for the miraculous in connection with the sun has also had its tragic side, regarding those people who have seriously damaged their eyes because of a desire to see something miraculous. E. Michael Jones recounts his own meeting with two sisters who were fellow pilgrims to Medjugorje, one of whom, on hearing that a friend of hers had seen the sun spin, decided the next day to stare at the noonday sun, until, as she related, "an arrow of pain" hit her eyes and "everything went orange." The result was permanent eye damage due to scarring of the retina.[305]

Miraculous Cures at Medjugorje?

As regards talk of miraculous cures at Medjugorje, this, too, seems to have been greatly exaggerated. A dossier of over fifty alleged cures, compiled by Fr Ljudevit Rupcic, joint author with Fr Laurentin of the bestselling Medjugorje book mentioned earlier, was presented to Dr Mangiapan, the head of the medical bureau at Lourdes, but his conclusions were negative. In the April 1984 edition of the *Association Medicale Internationale de Lourdes,* he stated that the cases he had been presented with were described very briefly and without adequate supporting evidence: "They are never confirmed ... by an objective medical examination (...) rarely is the duration of the cure mentioned ... (nor) are the treatment, the diagnosis or the grounds for any prognosis indicated. In conclusion, if we are to follow the norms of the Bureau, this entire dossier is of no practical value and as such would not give grounds for an argument in favour of the apparition."

One of the problems with assessing claims of cures is that there are often conflicting reports about them. An example of this is the case of a man who had allegedly been told by Ivan that his medical operation would be a success. The Archbishop of Belgrade informed Bishop Zanic that, while he was in hospital in May 1984, he had shared a room with this person, who was named Marko Blazevic, and who was waiting for a cardiac bypass operation. He told the Archbishop that Ivan had assured him that his operation would be successful, and it seems that the whole hospital knew about this prophecy. The unfortunate sequel is that Blazevic died immediately after his operation. But according to Fr Rupcic, it was actually the man's daughter, Melanie who spoke to Ivan about her father, and that Ivan did not promise a cure on behalf of the Gospa.[306]

There is also the case of the alleged cure of Venka Bilic-Brajcic, a woman suffering from cancer. After a mastectomy in 1980, and radiation treatment, scabs began to appear on one of her breasts. Her sister urged her to pray to the Gospa, and according to Frs Laurentin and Rupcic she began to feel better, returned to Medjugorje to give thanks, and also submitted medical documents in September 1982. However, sadly, she too died, in June 1984. An even more famous supposed miracle involved Diana Basile from Milan, who was allegedly cured of multiple sclerosis, and attendant blindness in one eye, in May 1984. This event received a great deal of publicity, but when Bishop Zanic arranged for the medical records of the case to be sent to the medical bureau at Lourdes, Dr Mangiapan responded that, because multiple sclerosis can go into spontaneous remission, it was very difficult to verify whether a cure had really taken place.[307]

This was also the experience of Randall Sullivan, author of the bestselling—but largely uncritical—*The Miracle Detective*, a book mainly devoted to Medjugorje. Sullivan, in investigating accounts of alleged cures at Medjugorje, was forced to admit that he "could not help but notice how many of them involved either MS [multiple sclerosis] or some other disease that attacked the nervous system. Difficult to diagnose and impossible to cure, such illnesses also are remarkably resistant to scientific study, making it very difficult to prove that a healing has been miraculous."[308]

It is interesting to note that Fr Rupcic, writing during the 1980s, describes the case of Diana Basile as not only "the one that has been most thoroughly examined," but also as "the most important among the healings in Medjugorje."[309]

We are clearly a long way here from the astounding cures of organic diseases which have taken place at authentic Marian shrines such as Lourdes.

The Australian investigative journalist, Terry Willesee, a Catholic, traveled to Medjugorje and was responsible for producing a video on the subject, in 1991, entitled *All I Need Is a Miracle*. Despite serious investigation he was not able to uncover any alleged miraculous events which could be substantiated as being of genuinely supernatural origin.[310]

To conclude, all the above evidence indicates that what has been happening on a day-to-day basis in Medjugorje, in terms of some of the activities of the visionaries, has often had more in common with what takes place in religious cults, than within a true and healthy Catholicism. Particularly as regards the bestowing of blessings, the contrast with Fatima could hardly be greater. Likewise, the mixture of ancestor worship with Catholic rituals, as found in the clan ceremonies carried out in Medjugorje, is surely a sign of an unhealthy religious atmosphere. Similarly, as regards the experience of many women in the locality, what would appear to be evidence of diabolical influence cannot be ruled out: when hundreds of women from a relatively small population seek exorcism then clearly something is wrong. If Our Lady really was appearing at Medjugorje they should have been turning to her, rather than the local "wise women."

As we have also seen, the claims for miraculous signs and wonders have been far from conclusive, and indeed, while many of them can be explained in natural terms, again there is a real possibility that some of them may be due to diabolical activity. Regarding the claims for miraculous cures, it is clear, too, that none of them can be accepted from a rigorous medical viewpoint. Regrettably, all of this is further evidence of a critically important aspect of Medjugorje which has rarely been exposed to proper public scrutiny.

15

The Church and Medjugorje

The Vatican and Medjugorje

During the 1980s, the apparently impressive reports about a religious revival emanating from Medjugorje had to be taken seriously. But it seems that, as time has gone on, the Holy See has adopted a more realistic approach, taking account of the various negative elements which have also become evident. No doubt, the Vatican also had to bear in mind the fact that, as the movement in favor of Medjugorje increased in popularity, attracting not just thousands, but in due course millions of pilgrims from all over the world, there was an increasing possibility that a negative judgment might lead to the formation of an alternative, breakaway Medjugorje-based "Church".[311] Certainly, as in so many areas of Church life which were proving contentious in the post-Vatican II era, the Holy See was keen to take a non-confrontational approach in trying to sort out problems, as, for example, those caused by dissident theologians. The same approach also seems to have been adopted with regard to alleged visions.[312]

In *The Ratzinger Report,* published in 1985, Cardinal Ratzinger, who replaced Cardinal Seper as the Prefect of the Congregation for the Doctrine of the Faith in the early 1980s, was queried by the Italian journalist Vittorio Messori, who asked him if he thought some sort of "clarifying statement" on Medjugorje from the Congregation was needed. The question arose because of the large number of pilgrims who were by then going to Medjugorje, and was also prompted by the ongoing conflict between the Franciscans and the local bishop. The first part of the Prefect's response was:

"In this area, more than ever, patience is the fundamental principle of the policy of our Congregation." He then went on to say that, "one of the signs of our times is that the announcements of 'Marian apparitions' are multiplying all over the world." Just prior to this, he had remarked that, "we certainly cannot prevent God from speaking to our time through simple persons and also through extraordinary signs that point to the insufficiency of the cultures stamped by rationalism and positivism that dominate us."[313]

From these words, it seems that Cardinal Ratzinger was at least open to the possibility that these reports of apparitions should be taken seriously, and moreover, according to Fr Michael O'Carroll, the Cardinal was here specifically speaking about Medjugorje. Given the support Medjugorje was receiving from theologians such as Fr Hans Urs von Balthasar, and Fr Laurentin, it would have been difficult for him to think otherwise at this stage, especially taking into account all the information circulating about Medjugorje at the time regarding its positive fruits. In respect of the conduct of pilgrims, conversions, fasting, and so on, much of this was apparently genuine in the early days.

In addition, in February 1985, Archbishop Franic had sent a report on Medjugorje to Cardinal Ratzinger, in which he gave his support to the Franciscans and particularly Fr Vlasic. He pointed to the great number of pilgrims and the other fruits, and characterized the letter circulated by Bishop Zanic as having "already caused scandal." In particular, he called for an "International Commission dependent on the Holy See itself, to evaluate the difficulties raised by His Excellency, the Bishop of Mostar." He made the same point further on, and said that action needed to be taken "before the Bishop succeeds in banning pilgrimages to Medjugorje definitively."

Meanwhile, Bishop Zanic had sent a letter of his own to the Secretariat of State at the Vatican, in January 1985, complaining about the books published by Frs Laurentin and Rupcic, and likewise about the activities of Archbishop Franic, saying that his attitude in supporting "all this propaganda … has appeared most improper and troublesome." He described the latter's archiepiscopal Curia as a "kind of Medjugorje Centre," and stated that the Archbishop had visited Medjugorje, preached there, and had given interviews in *Glas Koncila* to the Medjugorje Franciscans. He had also "visited the homes of the visionaries without any notification to the local bishop or Fr Provincial, as if these did not exist." He finished by saying: "I beg the Holy See to be good enough to issue enlightened directives on the subject."[314]

To return to Cardinal Ratzinger, Messori asked what other criteria the Congregation was using to judge these events, to which the Cardinal replied: "One of our criteria is to separate the aspect of the true or presumed 'supernaturality' of the apparition from that of its spiritual fruits." He then went on to speak of ancient pilgrimage sites which might not have much in the way of "scientific truth" about their traditions, but which were nevertheless spiritually fruitful at the time. He concluded by saying: "The problem is not so much that of modern hypercriticism (which ends up later, moreover, in a form of new credulity), but it is that of the evaluation of the vitality and of the orthodoxy of the religious life that is developing around these places."[315]

Vatican Concerns about Medjugorje

The great difficulty for the Church is that it cannot rush in and make a hasty judgment, and thus it has to be open to the possibility that any claimed vision may be genuine, at least initially, assuming that there are some good aspects present. And in the case of Medjugorje, the initial signs—prayer, fasting, conversions—did seem good, at least to the outside observer. It was only gradually that the negative aspects became apparent, and by then the whole Medjugorje movement had built up an appreciable momentum worldwide.[316]

Meanwhile, by the mid-1980s, the early hostility of the Yugoslav government was abating, as it adopted a different attitude towards Medjugorje. With pilgrim numbers increasing, it was realized that it was a potentially lucrative source of income, and thus from this time onwards, pilgrimages were encouraged. All this was taking place against the backdrop of the severe economic crisis which had developed following the death of Tito in 1980. The government was careful to ensure that accommodation costs were paid directly to it, but clearly there were many other ways that local people could make a profit, even though this financial activity mainly took place in the local currency, the dinar, which had no value outside Yugoslavia.[317]

By the mid 1980s, Bishop Zanic was very concerned about the way the whole phenomenon of the visions was developing, and the wider effect they were having in Croatia. He wrote a prophetic letter to this effect to Fr Laurentin on 25 January 1985, arguing that a "fierce frenzy has taken hold of many faithful who were good until now; they have become excessive and peculiar penitents ... One can look forward to a religious war here."[318] The hostilities which later broke out as Yugoslavia disintegrated indicate that Bishop Zanic's warning was no exaggeration, and that he was far more aware of the subtleties of the situation than some of his critics.

There was obviously some concern in the Vatican too, since, on 23 May 1985, a warning about Medjugorje was issued by Archbishop Alberto Bovone, Undersecretary of the Congregation for the Doctrine of the Faith, in the form of a letter sent to the Bishops of Italy. This letter indicated that official pilgrimages to Medjugorje should not be organized, while also deploring the publicity campaign surrounding the alleged visions, and the confusion that was resulting. Here is the entire text of the letter sent to the secretary of the Italian Bishops' Conference, Msgr. Egidio Caporello:

> Your Excellency, from many parts, especially from the competent Ordinary of Mostar (Yugoslavia), one can gather and lament the vast propaganda given to the "events" tied to the so-called apparitions in Medjugorje, for which pilgrimages and other initiatives have been organized that only contribute to the creation of confusion amongst the faithful and interfere with the work of the appointed Commission which is delicately examining the "events" under scrutiny. In order to avoid enhancing this mentioned propaganda and speculation going on in Italy, despite all that has been expressed and recommended by the Bishops' Conference of Yugoslavia, could this Presidency please suggest to the Italian Episcopate to publicly discourage the organizing of pilgrimages to the so-called centre of apparitions, as well as all other forms of publicity, especially written materials, which could be considered prejudicial to a sober assertion of the facts on the part of the Special Commission which has been canonically formed for this purpose. I take this opportunity to express the assurances of my highest regards...[319]

Clearly then, Cardinal Ratzinger's Congregation was concerned about the "vast propaganda" and "speculation" surrounding Medjugorje at this time.

A New Commission of Inquiry

Then, during the following year, on 2 May 1986, the enlarged commission of inquiry presented its verdict to Bishop Zanic, criticizing the alleged visions, and the following month he sent this report to the Holy See. However, this was not made public, and instead, on 18 January 1987, the formation of yet a third commission was announced, but this time at the higher level of the Yugoslav Bishops' Conference. According to the joint statement on this commission issued by Cardinal Kuharic and Bishop Zanic, this step was taken because the events at Medjugorje were increasingly having a wider impact throughout the Church, and moreover, the formation of this third commission was a Vatican initiative. This is clear from the third paragraph of the joint statement, which after pointing out that the CDF had been made aware of the most recent commission's work, said it had "urged that that work be continued at the level of the National Conference of Bishops."[320]

The immediate result was that the supporters of Medjugorje were able to claim that Bishop Zanic had been undermined and that the Holy See had removed the Medjugorje dossier from his jurisdiction, and this was the message that went out to the world, even though it was not actually the case. In reality, the situation was much more complicated, in that the transfer of the dossier released Bishop Zanic from having to make a difficult decision on his own, especially given the trying relationship he had with the Medjugorje Franciscans, while also allowing him to share the burden of responsibility with the Bishops' Conference.[321]

Pope John Paul II and Medjugorje

As regards the role of Pope John Paul II in this whole question, Fr Laurentin claimed, in 1997, that he had given the Pope a copy of his book on Medjugorje, and that this had influenced the pontiff. Similarly, John Paul II's sympathy towards movements involving young people was probably also a factor in the general mood of unwillingness to see Medjugorje condemned, in addition to the effect of the accounts then being circulated about its fruits. [322]

Moreover, we also have a report published in 1987, following the *ad limina* visit of the Venetian Bishops to Rome, during which they apparently asked the Pope what he thought about Medjugorje, to which he gave a non-committal response, while encouraging any spiritual fruits obtained through Medjugorje.[323]

However, the following year, 1988, Archbishop (later Cardinal) Pio Laghi, the former Apostolic Pro-Nuncio to the United States, stated in a letter that: "Although there have been made observations about Medjugorje attributed to the Holy Father or other officials of the Holy See, none of these have been acknowledged as authentic."[324] In any case, a Pope's *private* opinion on this or any other matter has no binding authority for the faithful.

Much the same can be said for the support given to Medjugorje by individuals such as Mother Teresa, and Fr Gabriele Amorth. While freely acknowledging Mother Teresa's outstanding holiness, this, of itself, did not make her an expert on Medjugorje. There is nothing to suggest that she had made any detailed examination of the facts and controversies surrounding it. Similarly, while acknowledging Fr Amorth's expertise as an exorcist, again, there is nothing to indicate that he has fully investigated Medjugorje. Indeed, it is clear from a 2002 interview he gave on the subject that he has been the leader of a Medjugorje prayer group since 1984, and was thus an early and, it would appear, a largely uncritical devotee of the visions.

Fr Sivric's Book on Medjugorje

1988 also saw the publication of a book in French by Fr Ivo Sivric, which highlighted the problems that emerged when Medjugorje was examined seriously. In 1989 it was translated into English, under the title *The Hidden Side of Medjugorje,* and as we have seen, it detailed, amongst other things, the original interviews between Fr Zovko and the visionaries, which revealed a great deal of hitherto largely unknown material about how Medjugorje had really begun. Fr Sivric was eminently qualified to write a book on Medjugorje, since it was his birthplace, and he was well acquainted with the local situation. In addition, he was a Franciscan, and so was fully aware of the nature of the problems involving some members of the Order and successive local bishops. After ordination in Yugoslavia, in 1941, he went to Rome for further studies, and then settled in the United States, teaching at Duquesne University and writing a number of books.

On hearing about the visions, he returned to his native country, and spent a total of about six months in Medjugorje at various times in 1983, 1984, and 1986. So he not only brought the right qualities to his studies, but had also benefited from his time abroad, which meant he had the ability to look at the situation from a broader perspective. Thus, for all these reasons, he was very well qualified to understand events in Medjugorje.

Fr Laurentin criticized this book in one of his periodic newsletters, but even so, he was obliged to admit that its "sources are fundamental. ... the numerous translated Croatian documents are a service to specialists. ...Thus, one can only congratulate him for having so carefully decoded and edited these probing interviews."[325]

We have seen in this chapter, then, that the position adopted by the Church has gradually clarified over time. To begin with there was an attitude of openness to the possibility that Medjugorje might be genuine: the initial signs seemed good—what could be wrong with calls to prayer, fasting, and a return to the sacraments? But that attitude was gradually replaced with one of greater caution, as some of the doubtful elements regarding Medjugorje began to emerge. By that time, though, the movement in its favor had grown to such proportions that Church authorities were faced with the dilemma of how to deal with the pastoral needs of the hundreds of thousands of pilgrims going there in good faith. Moreover, the political situation in Yugoslavia, and indeed Eastern Europe generally, was still causing concern. As a result, a definitive decision about Medjugorje has been consistently postponed, but surely such a delicate balancing act cannot be maintained indefinitely.

16

Medjugorje
Credibility Problems

Problems with Mirjana

Apart from the problems described above, the credibility of the visionaries has also come under increasingly close scrutiny as time has gone on. Regarding Mirjana, Fr Sivric comments about rumors as to her mental stability. He cites an interview between her and Fr Tomislav Vlasic, which was taped on 10 January 1983, pointing out that although most of this interview can be found in the book by Fr Svetozar Kraljevic, regrettably, in this source, "certain passages have been omitted or have had their sense mitigated."

Since Fr Sivric had a copy of the complete Croatian text of the original interview, he was able to compare this with the translated text and detail important omissions. These include some of Mirjana's thoughts on purgatory, heaven, and hell. The section on purgatory has poor souls from that place of purification allegedly knocking on the window of a sixth-floor apartment in order to ask for prayers—Mirjana explicitly claims that the Gospa told her this. As regards hell, we are told that: "The people begin feeling comfortable there."[326]

One remark that Fr Kraljevic did include from the interview was the claim that the visions at Medjugorje were "the last apparition on earth." When pressed on this point, Mirjana went on to say that: "It is the last time that Jesus or Mary will appear on earth."[327]

Certainly, there is evidence of some problems regarding Mirjana's mental state in the interview. At one point, Fr Vlasic asked her if she had been depressed after what had allegedly been her last meeting with the Gospa. To this she replied: "Terribly sad. At school ... everybody told me I'd gone mad. They laughed at me. I didn't want to talk to anybody. ... I've just wanted to sit by myself, alone. ... I start to cry, without knowing why."

In connection with this, it is perhaps worth noting that Fr Jordan Aumann lists "[c]onfusion, anxiety, and deep depression," as being amongst the recognized "signs of the diabolical spirit."[328]

The Credibility of Vicka

Regarding Vicka, the somewhat "difficult" side of her character comes across quite clearly in her talks with Fr Bubalo, as set down in his book, *A Thousand Encounters with the Blessed Virgin Mary in Medjugorje*. For instance, when he asked her about the nature of the holy water with which she sprinkled the Gospa on the third day, she responded thus: "Lord [!], why are you making like an Englishman? As though you don't know that in every christian home we have blessed salt, and also holy water."[329]

There are other examples of this type of thing found in the book, but suffice to say that she comes across as a difficult individual, one whose behavior is not consistent with what would be expected of a genuine Marian seer. Even Fr Vlasic could make a comment such as the following about Vicka: "this girl is choleric and has a brusque and sometimes aggressive style."

In another conversation, during which Fr Bubalo asked Vicka about her experience of heaven—which she alleged she had seen in a vision—he told her that somebody "once told me (and he was poking fun at it) that you said, telling of that Heaven, that Heaven has some kind of doors. What is your response now?" To this, Vicka replied: "Why the same as then! There where we stood with the Virgin there is some sort of tunnel, some sort of door, and next to them a man is standing. The Virgin said not everyone can enter. You need a *permit* there too. A narrow passage awaits everyone there."[330]

Whatever sort of reception people can expect at the gates of eternity, one thing is certain: permits will *not* be required to enter heaven!

Questions about Vicka can certainly be raised following an incident that took place on 14 January 1985. This involved a pilgrim
named Jean-Louis Martin, who, although initially enthusiastic
about Medjugorje, gradually came to have doubts, and decided to
put one of the visionaries to the test. Also present on this occasion
were Fr Pervan, who was the parish priest, Fr Barbaric, Fr Vego, and
Louis Bélanger. While Vicka was in an apparent ecstasy in the
apparition room at the church, Martin made as if to poke her in the
eyes with his fingers, and she reacted as if she had been startled,
fleeing the room accompanied by Fr Vego.

Vicka returned after a while, and then offered the quite incredible explanation that she had reacted in that particular way in order
to prevent the baby Jesus from falling, as she was under the impression that the Blessed Virgin was about to drop him. This incident
was captured on film and has been widely circulated. It is also true
that, from 27 January 1985, the apparition room was closed to the
public.[331]

Archbishop Franic mentioned this incident in a statement at
the meeting of the Yugoslav Episcopal Conference on 17 April
1985: "There is talk of a young Frenchman, who, we are told, put
his two fingers in front of the visionaries' [sic] eyes and they
reacted. ... I met this Frenchman in Medjugorje, he invited me to
his lodgings to let me see some video-cassettes, but I had not the
time to delay."[332]

Ivan and the "Sign"

In May 1982, Bishop Zanic sent two members of the investigative
commission he had set up the previous January, to question the
visionaries about the miraculous sign that had been promised. They
were asked to describe this sign but refused, prompting suspicions
that they had been tipped off. Mirjana was in Sarajevo at the time,
and she too refused to comply, leading Bishop Zanic to suspect that
somebody had contacted her by phone.

On this occasion Ivan Dragicevic was also absent, away at the
Franciscan seminary in Visoko, but when questioned separately he
readily agreed to write down details of the sign, which he did, and
his text, plus a copy, were sealed in envelopes and held at the
seminary archives and the bishop's office in Mostar respectively.

When all the visionaries, including Ivan, came to Mostar later in the year, on 3 August, they were asked by the Bishop to write down this "sign" on separate pieces of paper, but they refused, claiming they had a mandate not to do so from the Gospa.

Bishop Zanic increased the size of his commission from five to fourteen members in 1984, and Ivan was interviewed about the "sign" by three members of this enlarged Episcopal commission in March 1985. Fr Puljic, one of the commission members, asked Ivan if he had written anything about the "sign," to which Ivan responded: "No." Fr Puljic then asked him what he had put in the envelope at Visoko, to which Ivan replied: "I put a blank sheet of paper in the envelope; then I sealed it; then the Gospa appeared to me and she smiled."

Such an answer is clearly disturbing, since it implies that the Blessed Virgin would make a special appearance just to condone this deception.

But in reality, when the contents of the envelope from the bishop's Chancery were examined, in the presence of all the commission members, it was found to contain not a blank sheet, but a signed statement from Ivan, dated 9 May 1982. This included information about the sign, apparently dictated by the Gospa, that it would be, "a huge shrine in Medjugorje in memory of my apparitions and this shrine shall be [dedicated] to my person." Moreover, according to the statement, this shrine "will appear in the sixth month." This presumably meant June 1982. As is well known, though, to this day nothing of the sort has occurred.[333]

Archbishop Franic, during his statement made at the Yugoslav Episcopal conference on 17 April 1985, made the following remarks: "The case of Ivan Dragicevic is held by certain members of the Commission to be proof positive that everything that happens in Medjugorje is pure fantasy. We must distinguish Ivan the seer from Ivan the human being." He then went on to say that Ivan the seminarian had a "reverential fear" of his superiors, and was afraid he would be expelled if he wrote nothing.[334]

Marija's Messages – Her Retraction

Marija began giving out monthly messages from the Gospa on 25 January 1987. According to Wayne Weible, she would "write down the message and give it to Father Slavko Barbaric. It would then be checked thoroughly for adherence to Scripture and church doctrine, and in less than 24 hours, it would be transmitted to prayer groups and to others around the world."[335]

Had the Blessed Virgin Mary become so deficient in scriptural and doctrinal knowledge that her messages now needed to be vetted by Fr Barbaric? Is not this just more evidence that these statements are not supernatural?

Marija was also closely involved in a rather strange project which was promoted by Fr Vlasic and Agnes Heupel. On 25 March 1988, Fr Vlasic issued an "appeal" from near Parma, Italy, in which he claimed that, since 1985, "Our Lord and Our Heavenly Mother" had been speaking to him in his heart, "in a special manner," giving him "special communiqués," which involved the setting up of a religious community. As early as 7 October 1981, a little over three months after the visions began, Fr Vlasic had made the following request of the Gospa: "Should we found here a community just like that of St Francis of Assisi?" Obviously, then, such an idea had been in his mind for a long time. Agnes Heupel also claimed to have received a message from Jesus in support of this community of young people of both sexes, and the idea received an apparent endorsement from Marija in April 1988, who said that she had seen a vision of the Gospa and that she was supportive of the idea.

In any event, when this proposal for a mixed community was put to the Vatican, permission was not forthcoming. Marija then issued the following statement in a letter of 11 July 1988:[336]

> I feel morally bound to make the following statements before God, Our Lady, and the Church of Jesus Christ: ... The message of the text *An Invitation to the Marian Year* and the deposition which bears my signature is that I brought Our Lady's answer to Brother [sic] Tomislav Vlasic's question. That answer was supposedly: 'This is God's plan' In other words, it follows from these texts that I transmitted to Brother Tomislav Vlasic, Our Lady's confirmation and express approval of this work ... I now declare that I never asked Our Lady for any confirmation whatsoever of this work by Brother Tomislav Vlasic and Agnes Heupel ... My first statement ... does not correspond to the truth. Brother Tomislav Vlasic advised me, stressing the point again and again, that I, as a seer, ought to write a deposition which the world expected. [337]

Marija was due to marry her fiancée, Paolo Lunetti, in September 1993, and according to Wayne Weible, this "gave cause for concern among the Franciscans of Medjugorje. Would this marriage disrupt the flow of monthly messages, or the pattern of the apparitions, especially since Marija would be living in Monza, Italy?" Marija reassured them that she expected no change to her regime of daily visions, but concern remained because, "[t]he other visionaries who had married had settled in the village. Marija would be the first one to be living away from the direct spiritual guidance of the Franciscans."[338]

Vicka's Physical and Psychological State

In 1985, Vicka claimed to be receiving revelations about the life of the Blessed Virgin, and, more generally, about the future. She was also beset with headaches and black-outs—which went on for years—and which may indicate the sort of psychological strain she was under. It is certainly quite astonishing to read in an article by Fr Janko Bubalo, written in January 1986, that "Vicka lived a mysterious life of headaches and fainting which grew more and more difficult to bear and lasted longer and longer." These episodes were apparently impervious to medical treatment, even in Zagreb. Further on, Fr Bubalo tells us that her "fainting began to last longer and longer. Nearly every day it lasted fifteen hours or more," and she would only wake up for her encounter with the Gospa.

All of this indicates that Vicka's physical and psychological state was far from normal during this period. Indeed, as Joachim Bouflet points out, Vicka had at this time all the characteristics of an hysteric, being subject to strange illnesses which appear suddenly and which defy diagnosis. According to Mary Craig, these characteristics were also noticed by a group of psychiatrists who came to examine the visionaries in January 1986. They saw Vicka one afternoon "when she was in what her family described as a 'coma'," but which the psychiatrists described as an "hysterical stupor." In addition, one of the three psychiatrists "observed that she had a tendency to exaggerate for effect, always wanted to be the centre of attention, and was inclined to court popularity."

According to Craig, it was later claimed that Vicka had been suffering from a tumor on the brain, but that she was "cured on the

date foretold her by the Lady—25ᵗʰ of September 1988—and is now
in good health."[339] However, if she had been suffering from a brain
tumor, how does one explain the fact that it had not been revealed
by any of the previous medical examinations she had undergone?

This is what Fr Jordan Aumann has to say about the characteristics
required if we are likely to be dealing with genuine divine
revelations:

> The person who receives the revelation should be examined carefully,
> especially as to temperament and character. If the person is humble,
> well balanced, discreet, evidently advanced in virtue, and enjoys good
> mental and physical health, there is good reason to proceed further and
> to examine the revelation itself. But if the individual … suffers nervous
> affliction, is subject to periods of great exhaustion or great depression,
> or is eager to divulge the revelation, there is cause for serious doubt.[340]

Vicka's Ignorance of the Annunciation

In discussing the more ornate clothing worn by the Gospa during
important visions, Fr Bubalo asked Vicka if she could recall any
specific occasion, to which she replied: "I do recall, how could I
not! One of her feast days is marked in my mind, one that occurs
about the end of March or so." Fr Bubalo asked her if this was the
Annunciation, to which she replied: "I don't know. She told us
something about that day, but I don't remember." Fr Bubalo
responded to this uncertain reply as follows: "And it's not clear to
you what is commemorated on that day?" To this, the visionary
replied: "It is and it isn't. Don't let me jump off the deep end on
that one!" When Fr Bubalo then explained to her the significance
of the feast of the Annunciation, Vicka expressed relief as up to
then she hadn't been quite sure, but now she understood why the
Virgin had been so happy on that occasion: "I never saw her so
happy, not even on Christmas. Why she almost danced with joy!"

Fr Bubalo gave up on this particular line of questioning, but the
implications of this exchange are clear. It is surely difficult to
believe that somebody who was supposedly seeing the Blessed
Virgin on a daily basis was so ignorant of the importance of the
Annunciation. This is very significant, since a claim is made further
on in Fr Bubalo's book that Vicka had been receiving specific
instructions from Mary about her life, and we are led to believe that

these instructions had been going on for nearly three years. More-over, we are also asked to believe that the Gospa appeared to Vicka three or four times on certain days, and that up to 1985, she had appeared to her in thirty-eight different places.[341]

What, then, are we to make of the credibility of these particular visionaries? Whether it is Mirjana's reported psychological instabil-ity, Vicka's possible hysteria, her strange illnesses, and religious ignorance, Marija's humiliating retraction, or Ivan's "confusion" over the alleged sign, it seems clear from the evidence presented that they have almost nothing in common with genuine Marian seers, with the simplicity or holiness of St Bernadette or the children of Fatima.

Problems with the Religious Vows

Regrettably, the credibility of some of the Franciscans involved with Medjugorje has also been undermined by incidents in which it is alleged that the vow of chastity has been broken. While this would not constitute primary evidence against the visions—since given human frailty anyone can fall into sins of this kind—it would nevertheless indicate a further negative aspect which cannot be ignored.[342]

Similarly, serious sexual allegations were made against Fr Jozo Zovko, the parish priest in Medjugorje at the beginning of the visions, and as we have seen, one of the main Medjugorje promot-ers. These matters were brought to the attention of the Franciscan General, Herman Schalueck, and Fr Zovko was disciplined by Bishop Zanic in August 1989. He was also "disciplined a second time, in June 1994, this time under Bishop Peric, for pertinacious disobedience." Fr René Laurentin, in his *Dernières Nouvelles,* was forced to acknowledge that since the motives for the sanctions against Fr Zovko were not made public, they must have been serious.

The testimony of Marija Pavlovic, from 21 October 1981, that, according to the Gospa, Fr Zovko was, "a saint," looks regrettably and sadly suspect in the light of all this.[343]

It transpires, too, that in 1990, Fr Zovko was requested, by the Vatican Congregation for the Evangelization of Peoples, to move away from Medjugorje to a distant convent. But he only went as far as Siroki Brijeg, and still displayed evidence of disobedience by visiting Medjugorje. During the 1990s, he was involved in constructing, in the words of Bishop Peric, a religious house "of great proportions" in Siroki Brijeg without any ecclesiastical permission. In 1997, it was reported that up to 8 million Deutschmarks had been spent on this project, but it was unclear exactly where this money had come from.[344]

These very sad incidents further illustrate the "hidden" side of Medjugorje, a side which most pilgrims know absolutely nothing about.

17

Medjugorje and the War

The War in Yugoslavia

The Communist regimes in Eastern Europe began to unravel with great speed from 1989 onwards, a process which was definitively marked by the fall of the Berlin Wall in November of that year. By and large, this process was very peaceful, but the situation in Yugoslavia was different—and potentially explosive—given its rival groupings of Serbs, Croats, Slovenes, and Muslims, in a country divided along religious and ethnic lines. Franjo Tudjman became leader of a new political party in Croatia, the HDZ, but his program did not include guarantees for ethnic minorities within Croatia, and particularly for the Serbs. In Serbia, meanwhile, Slobodan Milosevic had been promoting an increasingly xenophobic policy as he rose to power. As nationalist feelings continued to grow all over Yugoslavia, conflict became inevitable, particularly in Bosnia-Herzegovina, which was very ethnically diverse and had a large Muslim population.[345]

Medjugorje and the Yugoslav Bishops' Conference

The findings of the Yugoslav Bishops' Conference on Medjugorje—the Zadar declaration—was officially published on 10 April 1991, and this clearly stated that, after nearly ten years of alleged visions, it could not be affirmed that "supernatural apparitions and revelations" had taken place. Equally, however, the bishops were concerned that pilgrims to Medjugorje, who, despite the dangerous situation in Yugoslavia, were still coming to the village, should have their spiritual needs catered for. The text of the declaration is as follows:

> On the basis of investigation up till now it cannot be established that one is dealing with supernatural apparitions and revelations. However, the numerous gatherings of the faithful from different parts of the world, who are coming to Medjugorje prompted both by motives of belief and certain other motives, require the attention and pastoral care in the first place of the bishop of the diocese and of the other bishops with him so that in Medjugorje and everything related to it a healthy devotion toward the Blessed Virgin Mary would be promoted in conformity with the teaching of the Church. For that purpose the bishops shall issue separate appropriate liturgical-pastoral directives. Likewise by means of their Commission they shall further follow and investigate the total event in Medjugorje.[346]

The declaration illustrated the dilemma faced by Church authorities: they could not pronounce in favor of the alleged visions because, as was stated, they could not find anything supernatural about them, but equally they also had to respond to the spiritual needs of those who believed in the visions in good faith.

Previously, it had been reported that the Pope had met with one of the Yugoslav Bishops, and assured him that a Vatican statement on Medjugorje would eventually be issued. According to John Thavis of the Catholic News Service, this meeting took place on 8 February 1991. Cardinal Ratzinger had made similar remarks to E. Michael Jones, who had put some questions to him during a visit to Dallas, Texas, on 7 February 1991: in agreeing with the stance of the Yugoslav Bishops, the Cardinal indicated that the statement would be issued soon. Later in the year, though, the civil war had apparently complicated matters to the extent that this statement was postponed. When asked about his own opinion on Medjugorje, Cardinal Ratzinger responded: "I can have no other opinion than that of the [Yugoslavian] bishops."[347]

The Zadar Declaration as Pro-Medjugorje?

But some supporters of Medjugorje then attempted to explain how the Zadar declaration could be seen, from their perspective, in a positive light. A good example of this comes from Fr Robert Faricy, who wrote about the work of the Yugoslav Bishops' commission as follows, saying that it "released an inconclusive report in 1990 that ... could not determine as yet whether the Medjugorje events were really from God in an extraordinary manner."[348]

This is a puzzling statement, and it is equally difficult to understand the following pronouncement from Archbishop Franc Perko of Belgrade, which was made in 1991:

> It is not true that the bishops' document ... states there is nothing supernatural about Medjugorje. The prelates wrote: '*non constat de supernaturalitate*' ["the supernatural character is not established"]. They did not write: '*constat de non supernaturalitate*' ["the non-supernatural character is established]. There is an enormous difference: the first cannot be interpreted definitively but is left open to new developments. This does not mean that I'm in favour of Medjugorje. I believe that we cannot make a definitive declaration but there are signs that perhaps there is, or has been, something supernatural about Medjugorje.[349]

That may have been the archbishop's own approach, and that of others on the commission, but is it really a logical position to take? On the face of it, it seems that the bishops' statement indicates their acceptance of the traditional Latin phrase *non constat de supernaturalitate*, that is, that there was no direct evidence of supernaturality, and thus it was not an express denial of supernaturality, as would have been the case if they had used the phrase *constat de non-supernaturalitate*. But having said that, in the real world, can it seriously be suggested that although there had been roughly three thousand alleged visions by this time, none of which could enable the bishops to state "that one is dealing with supernatural apparitions and revelations," nevertheless, the commission was genuinely holding out some hope that, perhaps after several thousand more visions, it would be able to come to a positive conclusion? Is that really a credible position to maintain?

In theory, the use of *non constat de supernaturalitate* could allow for further developments—but regarding Medjugorje is this at all likely? It *might* be possible if the commission had been dealing with a more "normal" claim of alleged apparitions, numbering in single figures, and one taking place over a short period, but surely not after ten years and thousands of alleged visions.

This becomes obvious if we use a more down-to-earth example to explore this situation. Supposing a person meets a new work colleague during a break and they get to know each other. Now, if after a week of such meetings, this person was to say that they could not affirm that anything that their new colleague had said during this time was true, then we could accept this as a reasonable situation. After all, a week is not a long time to get to know what another person is really like, and to be able to check up on what they have told us. But now, suppose that after working with this person for ten years, and talking with them every day, they were to turn around and say that they could not affirm that anything they had been told during this lengthy period was true, then unquestionably we would be in a completely different situation. In effect, they would be saying that they just could not trust the other person, and indeed were not even sure that anything they had been told was true. This type of example allows us to see the Zadar declaration in its proper perspective, and not through unrealistic, pro-Medjugorje, rose-tinted spectacles.

The Significance of the Zadar Declaration

It is important to note that the Yugoslav Bishops' decision had been supported by nineteen of their number, with only one abstention, that of Archbishop Frane Franic of Split, and with not a single dissenting vote. The Zadar decision was exceptional in that it is very unusual that a bishops' conference should have made such a declaration about alleged visions: usually this is the province of a single bishop. Thus, this was a very significant decision, because one of the spiritual powers conferred on bishops within the Catholic Church allows that, when a large number of them agree on a specific *spiritual* ruling, then it is to be assumed that they will be especially assisted by the Holy Spirit in proclaiming the truth.

What this means is that any ruling they come to will be more than just a product of their collective intelligence and experience as bishops—more even than any personal opinions they may have on the subject. The Holy Spirit will be assisting them in a special way to arrive at the truth, in ways that they may not even be consciously aware of.

This is illustrated by the teaching found in the Second Vatican Council document, *Lumen Gentium* (25), which states: "Bishops who teach in communion with the Roman Pontiff are to be revered by all as witnesses of divine and Catholic truth; the faithful, for their part, are obliged to submit to their Bishops' decision, made in the name of Christ, in matters of faith and morals, and to adhere to it with a ready and respectful allegiance of mind." This is obviously not to say that the Zadar declaration is on a par with, for example, official conciliar teaching, but it is still an authoritative verdict nonetheless. Regrettably, the great majority of Medjugorje supporters have interpreted the bishops' decision in a way which is contrary to a common sense reading of it.

Yugoslavia Disintegrates

Meanwhile, the unstable political situation, one of the factors which had hampered a straightforward Vatican decision on Medjugorje since the mid-eighties, was growing progressively worse as concerns about Communism were replaced by worries over a resurgent nationalism. This was increasingly reflected in violent incidents between the various ethnic groups, and acts of attendant ethnic cleansing, which were intensifying to the level of all-out war. From the Croat perspective, the Yugoslav army was acting exclusively at the behest of the Serbs, while for the latter an anti-Western, siege mentality was developing.[350]

Around the same time that the statement of the Yugoslav Bishops' Conference was issued, the political situation in the country began to come to a climax. Franjo Tudjman and Slobodan Milosevic met in early 1991, and decided between them that they would partition Bosnia-Herzegovina, with the Croats to take the northwestern section, the Serbs the southeastern section, with a Muslim buffer zone in the middle. On 25 June 1991, almost exactly ten years after Medjugorje began, both Croatia and Slovenia declared independence. The result of these declarations was that the Yugoslav army, essentially a Serb-run military, invaded Slovenia, thus initiating full-scale hostilities.

The Yugoslav Bishops had been due to ratify their Medjugorje directives arising from the Zadar declaration in a plenary session on 27 June 1991, but were prevented from doing so by the war. The ultimate result was that the thorny question of Medjugorje then devolved onto the four bishops who made up the Bishops' Conference of Bosnia-Herzegovina. Thus, it can be said that the violent dismembering of Yugoslavia was one of the factors which saved Medjugorje,[351] although undoubtedly even quite restrictive directives would not have dampened the ardor of many enthusiasts for the visions.

The European Community recognized Croatia and Slovenia as independent nations on 6 January 1992, followed a week later by the Holy See, and in April both the EC and US recognized Bosnia-Herzegovina, in a move which intensified the fighting in that region. This had a direct effect on Medjugorje, to the extent that the parish church was closed for services, remaining locked for nearly three months from April to June. According to E. Michael Jones, the reaction of the visionaries and their Franciscan mentors was to send an increasingly desperate series of faxes to George Bush demanding intervention on the part of the US, while Yugoslav jets screamed overhead.

It is certainly strange that the visionaries had not been somewhat better prepared for all this by their decade of daily encounters with the Gospa.[352]

Medjugorje's "Little War"

While all this was going on, away from the gaze of absent pilgrims, a regular "little war" was going on in Medjugorje. But the phrase "little war" should not be understood as indicating a lack of violence; rather the interclan feuds which broke out at this time were characterized by quite vicious atrocities and murders. Indeed, Mart Bax describes the area around Medjugorje as one where historically, "eruptions of human violence were the rule rather than the exception," and, quoting another author's words, which he makes his own, he describes it as a region "where the most primitive branches of the Serb and Croat tribes live."[353]

From late 1991 until July 1992, at which point the Croatian army "pacified" the region, Bax speaks of a *mali rat* ("little war") in Medjugorje, a conflict which led to a considerable number of deaths, missing persons, and people fleeing the area. As Bax puts it: "Whence this barbarization? How is it possible that after a ten-year reign of the Virgin Mary, referred to locally as the Queen of Peace, villagers started slaughtering each other?"

Those involved in the violence were not soldiers as such, but mostly rival groups of local people involved in the pilgrimage trade. It should be emphasized that this was not a Croat-Serb dispute, but one solely involving Croats. While the pilgrims flooded into Medjugorje during the eighties all was relatively calm, since there was enough profit for everyone. But once war broke out, this situation quickly changed as pilgrim numbers rapidly diminished. By the spring of 1991, the town was practically deserted, and since many of the villagers had gone into debt to finance the building of pilgrim accommodation, they demanded a fairer sharing out of what little business there was. But the financially dominant clan were not prepared to do this, and so violence ensued.[354]

Bax tells us that: "An estimated eighty people, almost sixty of whom were locals, lost their lives ... their mutilated bodies, usually hanging from a tree or ceiling beam, bore witness to the atrocious acts." He further informs us that: "The mutilations followed a fixed pattern, with more and more parts of the bodies being removed."

But eventually the violence subsided, and Bax was once more able to visit Medjugorje. He saw for himself that the pilgrimage business was reviving, under the "protection" of the Croatian army. Villagers were lavish in their apologies for the "inconvenience" the "war" had caused, while the pilgrims, for their part, were "very understanding," and were glad that "these people could live in freedom again," and that "the Message of Peace had triumphed."[355]

Once again, the contrast between the general atmosphere surrounding these events at Medjugorje, and Fatima, could hardly be greater. Sr Lucia's second volume of memoirs clearly shows the wonderful atmosphere in her home village of Aljustrel, which was not far from the site of the apparitions at the Cova da Iria. It was a place where genuine Christian love of neighbor reigned, and the idea that the inhabitants would engage in violence or vendettas against each other was completely unthinkable. Where there was violence it came from the government in its persecution of the Church, but this was an exterior violence and nothing to do with the people of Aljustrel.

To put all this violence in context, suppose, by the wildest flight of the imagination, that the piety stallholders, taxi drivers, and café owners of Lourdes or Fatima should suddenly start attacking each other with knives and guns—imagine the absolute scandal this would cause. Is it really possible to believe that Our Lady would have appeared in Medjugorje, knowing that within a decade this type of inter-communal violence would actually be taking place there? If the Blessed Virgin had really appeared in Medjugorje, and was continuing to do so on a daily basis, the very least that we could expect is that the centuries-old feuding in the area would have ceased, and that those involved in the violence would have been converted.

The Real War comes to Medjugorje

The disturbing way the war as a whole was affecting Medjugorje also became apparent in the early nineties; it seems that there was even a factory there that was turning out hand grenades. In addition, radical rightwing Croat HOS forces based in the town, along with more regular HVO [Bosnian Croat army] forces, were attracting neo-Nazis from all quarters to fight alongside them—swastika pins were on sale alongside rosaries in the piety stalls of Medjugorje.[356]

A common claim made by Medjugorje supporters is that the divine origin of the visions is indicated by the fact that the village itself was not seriously affected by the war, in contrast say to Mostar, which was devastated. This is to ignore the fact that wars, by their very nature, are chaotic, and that particular locations may well escape damage essentially because they are not of strategic importance. If this argument is taken to its logical conclusion, then we would have to say that the famous Benedictine monastery at Monte Cassino in Italy, which was severely damaged during the Second World War, was somehow a place of infidelity, of God's *disfavor*. In fact, it was destroyed by warfare on two previous occasions, and also by an earthquake in the 14th century. Thus, whether or not a particular religious location is destroyed during a war is neither here nor there as regards authenticity, and this is just another example of a very weak argument being used to prop up Medjugorje.

By the early nineties, then, it began to look as if Medjugorje was in a state of decline: Yugoslavia was rapidly fragmenting as the vicious civil war took its course, and the Yugoslav Bishops had clearly indicated that there was nothing supernatural about the visions. Somehow, though, once the war was over, the pilgrims returned, and this is surely one of the most inexplicable aspects of the whole affair. Negative factors which would have been enough to destroy any normal enterprise many times over have been shrugged off by Medjugorje enthusiasts, with barely a ripple of concern being expressed.

18

Clarifying the
Case of Medjugorje

The Poem of the Man-God and the Visionaries

The Poem of the Man-God, the "life of Christ" by Maria Valtorta, was placed on the *Index of Forbidden Books* in 1959, but it still managed to impinge on Medjugorje in 1991. When the *Index* was effectively revoked following Vatican II, previously banned works like *The Poem* were given a new lease of life, and it was particularly popular with Medjugorje supporters. However, Cardinal Ratzinger had written to Cardinal Siri with respect to the *Poem of the Man-God,* in January 1985, saying: "After the dissolution of the Index, when some people thought the printing and distribution of the work was permitted, people were reminded again in *L'Osservatore Romano* (June 15, 1966) that, as was published in the *Acta Apostolicae Sedis* (1966), the Index retains its moral force despite its dissolution."

Marija Pavlovic appeared, with Fr Slavko Barbaric, on a call-in TV show from New Orleans entitled *Focus.* During the program, a caller asked what Our Lady had said about *The Poem of the Man-God,* and Marija responded in Italian, *si può leggere,* that is: "You can read it." Realizing belatedly that this was probably not a good answer, she turned to Fr Barbaric for help, and he attempted to rescue the situation by suggesting that viewers might like to consult their local bishop about Valtorta's work.[357]

It is clear that amongst the other visionaries, Vicka also had a similar approach to this work, which has been described—with good reason—as a "vulgar, blasphemous, and fraudulent 'revelation'. " In an interview, when asked about this, she said: "Marija asked the Virgin about that book, and the Virgin said that she should read that book, because it is like a poem between God and man."[358]

Surely this is another indication that Medjugorje is not supernatural, since it is impossible to believe that the Blessed Virgin could have suggested that dangerous nonsense such as the *Poem* was suitable as spiritual reading.

Bishop Peric, the Pope, and Medjugorje

In early May 1992, Bishop Zanic's Episcopal palace in Mostar was shelled by artillery and destroyed. He was forced to flee and finally reached Rome, where he asked the Pope to be relieved of his duties, and that Ratko Peric be named as his successor.[359]

The Pope had been due to visit Sarajevo in September 1994, but just before he arrived, the Serbs shelled a spot very close to where he had been scheduled to celebrate an outdoor Mass, and this part of the trip was cancelled. According to E. Michael Jones, this happened after the visionary Marija Pavlovic had proclaimed a message from the Gospa, on 24 August, to the effect that the Pope *would* be arriving there as planned.[360]

Bishop Ratko Peric attended the Synod of Bishops in Rome in October 1994, and made a public plea for help in resolving the question of Medjugorje. He stated that many ecclesial problems were evident at Medjugorje, including unauthorized religious communities establishing themselves in the town, and religious buildings being erected without permission—such as the giant pavilion behind the local parish church of St James—as well as difficulties caused by the local Franciscans acting illicitly.

Jones reports that street protests against the Bishop were organized in Mostar by supporters of the Franciscans, and the situation became so bad that, as we have seen, on 2 April 1995, "the Bishop was attacked by a mob in his chancery, and his pectoral cross was ripped from his person. He was then beaten up, forced into a waiting car, driven to an illicit chapel run by the Medjugorje Franciscans, and held hostage for 10 hours. It was only when the

Mayor of Mostar showed up with UN troops that the Bishop was released."[361]

Fr Laurentin confirms that this incident did take place saying: "When Bishop Peric annexed the Franciscan parishes around Mostar, the Croatians wrongfully kidnapped him. No one was able to stop them, except for the Franciscans, I am told."[362]

How could the Franciscans conceivably have consented to such an outrage? What does this further incident reveal about the whole Medjugorje phenomenon?

The following statement from Pope John Paul II, as reported in the 18 September 1996 edition of *L'Osservatore Romano*, would appear to be a criticism of the spirituality which has developed out of alleged visions like Medjugorje, and represented his more recent thinking on the subject: "Within the Church community, the multiplication of supposed 'apparitions' or 'visions' is sowing confusion and reveals a certain lack of a solid basis to the faith and Christian life among her members."[363]

Circulating Accounts of Alleged Visions

The 4 December 1996 edition of *L'Osservatore Romano* carried a notification from the Congregation for the Doctrine of the Faith, principally on the questions raised by the case of Vassula Ryden; but it also contained a second section giving important general information relevant to the whole problem of alleged visions:

1) The interpretation given by some individuals to a Decision approved by Paul VI on 14 October 1966 and promulgated on 15 November of that year, in virtue of which writings and messages resulting from alleged revelations could be freely circulated in the Church, is absolutely groundless. This decision actually referred to the "Abolition of the Index of Forbidden Books" and determined that—after the relevant censures were lifted—the moral obligation still remained of not circulating or reading those writings which endanger faith and morals.

2) It should be recalled however that with regard to the circulation of texts of alleged private revelations, canon 823 §1 of the current Code remains in force: "the Pastors of the Church have the ... right to demand that writings to be published by the Christian faithful which touch upon faith or morals be submitted to their judgment."

3) Alleged supernatural revelations and writings concerning them are submitted in first instance to the judgment of the diocesan Bishop, and, in particular cases, to the judgment of the Episcopal Conference and the Congregation for the Doctrine of the Faith.

Regarding the belief amongst many Medjugorje supporters that "writings and messages resulting from alleged revelations" can be circulated freely in the Church, it is clear that this is incorrect. In reality, all such texts should be submitted to the "Pastors of the Church," for their judgment, which in this case means the local Bishop, and if necessary an even higher authority. This has certainly not happened with many of the books supportive of Medjugorje, to say nothing of the periodic messages emanating from some of the visionaries.

Even as long ago as the 1950s, the Church had begun to warn ordinary Catholics about the dangers of a too credulous approach to accounts of visions. This is what Cardinal Ottaviani wrote on the subject, as reported in *L'Osservatore Romano* of 14 February 1951:

> Fifty years ago who would have believed that the Church today would have to put her children, and even her priests, on their guard against stories of visions, false miracles and of those so-called preternatural occurrences which from one country to another, from one continent to another, everywhere indeed, attract excited crowds. ... We have for years been in the presence of a revival of a popular passion for the marvellous, even in matters of religion. Crowds of the faithful assemble in places where apparitions or miracles are supposed to have happened; but at the same time they desert their churches, the Sacraments, the hearing of sermons. ... The Church certainly does not wish to hush up the wonders wrought by God. She only desires the faithful to distinguish clearly between what comes from God and what does not come from God and may come from our adversary who is also His. The Church is the enemy of false miracles.

Some Guidelines for Discernment

Fr Jordan Aumann OP, in his *Spiritual Theology,* speaks of there being three different "types" of spirits which can affect us, that is the divine spirit, the diabolical spirit, and the human spirit. God always inclines us towards good, the devil always inclines us towards evil, while our own human spirits can be influenced either way.

While the devil, or a diabolical spirit, cannot, for example, pro-duce any genuinely supernatural phenomena, such as raising the dead or predicting the future, evil spirits can produce corporeal or imaginative visions, or false ecstasies. They can also cure diseases due to diabolical influence, or cause individuals to hear sounds or voices.[364]

It is clear from the Bible, that there have been instances when, by means of diabolical power, individuals have been able to mimic miracles. Thus, as we can read in Exodus, chapters 7 to 9, Pharaoh's magicians and sorcerers were able to imitate some of the miraculous deeds done by Moses and Aaron. But there was a limit to their power.

Fr Aumann also speaks of the following characteristics which can be taken as "general signs of the divine spirit." Amongst these he includes a tendency towards truthfulness, and also what he describes as "gravity," that is the idea that: "God is never the cause of things that are useless, futile, frivolous, or impertinent. When his spirit moves a soul it is always for something serious and beneficial."

As we have seen, it is highly questionable if truthfulness or grav-ity are words that could be justly used in describing many aspects of Medjugorje.

In the same way, Fr Aumann speaks about the quality of *docility,* namely the principle that: "Souls that are moved by the spirit of God accept cheerfully the advice and counsel of their directors or others who have authority over them. This spirit of obedience, docility, and submission is one of the clearest signs that a particular inspiration or movement is from God. This is especially true in the case of the educated, who have a greater tendency to be attached to their own opinions." He also has this to say about the quality of *humility* regarding those claiming divine favors: "The Holy Spirit always fills the soul with sentiments of humility and self-effacement. The loftier the communications from on high, the more profoundly the soul inclines to the abyss of its own nothing-ness. Mary said, 'I am the servant of the Lord. Let it be done to me as you say.' "

If we apply these criteria to both the visionaries and some of their associates, then clearly they cannot be said to have been acting with any great spirit of docility or humility with regard to the bishops of Mostar.[365] Similarly, it is hard to believe that another quality he lists, that of *self-abnegation,* is a defining characteristic of the visionaries, given their strong tendency to court publicity.

Regarding "signs of the diabolical spirit," Fr Aumann lists the following points as being worthy of attention, and particularly, a *spirit of falsity,* since, because "[t]he devil is the father of lies," he can cleverly conceal "his deceit by half-truths and pseudo-mystical phenomena." He also speaks of *obstinacy* as being one of "the surest signs of a diabolical spirit," while "constant indiscretion and a restless spirit" are equally amongst his contra-indications. Similarly, both a s*pirit of pride and vanity,* and *false humility,* come in for censure. The former is apparently characteristic of those who are "[v]ery anxious to publicize their gifts of grace and mystical experiences," while the latter "is the disguise for their pride and self-love."[366]

The reader can make his or her own judgment as to how well the above description fits the activities of the Medjugorje visionaries.

The Position of the Church on Visions

This is an opportune moment to review the position of the Church on the whole area of visions and apparitions. The various approved Marian apparitions, such as Lourdes and Fatima, are classed as "private" revelations, in that the public Revelation to and through the Church was completed during Apostolic times, and is now closed. All that the Church has done since then is to develop and clarify those public truths, and Catholics are bound to believe them as truths of the Faith. Private revelations, however, including the approved Marian apparitions, are given to an individual or group for their own good or that of others; Catholics are not obliged to believe in them, and they do not add to the sum total of public Revelation,[367] as the *Catechism of the Catholic Church* (67) makes clear:

> Throughout the ages, there have been so-called 'private' revelations, some of which have been recognized by the authority of the Church. They do not belong, however, to the deposit of faith. It is not their role to improve or complete Christ's definitive Revelation, but to help live more fully by it in a certain period of history. Guided by the Magiste-

rium of the Church, the *sensus fidelium* knows how to discern and welcome in these revelations whatever constitutes an authentic call of Christ or his saints to the Church.

There is always the danger of illusion or deception in visions or apparitions, and that is why the Church, in the person of the local bishop initially, has always been reluctant to accept them without a great deal of scrutiny. In approving particular private revelations, the Church is only proposing them for assent on the basis that they are worthy of an act of human faith, based on human testimony. The classic view on this matter was expressed by Pope Benedict XIV (1675–1758) as follows: "Although an assent of Catholic faith may not and can not be given to revelations thus approved, still, an assent of human faith, made according to the rules of prudence is due to them; for, according to these rules such revelations are probable and worthy of pious credence."[368]

It could be remarked in passing that Benedict XIV wrote in the period before the major modern Marian apparitions, and there has been some development in thinking since then. That is particularly so if we recognize the special nature of the messages received and transmitted by the various more recent Marian seers, which seem to go beyond purely "private" revelation. At the very least, they seem to be a special case of such revelation, since they form a series which has been of great importance in strengthening the Church in modern times. They certainly differ from the various private revelations to individual saints, which have been concerned with, for example, the foundation of a religious order. That is, such revelations concern only part of the Church, whereas the major Marian apparitions have been taken up by the Church as a whole, and so can, in some sense, be described as "public."

Discernment of Genuine Revelations

As Fr William Most states, "Some private revelations of our own times, such as those at Fatima, are directed to all Christians, not only to one individual; still they are technically called private, to distinguish them from that revelation which closed with the death of St. John."[369] Thus, we have to distinguish between those revelations made to individuals, for their own good, and those meant for the whole Church. Fatima and Lourdes certainly fall into the latter category, and, given the miraculous events surrounding them, which are evidence of the divine, these seem to call for more than a simply "human" faith, even if it does not appear that they demand a truly "theological" faith.[370]

The question also arises as to how certain we can be that an apparition really comes from God. In the Old Testament period, prophets such as Elijah appeared and claimed to speak in the name of God, apparently proving this by miraculous signs accepted by the people. These signs were necessary because of the presence of false prophets, and so a process of discernment was needed. Likewise, Christ proved the divine nature of his person and mission by performing miracles. This is the view of the French spiritual writer, Fr Poulain, on how much credibility we should give to revelations and visions generally, and, by extension, this also applies to Marian apparitions: "When a miracle is performed, and it is stated that it is worked with this intention, [as a sign] or when circumstances show this to be the case, it is an undeniable proof of the divine nature of the revelation. A prophecy fulfilled will be the equivalent of a miracle, if it was couched in definite language and could not have been the result of chance or a conjecture of the Devil."[371]

The miraculous healings at Lourdes seem to fulfill these criteria, while at Fatima, there was both a fulfilled prophecy and a miraculous sign in the foretelling and actual occurrence of the miracle of the sun. This indicates that these Marian apparitions really did come from God, and so we can be *morally certain* they are worthy of belief. In contrast, however, regarding Medjugorje, as we have seen, there is no clear-cut evidence of miraculous signs or genuine prophetic utterances.

The Role of the Local Bishop

The decision as to the authenticity of an apparition rests in the first place with the local bishop, who is the "father in Christ" of his own diocese. If, after sufficient study, there is solid evidence to support the apparition, in terms of the facts surrounding it and the activities of the seer or seers, and likewise regarding such matters as miraculous healings, then the bishop is empowered to issue some form of edict declaring the authenticity of a particular apparition. While such a statement is not infallible, and no one is absolutely obliged to believe in that particular apparition, the position of the bishop as the spiritual ruler of the diocese does mean that his decision should be respected. The two extremes to be avoided are excessive credulity, which believes every report of an apparition, and excessive skepticism, which holds apparitions almost in contempt.

The attitude of the bishop, of course, also holds good with regard to alleged visions which show clear signs of being false, including Medjugorje. As we have seen, the position of the successive Bishops of Mostar has been negative, and these have not been arbitrary decisions which can be ignored, although unfortunately that seems to have been the attitude of most Medjugorje supporters.

Over time, the papacy may grant special privileges to particular shrines, and those are a sign of further approval by the Church as a whole.[372] One such liturgical sign is the granting of a feast day, as, for example, that of Our Lady of Lourdes on 11 February. In recent times, as already indicated, popes such as Paul VI and John Paul II have visited a number of Marian shrines, thus giving them the highest possible level of approval. In sum then, the Church has consistently taken a very cautious attitude towards Marian apparitions, with only a very small minority of such reported events being accepted. Episcopal approval is the first step in such acceptance, but other factors such as general Church approval, expressed in the building of a basilica, for example, or a papal visit, would also seem to be important if an apparition is to be fully acknowledged.

Bishop Peric on Medjugorje

Bishop Peric was interviewed by the French writer Yves Chiron in the journal *Présent,* dated 25 January 1997, and was at pains to emphasize that the conclusions of the Zadar declaration of 1991 still held good—that it could not be affirmed that "supernatural apparitions and revelations" had taken place at Medjugorje. Similarly, he made it plain that there had been no recognition of any cult there as a preliminary to recognition of the alleged visions themselves. He also pointed out, contrary to statements made by certain authors, that the inquiry into the visions had *not* been removed from his authority to that of the Holy See.

Bishop Peric commented on his parochial visits to Medjugorje as follows:

There are many disorders there. There are Franciscan priests there with no canonical mission; religious communities have been established without the permission of the diocesan bishop, ecclesiastical buildings have been erected without ecclesiastical approval, parishes are encouraged to organize official pilgrimages, etc. Medjugorje, considered as a location of presumed apparitions, does not promote peace and unity but creates confusion and division, and not simply in its own diocese. I stated this in October 1994 at the Synod of Bishops and in the presence of the Holy Father, and I repeat it today with the same responsibility.

He further remarked that he did not see the need for any new commission of inquiry, and moreover, the Congregation for the Doctrine of the Faith had upheld his general position in letters to two French bishops, sent in July 1995 and March 1996. In these, after citing the 1991 Zadar declaration of the Yugoslav Bishops Conference, the text of the CDF letters had continued as follows: "[O]fficial pilgrimages to Medjugorje, representing it as a place of authentic Marian apparitions must not be organized either on a parish or diocesan level, because this would be a contradiction of what has been affirmed by the bishops of the ex-Yugoslavia in their previously cited declaration."[373]

The Pope was finally able to make his postponed visit to Sarajevo in April 1997, but during his homily, he made no mention of Medjugorje. Rather, he restricted his remarks to the Marian shrine at Hrasno, about twenty-five miles southeast of Medjugorje; on 9 May he sent a telegram to Bishop Peric, in which he praised the shrine at Hrasno, as a true centre of Marian devotion.[374]

In October 1997, in response to a letter from Thierry Boutet of the French organization *Famille Chrétienne,* ("Christian Family"), Bishop Peric stated that:

On the basis of the serious study of the case by 30 ... [academics], on my episcopal experience of five years in the Diocese, on the scandalous disobedience that surrounds the phenomenon, on the lies that are at times put into the mouth of the "Madonna," on the unusual repetition of "messages" for over 16 years, on the strange way that the "spiritual directors" of the so-called "visionaries" accompany them throughout the world making propaganda of them, on the practice that the "Madonna" appears at the "fiat" (let her come!) of the "visionaries," my conviction and position is not only *non constat de supernaturali-*

tate [the supernaturality has not been proven] but also the other formula *constat de non supernaturalitate* [the non-supernaturality is proven] of the apparitions or revelations of Medjugorje. [375]

Franciscan Disobedience Continues

On 22 June 1997, the Catholic Information Agency in Zagreb published an important document signed by Don Ante Luburic, the Chancellor of Mostar diocese, which detailed further examples of Franciscan disobedience to Bishop Peric. He outlined some aspects of the history of the problem, before giving specific examples, including churches which had been built and blessed by the Franciscans without the knowledge of the Bishop, and in contradiction of Canon Law. He also mentioned the fact that more than forty Franciscans did not have the necessary faculties for pastoral work in the diocese. In particular, he mentioned the case of those parishioners, who with the knowledge of the Franciscans, had bricked up the entrance of the church at Capljina, to prevent the bishop from sending secular priests to the parish. Similarly, he gave details of the numerous "religious" communities, including the Charismatic "Beatitudes" community, which were operating at Medjugorje without the permission of Church authorities. [376]

The situation worsened at Capljina, Fr Vlasic's old parish, when, on 5 October 1997, an unknown "Bishop" conducted a confirmation ceremony at the church. He apparently spoke in German, and one of the Franciscan priests acting illicitly at the parish translated for him. It does not seem that the Sacrament was validly conferred on this occasion, and it is certainly highly irregular for any bishop to attempt to confer confirmation in another diocese without the permission of the local Ordinary, to say nothing of doing so in a church whose main entrance had been bricked up. Fr Laurentin confirms that this incident did indeed take place [377] On 23 March 1998, the Congregation for Religious in Rome confirmed decrees dismissing two of the priests involved at Capljina, Frs Boniface Barbaric and Bozo Rados, from the Franciscan Order. [378]

The Letter to Bishop Aubry

In May 1998, Archbishop Tarcisio Bertone, Secretary to the Congregation for the Doctrine of the Faith, responded to an enquiry from Bishop Gilbert Aubry of Saint-Denis de la Réunion, on the question of Medjugorje. This response has been taken by many adherents of Medjugorje as providing support for their position, but on examination it will be seen that this is certainly not the case.

The first point to make is that this was a purely personal letter, addressed to one bishop, and not meant as a general response for the whole Church; despite this, Archbishop Bertone speaks of the "so-called apparitions of Medjugorje," thus indicating that the Holy See has not in any way approved of the claimed visions. Furthermore, the Archbishop says that it is impossible for him to answer all the questions put by Bishop Aubry on matters such as pilgrimages and the "pastoral care of the faithful who go there," because "the Holy See does not ordinarily take a position of its own regarding supposed supernatural phenomena as a court of first instance."

This is a very important point, because it confirms that the Holy See is not going to override the authority of the local bishop in these matters unless there are very good reasons for doing so. And clearly, with regard to Medjugorje, no such reasons for overriding Bishop Peric exist—otherwise they would have been indicated. Neither has the Congregation overridden the essentially negative judgment on Medjugorje by the Yugoslav Bishops' Conference at Zadar in April 1991.

Archbishop Bertone then went on to speak about the "credibility" of the "apparitions" in question, stating that the Congregation accepts the Zadar declaration made by the Yugoslavian bishops in April 1991, that is, that supernatural events at Medjugorje cannot be affirmed. The Archbishop then indicated that if the case were to be re-examined this would be under the aegis of the Episcopal Conference of Bosnia-Herzegovina, and it would be for this body "to make any pronouncements that might be called for."[379]

The Archbishop indicated that Bishop Peric's statement to Thierry Boutet, as detailed above, that is, that the "non-supernaturality" of the visions or revelations of Medjugorje is "proven," was the "personal conviction" of Bishop Peric. But this does not mean that he was dismissing or contradicting the latter—he was merely stating a fact, while at the same time acknowledging that Bishop Peric was perfectly entitled to express such a conviction.

Finally, with regard to pilgrimages to Medjugorje, Archbishop Bertone reiterated the fact that "private" pilgrimages were allowed, providing "they are not regarded as an authentication of events still taking place."[380]

So, once again, the negative aspects of Medjugorje become clear when the facts are examined. The widespread circulation of Medjugorje messages and books has led to many disorders. By rights, all of these writings should have been submitted to lawful Church authority. Bishop Peric's forthright interviews on the subject of Medjugorje, in which he details the problems which have arisen there, make his position very clear. Similarly, the association of the Medjugorje message with a work which was previously on the *Index of Forbidden Books* is a serious stumbling-block. When one recalls the blatant disobedience of the Franciscans at Capljina, and also the personal assault on Bishop Peric, surely the grave misgivings expressed by those critical of Medjugorje have been fully vindicated.

19

The Good and Bad
Fruits of Medjugorje

Good Fruits in the Early Years

It would be wrong to claim, however, that there have been no good fruits arising out of Medjugorje, at least as far as the early years were concerned. For example, Fr Sivric details the activities of a group of four Franciscans from a small monastery seven or eight miles away, who, right from the beginning, came to Medjugorje practically daily to hear confessions, and had indeed heard tens of thousands of confessions as part of their ministry there. On the bigger feasts, when the crowds were even larger than usual, these priests were joined by other Franciscans from even further afield.[381] What is particularly impressive, of course, about the Sacrament of Reconciliation, as celebrated at Medjugorje, is the sad fact that many confessionals in the developed countries are largely empty of penitents.

Undeniably, Medjugorje exerted a great attraction for people, and particularly young people, from a very early date. Sr Lucy Rooney tells us that: "On the feast of the Exaltation of the Cross in 1983 (celebrated on a Sunday), over 100,000 came, over half of them young people. Transport being forbidden, they came mostly bare-footed, walking to the isolated village and climbing up the rocky mountain to the great cross on the ridge." She also tells us about the situation on 24 and 25 June 1984, the "third anniversary" of the beginning of the visions, when: "So many pilgrims came from overseas that Masses were said each day in Italian, German, French and English, as well as Croatian. The majority of people were from Yugoslavia itself. They came on foot with no plans to stay anywhere, carrying what they would need for a night or two in the open."[382]

The Good Fruits Analyzed

However, just because many people came to Medjugorje then, and continue to do so, this does not of itself guarantee authenticity. The events at Necedah involving Mary Ann Van Hoof, who at the age of 40, in 1949, began to claim that she was seeing visions of the Virgin Mary, are a good indication of this. Nothing in anything she said was particularly credible, but she succeeded in deceiving large numbers of people.

The origin of her visions was almost certainly diabolical, given that her parents had been immigrants from Transylvania where they had dabbled in spiritualism—a career her mother continued in the United States, running a "spirit cabin" at Kenosha, Wisconsin. Mary Ann had acted as her assistant and was familiar with the activities of spirit mediums. It seems, too, that her mother was present during her daughter's later visions. When the La Crosse Diocese investigated the case, it transpired that neither Mary Ann, nor her husband, Fred Van Hoof, had been particularly zealous Catholics, and that they hadn't received the sacraments regularly until *after* the visions began. Almost unbelievably, too, for a supposed Marian visionary, it seems that she "detested Catholics and referred to them in derogatory terms, especially her husband's family whom she labeled, 'those damn Catholic farmers'."

In any event, as news of her prophecies and revelations spread, pilgrims began to come in increasing numbers to the Van Hoof's Necedah farm, despite the strongly negative stance taken both by the local Ordinary, Bishop Treacy, and Cardinal Stritch. It is estimated that up to 100,000 people were present at the farm on 15 August 1950 for the feast of the Assumption.[383] This in itself is surely a clear indication that crowds coming to an alleged pilgrimage site offer no guarantee of authenticity, and thus a warning that the number of pilgrims going to Medjugorje is no indication as to its real status.

Fr Michael O'Carroll was one visitor to Medjugorje, in 1986, who was obviously greatly impressed by what he saw: "The parish of Medjugorje is the first patent miracle of Our Lady, Queen of Peace. The parishioners are a case history. Their dissensions, at one time acute, have vanished. Their prayer is of a kind seen nowhere in the world." He also claimed that: "The apparitions have sparked off a spiritual revolution in the parish of Medjugorje. Again, never has a whole community been so affected and transformed and brought to such a pitch of fervour."[384] Fr Laurentin similarly lavished praise on Medjugorje, saying that, "because of false news having been published about it, we wish to stress that the parish of Medjugorje is the most normally operated in the world."[385]

These are the views of foreigners who had been drawn to Medjugorje from overseas, but Fr Sivric's investigations told a different story. The reader will recall that he was born and bred in Medjugorje, and was thus well equipped to assess the real situation. While conceding that in the early days there certainly was a change of attitude amongst many of the local people, according to his researches it seems that over time they began to grow blasé, possibly because the threats issued in the name of the Gospa had progressively lost their impact. While acknowledging that there had been some improvements, he pointed to the persistence of "malicious and vindictive gossip." This was akin to Mark Waterinckx's experience in the eighties, when during his long stays in Medjugorje he frequently witnessed parishioners quarrelling, despite stories of there being a new spirit in the village.[386]

In fact, Fr Faricy was forced to acknowledge that by 1986 the religious situation in Medjugorje had deteriorated, with fewer people attending the evening Mass and rosary.[387] Regarding the activities of those pilgrims who came to Medjugorje in the early years, Mary Craig describes how one observer assessed the situation: "A lot of them weren't interested in praying. What they enjoyed doing most was looking at the sun and applauding the visionaries whenever they appeared."[388]

Wayne Weible was certainly disappointed with the way things had turned out at Medjugorje in comparison with the early days. He talks of how in the years that followed, a marked decline set in as its:

pristine atmosphere began to show signs of pollution: Pilgrimages began to include curiosity seekers and those who came strictly as tourists. Travel agencies ... [were] anxious to cash in on the growing popularity of the region, ... The presence of the Virgin each evening became almost commonplace for many villagers ... Medjugorje had become a place of material opportunity for many. New entrepreneurs were coming to the village in droves. Their demeanor was that of rapacious wolves disguised as converted sheep, as they attempted to cash in quickly on the desires of those in search of miracles. Cafes and souvenir stands sprang up almost overnight, along with hotels and barracks. There was constant construction as villagers continued to build additional rooms onto their homes to house pilgrims. Many villagers who had responded so fervently in the beginning months of the apparitions were now busy making money as they had never made it before. They were too busy to attend evening Mass, or to pray a family rosary, or to fast on Wednesdays and Fridays as requested by the Virgin.[389]

Some Genuine Good Fruits?

Undoubtedly, though, there have been individuals and groups present in, or associated with, Medjugorje who have benefited from this. One example of this involves Moira Noonan, who, in her book *Ransomed from Darkness*, recounts her experiences as a New Age teacher—but one who eventually came back to the Catholic faith. This seems to have occurred to some extent through her contacts with Medjugorje. The negative side of all this, however, is that, in the words of Noonan, "an enormous false Mary movement," has grown up, principally through the writings of Sondra Ray, a well-known new-age practitioner, who has promoted the idea that the Blessed Virgin is a goddess who can be "channeled" in a spiritualistic fashion.

In any event, Noonan claims that while engaged in a spiritualistic "table rapping" session, she heard an "inner voice" from the "Queen of Peace" giving her an intuition that what she was doing was wrong. But she also tells us that she had started to wear a miraculous medal that had been left to her by her deceased grandmother. Other incidents seemed to be pointing her towards Marian devotion, including one where she was physically prevented from using her New Age crystals by an invisible force, and again heard an inner voice, this time telling her to pray the rosary. She was also led to go to confession, the first time she had received this sacrament in 25 years.

She now began to live a sincere Catholic life centered on Mass, prayer and spiritual reading, but breaking with her past was a long and difficult process. She finally managed to go to Medjugorje, where she went to confession to a priest with experience of the New Age movement. Her first confession to him lasted for 2½ hours, and in subsequent meetings with him she was gradually led to renounce all her past spiritualist activities, and was thus able to make a truly fresh start.[390]

While applauding this outcome, the point clearly needs to be made that it was her participation in the Sacrament of Confession at Medjugorje which was the crucial part of her spiritual healing, rather than actually been present in the place itself. We also have to take into account the fact that she was wearing a miraculous medal. But having said that, it does seem possible that she did receive some extraordinary supernatural help to bring her back to the right road. This has to be understood, though, in the context of her overall situation. It may well be that God had infallibly foreseen that it was only by means of her coming into contact with Catholics associated with Medjugorje that it would be possible for her to free herself from her New Age involvement. In other words, in an extreme situation like this, it might be necessary for God and the Blessed Virgin to have intervened miraculously in her life, given that she was so deeply involved in occult practices. However, this obviously does not imply a blanket endorsement of everything to do with Medjugorje.

Another example is the international youth movement, Youth 2000, whose origins have been linked with Medjugorje. But it emerges that the original impetus for the movement came to Ernest Williams while he was in Fatima in 1989, immediately following the World Youth Day at Santiago de Compostela—although the first Youth 2000 Festival of Prayer was actually launched in Medjugorje the following year. In any event, it is clear that more recently Youth 2000 has been at pains to distance itself from Medjugorje. In the CTS booklet on the movement, in the question-and-answer section, the following statement appears: "Ernest Williams, and many other young people who ran the first retreats in

England, have visited Medjugorje. However, Youth 2000 has no official connection to Medjugorje and awaits the definitive ruling of the Church."

In fact, the spirituality of Youth 2000 has far more in common with the message of Fatima than that of Medjugorje, as a further quote from the CTS booklet indicates: "The charism of Youth 2000 is to draw young people through the Immaculate Heart of Mary to a deep and lasting union with the Eucharistic Heart of Jesus." At Fatima, Our Lady spoke of God's wish to "establish in the world devotion to my Immaculate Heart." As we will see, the Medjugorje messages make virtually no mention of this devotion.[391]

Emotional Enthusiasm

What, then, of those foreign pilgrims who have come to Medjugorje, and claimed conversions and other spiritual benefits? The first point to note is that God does not deny his graces to those who go to a place of alleged visions in good faith to pray, attend Mass, join in the Rosary and go to Confession. The people who go to Medjugorje are clearly open to God's grace, otherwise they would not have gone in the first place. But having said that, we have to beware of transitory spiritual conversions which do not last, and also of emotional feelings of self-satisfaction, which may lead individuals to believe that they are part of a spiritual élite, and thus better than the ordinary Catholic. The question then becomes: do those who have experienced a conversion at Medjugorje return home and show that their lives have been changed through becoming seriously involved in the day-to-day low-key work of building up the Church? Or are they more interested in trying to get other people involved in believing in alleged visions which have not been recognized by the Church?

Some of those caught up in the enthusiasm over Medjugorje were very influential:

> By chance, John Hill, a Boston millionaire and lapsed Catholic, heard an audio-cassette about Medjugorje, and instantly dedicated his entire fortune to promoting the messages. Setting up a Center for Peace in Boston, he dispatched a team to make an hour-long television film, began organizing monthly charter flights for pilgrims and arranging for

the free distribution of booklets, video and audio cassettes, in a variety of languages to people all over the world.[392]

What has certainly happened is that the large number of pilgrims returning from Medjugorje has precipitated an explosion in the number of major worldwide centers promoting the visions, as well as a vast number of smaller local groups often producing their own newsletters and literature. In addition, the fact that the visionaries have been very ready to travel, and can apparently experience "visions on demand," has greatly helped to promote Medjugorje. For all these reasons, and more, Medjugorje captured the imagination of many Catholics during the 1980s, when, for various reasons, people wanted something new, something exciting, something more than they were getting from their ordinary parish life.[393]

Wayne Weible indicates the impact Medjugorje was having on the Church at this time:

> The month before the eight[h] anniversary celebration in Medjugorje, the first national conference in the United States on Medjugorje was held at the University of Notre Dame, in Indiana. More than 5,000 followers of the apparitions came to enjoy three days of retreat into holiness—very much akin to what takes place during pilgrimage at Medjugorje. ... Within two years, similar conferences were springing up throughout the United States. Franciscan priests stationed at the parish in Medjugorje, and several of the visionaries themselves, were now coming to speak at these conferences, bringing their experiences to thousands who could not personally go to Medjugorje. Many skeptical and cautious priests and bishops who had journeyed there now urged the faithful to listen to and live the messages.[394]

Modern communications, initially via the telephone and fax machine, and later via the Internet, mean that the Medjugorje messages can now be instantly flashed around the world. This is something new, and has given many people a sense of belonging which, for them, was lacking in the institutional Church. They feel as though they are part of an extended Medjugorje family, and the monthly messages encourage this feeling.

This recent technological revolution, involving the Internet particularly, but also television, video, and the Press, has meant that the visionaries and their supporters have been able to largely bypass Church authorities and the traditional forms of regulation and control which they have exercised. They have been able to take their message direct to potential pilgrims worldwide.[395]

No Personal Messages

Undoubtedly, one of the biggest reasons people have been drawn to Medjugorje, or to events involving the visionaries, has been the belief that the Blessed Virgin has been appearing on a daily basis, and that it may even be possible to receive a personal message from her, or see some sign. As we have seen above, though, St John of the Cross warns that the desire for revelations is very dangerous, and is almost guaranteed to lead to serious problems.

We can see this from the following section of an address by Fr Gianni Sgreva, given at the National Medjugorje Conference held at the University of Notre Dame in 1991. He told the audience how on the

> evening of December 4, 1985, I was taking off my priestly vestments in the sacristy of Medjugorje. Marija Pavlovic approached me and said, "Father Gianni, the Madonna spoke of you this evening." Immediately I answered, "What did she tell you?" "No, I won't tell you right away. You have to put yourself in prayer and recollection." I was left a little upset in the face of Marija's words. But I agreed to go with her together in prayer the following day. Then Marija gave me the message of the Madonna. Our Lady said: "Tell Gianni that I want to speak to him personally." I did not believe it. I told her, "If you see Our Lady again this evening, say to Our Lady that Fr. Gianni wants only facts and signs, and few words." But there was one thing that I liked right away. It came to my mind immediately that Our Lady said my name then."

Fr Sgreva goes on to say that "fruits and signs began right away," and that these prompted him to ask Marija to ask the Gospa if these signs were genuine. Not surprisingly, he was told that they were.[396]

This was not the only occasion on which Marija gave a "personal" message allegedly from the Gospa to a particular individual. As already noted, Archbishop Franic was also guilty of this type of indiscretion. On 17 December 1984, he tells us that he "asked Marija if I would be imposing too much if she were to ask Our Lady if there was a message for me. I expressly said I would be happy if she would give me some admonition for my conversion, if she would point her finger at my weaker points and tell me where I need to be careful and where I need to improve."[397]

The Archbishop received the "message" that he should expect "greater sufferings" in the future.

The problem is that we don't find this type of thing—personal messages for individuals—in the accounts of the approved apparitions of Our Lady. She has certainly given instructions to individuals through the seers, that they should carry out a particular action to do with the establishment of a shrine, for instance, but this idea of the Blessed Virgin acting like the personal spiritual guru of particular individuals is just not present.

Suspect Incidents at Garabandal

However, a similar type of thing did happen at Garabandal. We read of how "a totally skeptical priest ... arrived wearing street clothes. He watched one of the children approach him. She offered him a crucifix to kiss several times. 'If this is genuine' he thought to himself, 'let the child come to.' In an instant the visionary emerged from her ecstasy, smiled at the priest and turned to go home."

A further incident concerned another skeptic who: "During one vision, ... thought to himself: 'For me to believe this, the child will have to take my rosary from its case and hand it to me.' The visionary immediately approached him, handed him his rosary and, to everyone's astonishment, said, 'You didn't believe before, but now you do.' "[398]

Such incidents were by no means uncommon at Garabandal, and the mistake that such individuals made was to look for signs to indicate that the visionaries were genuine. The problem is that such an attitude is presumptuous and leaves the way open for diabolical involvement.

Thus, the attitude of those Medjugorje visionaries who have offered signs and messages to individuals, supposedly from the Gospa, is totally at variance with what has happened during approved apparitions.

Dangerous Desire for the Miraculous

Generally speaking, we can say that this desire for the "miraculous" can partly be explained as the effect of a sort of spiritual lethargy which results in people not wishing to make the effort to pray as a means of discovering God's will, but rather to look for shortcuts and quick answers. However, believers should realize that it is contrary to faith to expect God or the Blessed Virgin to personally impart some sort of message to them. They are not there simply to do our bidding. It doesn't work that way. The whole history of the Church makes this abundantly clear. Rather, we have to live by faith, and not by signs, wonders or messages. The very sobering words of Christ on this subject were that it was an "evil and adulterous generation [that] seeks for a sign." (Matt 16:4)

Medjugorje devotees should thus ask themselves this crucial question: do I believe in Medjugorje because my rosary has changed color, or because I have seen the sun spinning, or because alternatively, I have had a genuine spiritual experience which has had a lasting effect? If the main focus has been on the former aspects, rather than the latter, then obviously that is inconsistent with the authentic way the Faith should be lived.

Ultimately, it seems that many Medjugorje supporters have come to believe the mistaken position that what counts is their personal opinion, rather than an objective discernment of the true facts. This would appear to be the only rational way of explaining why otherwise sensible Catholics can completely disregard the consistent stance of the Bishops of Mostar on Medjugorje—a stance which has been implicitly upheld by the Apostolic See. And there is likewise the serious worldwide problem of all the alleged visionaries who have also been claiming to see the Blessed Virgin in the wake of Medjugorje, many of these being people who have been there.

Paolo Apolito lists the following individuals as being amongst those claiming to have started to receive their own revelations either following a visit to Medjugorje, or through some more general contact with it: Veronica Garcia; Br David, a Franciscan; Fr Jack Spaulding; Gianna Talone; Estela Ruiz; Lena Shipley; Alfredo Raimondo and Patricia Soto. And he also makes the very pertinent point, that whereas prior to the modern era, with its explosion of visionary claims, individuals claiming such experiences would almost certainly have been shunned by the average Catholic, now they could expect to be treated as celebrities.[399]

Christ's Teaching on Good Fruits

On this question of the fruits arising from Medjugorje, reference is often made to the statement of Christ in the Gospels on the subject, with the implication that what has happened there is in line with his teaching:

> Beware of false prophets, who come to you in sheep's clothing but inwardly are ravenous wolves. You will know them by their fruits. Are grapes gathered from thorns, or figs from thistles? So, every sound tree bears good fruit, but the bad tree bears evil fruit. A sound tree cannot bear evil fruit, nor can a bad tree bear good fruit. Every tree that does not bear good fruit is cut down and thrown into the fire. Thus you will know them by their fruits. (Matt 7:15–20)

Yet a careful reading of the text makes it plain that Christ was *not* expressly talking about the spiritual fruits that might result from the actions of particular individuals, but rather was telling us to look carefully at the way those individuals themselves actually lived. The text is about false prophets, and Christ says we will know *them* by their fruits. This does not absolutely exclude the genuine good fruits which might proceed from the actions of individuals who themselves are not trustworthy, but it does seem that the emphasis being made here is on the activities of those individuals themselves, and not on any movements they might initiate.

Jesus gave us another solemn warning about "false prophets," which has been recorded in St Matthew's Gospel. Although this refers specifically to the "end times," it can also be applied throughout Church history, including our own period: "For false Christs and false prophets will arise and show great signs and wonders, so as to lead astray, if possible, *even the elect.*" (Matt 24:24)

Yes, even the "elect," which as regards Marian apparitions, indicates those people with a genuine devotion to the Blessed Virgin; even they can be led astray by false prophets.

If we apply the "good fruits" criterion to Medjugorje as it should essentially be applied, that is to the visionaries and their Franciscan associates, then as this book has clearly indicated it is obvious that they have been less than satisfactory. To take just a few examples, whether it is Vicka's "bloody handkerchief" story, or her activities as regards the laying on of hands, or the incident of the alleged dropping of the Baby Jesus by the Blessed Virgin, obviously the fruits in her case are suspect. Similarly, the threatening letter written by Ivan's hand to Bishop Zanic gives grave cause for concern, as does the mental state of Mirjana, and the retraction of Marija's support for Fr Vlasic's idea of a community.

Regarding the Franciscans most involved with Medjugorje themselves, their long-running state of disobedience, both as regards the local bishop and the Holy See, is surely a very bad fruit. More recently, this disobedience has been expressed by other Franciscans through the erection of churches without permission, as well as irregular Confirmations. And as we will see shortly, the lifestyle of those principally involved in Medjugorje, as it has unfolded over the years, is a far cry from the poverty and simplicity one would expect of genuine seers or their associates.

This is what Fr Laurent Volken says on this point: "Disobedience is a negative criterion of discernment and emphasized by theologians. And one of the reasons which bishops and other ecclesiastical authorities have given for condemning this or that apparition has been precisely the disobedience of the visionaries or even of members of the Church who believed in the apparitions in question and disobeyed the instructions given upon the matter."[400]

Thus, by the standards of Christ's teaching on good fruits it is hard to avoid the conclusion that both the visionaries and their Franciscan associates cannot be said to have lived up to either its spirit or letter.

False Prophets

There seems to be a reluctance in some Catholic circles to believe that those involved in either receiving or promoting alleged visions or messages can possibly be acting from anything other than the highest motives. Sadly, such well-meaning but naïve support for Medjugorje has led many sincere people astray. It is an unfortunate fact that throughout Church history there have been false prophets and false visionaries at work. Where there is a group of religious enthusiasts, it is hardly surprising that out of self-interest people will be attracted to them purely for financial gain.

Is it really conceivable that these types of activities should have suddenly ceased following the Second Vatican Council? The answer is obviously no, and indeed all the evidence suggests that the situation has grown markedly worse since Vatican II, and this is only a reflection of the state of the secular world where the incidence of fraud of all types has exploded in recent years.

To use a concrete example, suppose a person has a $10 bill or a £10 note in their possession. How do they know that it is not counterfeit? Suppose it is believed that forgers have been working in the area, and that there is a possibility that an appreciable amount of forged currency is in circulation. The person has two basic options: they can either take the suspect note to the bank and have it checked, or they can just pass it on to the next person. They might argue that if that person accepts it then they will assume it is good, and if they don't, then they will regard it as a forgery. But that is faulty from a moral perspective. If someone has good reason to believe that a banknote is forged then it is their *duty* to have it checked.

If we apply this to the question of true and false visions, then it is obvious that checking the note with a bank is like finding out what the official spokesman of the Church—the bishops—have said about a particular vision. But just ignoring the status of the vision and relying on the alleged good fruits is like passing on the note the next time we shop—all that concerns us is whether or not the shop accepts it, and not whether it is forged or genuine. It might be said that a few forged notes in circulation are not going to do much harm, and that is true enough. But if the forgeries reach a certain percentage of the money in circulation then it will start to lose its value—the principle of bad money driving out the good comes into play. If the process goes on unchecked, ultimately the economy of the nation concerned will collapse, because its money will become totally worthless.

Modern False Visions and Visionaries

Something like this has been happening with regard to visions. False or unapproved visions have been driving out the true. Yves Chiron lists seventy-one apparitions that are alleged to have arisen following Medjugorje, between 1981 and 1991. Of these, only Kibeho in Rwanda and San Nicolas in Argentina have gained any sort of support from the local bishop, while twelve were judged negatively, and no decision was taken about the others—which in effect means that they were not pronounced to be authentic.[401] It should be noticed that this list is far from exhaustive, and in the intervening period there has been no slowdown in the number of alleged visions being reported. Yet, for many people, the very fact that all these reports are proliferating is a sign that the Blessed Virgin must indeed be appearing all over the world. What this means in practice is that many Catholics seem to have lost the ability or even the notion of seeking to discern between true and false visions.

But even Fr Laurentin, the foremost modern supporter of practically every conceivable allegedly "supernatural" event, has, in his *Apparitions of the Blessed Virgin Mary Today,* an appendix entitled: "Apparitions without credibility." These include Bayside in New York, where Veronica Leuken claimed to be receiving heavenly messages for many years, including the preposterous notion that Pope Paul VI had been replaced by an impostor whose features had been altered by plastic surgery. He also mentions an alleged female visionary at Belluno in Italy in the 1980s, and events involving a priest called Don Vincenzo and another female visionary, Maria Fioritti, who began to allege visions at Pescara following a visit to Medjugorje in 1987. Great signs were promised, and it was claimed that Pescara would be the conclusion of Medjugorje, and the "greatest apparitions in history." Fr Laurentin describes this as "sensationalism" which "contradicts the messages of Medjugorje."

The French priest also deals with William Kamm, the German-born Australian visionary who styles himself as the "Little Pebble," and who has been claiming visions, including various unfulfilled prophecies and warnings for many years. None of his claims has been given any credence by successive local bishops. Similarly, Fr Laurentin discusses the case of Marie-Paule Giguère, the founder of the Army of Mary in Quebec, Canada. This flourished during the 1970s, and even received local episcopal approval for a while, but "serious errors," including the idea that the foundress was the "mystical reincarnation of Mary," became manifest after some time, and the organization was dissolved in 1987.[402]

Nor are these the only alleged visions which by any standard must be regarded as false. There have been a great number of such incidents since Vatican II, particularly in the wake of Medjugorje, and thus the alleged events in Bosnia-Herzegovina have to be seen against this backdrop of a large numbers of false or at best questionable visions.

Finally, we have to confront the startling fact that some of those involved in investigating Medjugorje have received death threats. Fr Sivric did not return to Medjugorje in later years because of such threats, while E. Michael Jones tells us that he "got a call from a man in England warning me that if I went back to Bosnia, the Franciscans were going to have me killed."[403] Would a genuine Marian apparition give rise to this sort of thing? These are some of the "fruits" of Medjugorje which, not surprisingly, we don't hear very much about.

We can say, then, that although there was evidence of good fruits arising from Medjugorje in the early days, particularly as reported by outsiders, those more familiar with the local culture, such as Fr Sivric, were more critical. In addition, orthodox organizations such as Youth 2000 have distanced themselves from Medjugorje. The danger of excessive emotional enthusiasm for Medjugorje has become clear, particularly in the mistaken belief that the Blessed Virgin has been appearing daily to the visionaries. Similarly, the problems engendered by an excessive desire for revelations, especially as expressed by writers such as St John of the Cross, have not been understood by Medjugorje supporters.

We have seen, too, that Christ's teaching on good fruits indicates quite clearly that the focus should be on the behavior of the individuals in question, and not on any movements they might initiate. Investigations along these lines have shown that the "fruits" exhibited by the Medjugorje visionaries and their Franciscan associates have left much to be desired. The strange reluctance of many Catholics to acknowledge that there is even a possible problem as regards false prophets has also been explored, as has the clear evidence that the vast majority of alleged visions reported in recent years are almost certainly false.

In sum, despite a number of positive points in its favor, the overall picture as regards good and bad fruits surely indicates that Medjugorje must be judged in a negative light.

20

Medjugorje:
Problems and Dangers

Focusing on Negative Elements

Apart from the considerations discussed in the last chapter, the attraction of going on pilgrimage to a shine where Our Lady is allegedly appearing every day has proved irresistible for many. But one of the consequences of this development has been a general devaluation of Marian piety, and as a result all sorts of strange ideas have begun to circulate freely in the Church. For instance, there has been the focus on supposed "signs and wonders," on rosaries changing color, or the sun spinning, rather than on the real heavenly message of prayer and penance given at Fatima. Or in some cases, where these ideas have been taken up, they have been pushed to extremes, so that people fast excessively, or spend long hours in prayer, to the detriment of the duties of their state in life or their family commitments. The sound Catholic principle of observing a sensible balance has often been lost.

Denis Nolan effectively admits that there have been problems in this area, saying, "it may be true that some have gone to Medjugorje seeking some kind of supernatural titillation. There may be pilgrims who seek signs and wonders and who are disappointed if they do not end up with gold rosaries and a private apparition."[404]

Wayne Weible has this to say on this general point:

Many pilgrims who had experienced a life-changing conversion through Medjugorje were now busy following after every claimed visionary and locutionist. They seemed driven by an insatiable thirst to know every possible detail about any supernatural event. The monthly messages given to Marija were now awaited more out of curiosity about what new things might be said, rather than out of a desire to learn from them and make them part of daily life."[405]

Similarly, there has been too great a focus on apocalyptic elements, such as warnings, chastisements and signs, and particularly on the notion that the Second Coming of Christ is quite near. Apart from the fact that this type of message has been frequently advocated by false prophets, it is quite contrary to the genuine message of Fatima. It is true that the secret of Fatima does contain elements pointing to the future, but there is a complete lack of sensationalism. Rather, the emphasis is on what we can do to follow Our Lady's requests, so as to bring about the triumph of her Immaculate Heart, and not on a sort of fatalism which sees unavoidable impending disaster around every corner. The fact is that the Blessed Virgin said nothing at Fatima about the Second Coming of her Son, but she did promise the world a period of peace provided that people complied with her requests. This period of peace may well be preceded by possibly great upheavals, but it would be wrong to describe the message of Fatima as apocalyptic or eschatological in the traditional sense of these words, that is as related to the end of the world.

The Danger from False Prophets

To return to Christ's teaching on false prophets, this also supplies the answer to those who might argue that it is unfair, or lacking in Christian charity, to bring up any negative points about the visionaries or the Franciscans. Unless people are informed about the nature of the activities of these individuals, how can they judge whether they are true or false prophets? If somebody begins to act as a visionary, or becomes closely associated with such a person, then they must expect to be submitted to a searching personal examination. Unless we examine their fruits—that is their actions and words—in some detail, it will be impossible to come to any balanced, objective conclusions about them. If the person is a genuine seer then any such investigation will only make this apparent, and they will grow in humility, as was the case with the little children of Fatima.

But if they are false prophets, if they exhibit pride or deceit, if the visitations, visions and messages which they say they are receiving, in truth do not come from heaven, then for their own good the ordinary believer needs to be protected from unwittingly accepting communications which are not divine. It is for this reason that the Church has clear rules which stipulate that the claims made by any visionary must first of all be approved and accepted by the local Ordinary as being of divine origin, before people may officially promote them.

The Lifestyle of the Medjugorje Visionaries

Joachim Bouflet reproduces a non-exhaustive list of the various journeys which were undertaken by the Medjugorje visionaries between 1990 and 1998. They visited countries all over the world, but the emphasis was on the United States and Europe. He details twenty-six "apostolic" journeys undertaken by Vicka, with twenty-three by Ivan, followed by Marija with seventeen, while Jakov, Mirjana and Ivanka made twelve between them.[406] Contrast this with the behavior of the seers of approved apparitions, such as St Catherine Labouré, St Bernadette, or Sr Lucia, who scarcely stepped outside her convent in Coimbra after 1948! Even if we consider the children at Beauraing and Banneux, who, like the Medjugorje visionaries, did not become professed religious, it is nevertheless the case that they certainly did not travel all over the world. Rather, they stayed out of the limelight living quiet lives.

As regards the lifestyle of the Medjugorje visionaries, according to E. Michael Jones, in the late 1990s, Ivan Dragicevic was driving an expensive BMW car and living in a large mansion not far from the site of the alleged first vision, having married Loreen Murphy, "Miss Massachusetts," a former Beauty Queen. Mirjana Dragicevic was living in a similar dwelling right across the street. In addition, it was clear that the overweight Ivan was not following the bread and water fast of the early days, and in general, it is apparent that his globetrotting activities are less than edifying in comparison with the way the seers of recognized Marian apparitions have behaved.[407]

The following extract from a report in *The Sunday Times (London)*, dated 29 December 2002, gives an update on the status of some of the visionaries:

Three of the six "seers", as they are known, have stayed in the town and their prosperity has risen to reflect the Madonna gold rush. Two of them, Jakov Colo, 31, and Mirjana Dragicevic-Soldo, 37, live in smart executive houses with immaculate gardens, double garages and security gates. On the other side of town the residence of Ivanka Ivankovic-Elez, 36, is even more sumptuous, with a brand new tennis court. All three refused to discuss their experiences and the huge wealth it has generated. Local Franciscan monks [sic] who gave credence to the visions preferred to say nothing, demanding that any questions be sent by fax.[408]

Under the heading, "Ivan Dragicevic's Speaking Schedule 2005," a prominent Medjugorje website has the following information:

Our Lady has appeared to Ivan every day since June 24, 1981, and has, to date, confided nine secrets. Ivan married in 1994 and has two beautiful children. ... Ivan and his family spend May-September in Medjugorje and the rest of the year in the US spreading Our Lady's messages in parishes around the country. Important Note: During their time in Medjugorje, Ivan's family offers a personal prayer experience for a limited number of pilgrims in their home in Medjugorje.

Visitors to the site are then invited to, "Click For Details, and a Schedule."[409]

Medjugorje – Why So Popular?

One of the enigmas about Medjugorje is why it has proved to be so incredibly popular with so many Catholics, despite all the negative points which have been detailed above. One answer, it seems, is that many people *want* to believe in Medjugorje, and simply assume Our Lady is appearing there daily, as it is claimed, without taking the trouble to investigate whether or not this is true. The reality is that people can quite easily be tempted to *believe what they want to believe*. As Kevin Orlin Johnson says, for people in this enthusiastic frame of mind, with a pre-disposition to believe, there are only two possible verdicts on an alleged apparition, that is, either "yes," it is true, or alternatively it is probably true but "not yet proven." Thus, there is a failure to consider the very real possibility that the vision in question may well be false.

Johnson also comments on the mistaken perception that if enough people go to a particular site, then the Church will be obliged to reverse a negative judgment and call it positive. As he says, this is to mistake the Church's traditional approach for one where "reality can be determined by vote," and this attitude may well be due to "culpable negligence," regarding Church teaching on these matters.[410] Such negligence may include an unwillingness to recognize that official ecclesiastical statements on a particular vision do have real meaning, and cannot be disregarded just because they don't fit in with our own point of view. Conversely, there is also a lack of understanding that no matter how many priests, bishops, or even cardinals, believe in a particular alleged vision, that, of itself, does not make it true. Ordinarily, it is only the bishop of the particular diocese in question who has the authority to pronounce upon what is going on there. In fact, to organize pilgrimages to Medjugorje is to go against the express wishes of successive bishops of Mostar.[411]

There is also the danger of people becoming addicted to the spiritual experiences generated by a visit to Medjugorje. This is particularly the case if the person who has been converted at Medjugorje was previously a lukewarm or non-practising Catholic. If they experience signs and wonders such as their rosary turning to gold, they may find it very difficult to question the authenticity of the happenings at Medjugorje. One hears of people whose whole spiritual life revolves around the messages from various alleged visionaries, and who travel from one place to another to satisfy a craving for these phenomena.

However, one reason for this particular quest amongst many believers today, is the undeniable fact that there is a spiritual vacuum in the Church, a vacuum which has arisen due to various factors. Many people get caught up in visions because they have a genuine thirst for the supernatural, and, not readily finding it in the Church, are driven to look for it elsewhere, as in the area of alleged visions such as Medjugorje. This is a point which is dealt with in more detail below. There are also many people today who have become bound up in a quest for religious novelties, and this is essentially the Catholic counterpart of what we see in society as a whole: that is a restlessness and unease which can only be satisfied by new and exotic experiences. For such people the timeless truths of Fatima are not exciting enough—they need a ceaseless round of new messages or they are apparently not happy.

Medjugorje from Heaven's Perspective

Let us attempt to look at this situation from Heaven's perspective. We all have free will, so while it is possible it is not likely that there is going to be any dramatic supernatural intervention to prevent the visionaries from continuing their activities, in opposition to the directives of the Bishop, nor will anything miraculous be done to prevent people going on pilgrimage to Medjugorje. In many cases, pilgrims going there may well be lapsed, or even living a sinful life. Given the condition of the Church, as in the case of Moira Noonan, God may well foresee that, for a particular individual, a visit to Medjugorje may be the only chance they will have to be converted. The visions and messages are not approved, but the vast majority of pilgrims go there in all sincerity, and thus we can surmise that, in such genuine cases, God will grant the necessary graces of conversion. And this, of course, is to say nothing of the effects of the prayers and sufferings of their friends and relatives, who in some cases may have been interceding on their behalf for years.

However, in many cases, when such people are converted, after a time they realize the deficiencies of some aspects of Medjugorje spirituality, and move on to a properly regulated mainstream Catholic life, focusing more on prayer and the sacraments, and less on spiritual experiences. That is, they begin to live by faith, rather than by means of "signs and wonders." We might compare this situation to that of a person who enters the unheated porch of a house on a bitterly cold day. Compared to the temperature outside, the porch feels warm, but if they remain in the porch for too long they soon feel the cold again, and have to move into the house itself. Medjugorje, taken as an overall phenomenon, can thus at best be regarded as a sort of porch or vestibule of the Church proper, a sort of halfway house; but it is not a place where one should remain, spiritually, for any length of time.

Another very powerful influence in favor of Medjugorje has been the Catholic media, which with very few exceptions has been reluctant to criticize Medjugorje in any way. It seems that many of those involved in the media have been afraid of losing readers if they publish anything even remotely critical. Similarly, editors have been reluctant to lose advertising revenue from those promoting pilgrimages to Medjugorje. This, of course, is to say nothing of those who have a vested interest in promoting Medjugorje, through publishing books, or organizing conferences and pilgrimages, activities which have naturally generated a great deal of money.

A further source of support—which at first sight might seem rather surprising—has been the secular media. For the most part, instead of the hostility which is usually shown towards all things Catholic, their approach to Medjugorje has been almost benevolent. Denis Nolan quotes excerpts from newspapers, magazines and journals ranging from the *Wall Street Journal* to the *Reader's Digest,* and television programs ranging from NBC's *Inside Edition* to the *Oprah Winfrey show,* none of which have apparently had anything particularly critical to say about it.[412] It could be argued that this in itself is rather suspicious: Christ told those of his "brethren" who did not believe in him that: "The world cannot hate you, but it hates me because I testify of it that its works are evil." In other words, the Church, which is the body of Christ, can really only expect antagonism, even hatred, at the hands of the world—of which the secular media is the "conscience"—and yet Medjugorje has been treated with what amounts to kid gloves by the media.

Medjugorje and the Crisis in the Church

In some respects, the desire for people to go to Medjugorje is understandable in the light of the serious problems that the Catholic Church in the West has been experiencing in recent years. Up until the Second Vatican Council, Marian devotion in the developed countries was strong and healthy. Organizations such as the Blue Army and the Legion of Mary thrived, and the rosary was a solidly rooted devotion. But following the Council, various liberal groups, with an agenda of their own, and acting in the alleged "spirit" of Vatican II, managed to foist their own ideas on ordinary Catholics in the United States and Europe. Distorting the true meaning of conciliar documents such as *Lumen Gentium,* they succeeded in virtually eliminating Marian devotions from many churches. As a result, many traditionally-minded Catholics suddenly found themselves strangers in their own Church. This created a spiritual vacuum which various groups and individuals, including alleged visionaries, have been quick to fill.

The devotional and liturgical life of many parishes is still sadly inadequate, and thus numerous people are drawn to Medjugorje because they are looking for something with a more profound spirituality. However, as previous chapters of this work have demonstrated, the tragedy is that the spirituality they will encounter at Medjugorje will not in the end prove to be a "healthy devotion toward the Blessed Virgin Mary ... promoted in conformity with the teaching of the Church." This is because "it cannot be established that one is dealing with supernatural apparitions and revelations." As we have seen, both of these quotations come from the Yugoslav Bishops' Conference Zadar declaration of April 1991.[413] Believing in visions which have not been approved by the Church—and which all the available evidence indicates are false—cannot be good for one's spiritual health in the long term. The counterpart to believing in Medjugorje is neglecting to profit from the genuine apparitions of Mary, and in particular Fatima. Unless one has moral certainty that a series of apparitions is genuine, then one is on very dangerous ground in believing in them.

As indicated above, the picture which emerges if we analyze the good fruits that are claimed for Medjugorje, is that these were certainly present to some extent in the early years. But as time has gone on, they have been noteworthy largely because of their absence. While there is much misunderstanding regarding exactly what Christ meant by this term, a correct analysis of his teaching indicates that we are meant to look mainly at the activities of those claiming visions, or those closely supporting them, rather than at any general religious enthusiasm which might be generated. In this sense, the evidence which we have been considering in earlier chapters of this work demonstrates that the fruits at Medjugorje cannot be said to have been good.

Furthermore, it is clear that within the general Catholic community, there is a widespread failure to realize that the fabrication of visions is a distinct possibility, or that the devil might well be involved in originating or sustaining them. This is what St John of the Cross says on this general point:

> among locutions and visions there are usually many that come from the devil. For he commonly deals with the soul in the same manner as God does, imparting communications so similar to God's that, disguised among the flock like the wolf in sheep's clothing, his meddling may be hardly discernible. Since he says many things that are true and reasonable and turn out as predicted, people can be easily misled, thinking that the revelation must be from God since what was predicted truly comes about.[414]

In the past, Catholics were warned about the wiles of Satan, and of the need to remain wary about apparently miraculous events, but in recent years, the Church's traditional caution in this area has been sadly neglected.

A Diabolical Atmosphere

Given, then, all of the evidence discussed previously, how is one to explain the origin of the Medjugorje visions? Regrettably, an impartial assessment of the facts clearly suggests the possibility, if not the probability, of a diabolical intervention. The Bible tells us that we should be sober and watchful, because, our "adversary the devil prowls around like a roaring lion, seeking someone to devour." (1 Pet 5:8). Satan is perpetually on the lookout to ensnare the unsuspecting or unwary. Most of the time, he can do little damage to us, providing we are in a state of grace and endeavor to resist his temptations. But if particular circumstances arise then problems may well begin.

As regards Medjugorje, these include the unstable family backgrounds and temperaments of some of the visionaries, which indicate that such persons would not be likely to receive communications from heaven. In addition, as already indicated, the fact that Ivanka's mother was recently deceased would have put her in a vulnerable emotional state, which might have predisposed her to see something. Moreover, we have noted, too, the possible influence of the evil atmosphere resulting from the vengeance killings that were so much a part of the local "culture," in addition to the previous worship of spirits in the area, and in particular the *location* of the visions, that is in a place associated with the wartime massacres at Surmanci near Medjugorje.

On this last point, Moira Noonan recounts a revealing incident. While still embroiled in New Age practices, she visited a spiritual "retreat center" in the northeast United States, which included a lake on the property. One hot summer's day while sitting on the lake shore she tells us that she "had the sensation that something was wrong. I felt that there was something very strange and forbidding about this lake." She attempted to shrug off this feeling by going for a swim out to a platform in the lake, but by the time she reached this, "the dark emotion I felt had completely overwhelmed me. ...It was as if I had been literally swimming through spirits. It was just eerie and it was sickening. It felt like I was swimming through blood, it was just so thick. I couldn't stand it."

When she got back she discovered that the white settlers of the area had massacred the native people who lived there—killing men and women and children—and then throwing their bodies into the lake.[415] The parallel with the massacre at Surmanci is clear and disturbing.

Putting all this together, we can see that when Ivanka and Mirjana went up Podbrdo, to smoke and listen to rock music, the strong possibility of a diabolical intervention cannot be ruled out.

A Diabolical Incident

That some of the visionaries were involved in occurrences which strongly suggest this is clear from the following examples. A strange incident involving Mirjana took place about a year after the initial visions, in mid-1982, and she recounted it to Fr Vlasic in January 1983. She tells us that as she was waiting in her room for her usual rendezvous with the Gospa:

> I knelt down, and had not yet made the sign of the cross, when suddenly a bright light flashed and a devil appeared. It was as if something *told* me it was a devil. I looked at him and was very surprised, for I was expecting the Madonna to appear. He was horrible—he was like black all over ... He was terrifying, dreadful, and I did not know what he wanted. I realized I was growing weak, and then I fainted. When I revived, he was still standing there, laughing. It seemed that he gave me a strange kind of strength, so that I could almost accept him. He

told me that I would be very beautiful, and very happy, and so on. However, I would have no need of the Madonna, he said, and no need for faith. "She has brought you nothing but suffering and difficulties," he said; but he would give me everything beautiful—whatever I want. Then something in me—I don't know what, if it was something conscious or something in my soul—told me: *No! No! No!* Then I began to shake and feel just awful. Then he disappeared, and the Madonna appeared, and when she appeared my strength returned—as if she restored it to me. I felt normal again. Then the Madonna told me: "That was a trial, but it will not happen to you again."[416]

This was clearly a frightening incident, but the biggest problem with this particular vision is that, unlike genuine Marian apparitions, where there is a clear distinction between the divine and the diabolical, here they are intertwined. Thus, in an overall sense, this type of manifestation is far more characteristic of the diabolical.[417]

This is evident from an incident which happened to Francisco of Fatima. In her memoirs, Sr Lucia does not tell us exactly when this happened, but it is clear that it was quite separate from one of the Blessed Virgin's apparitions. She tells us how one day the three of them went to a rocky place called Pedreira, and while the girls played and looked after the sheep, Francisco withdrew to pray nearby. After a while, Lucia and Jacinta heard him shouting and crying out to Our Lady, and they ran to find him, "trembling with fright, …and so upset that he was unable to rise to his feet." They asked him what had happened, and in a very frightened voice he told them that: "It was one of those huge beasts that we saw in hell. He was right here breathing out flames!"[418]

A Further Strange Incident

Marinko Ivankovic, speaking in February 1983, testifies to a strange event which took place, "on the Feast of the Madonna of the Angels," 2 August 1981, in a field near Medjugorje, one evening after Mass. This was apparently a well-known meeting place for prayer. The visionaries were present, and claimed that the Gospa had appeared to them, and would allow all those who wished to do so, to touch her. The people duly came forward and "touched" the Gospa, being told by the visionaries that they were touching her veil, her head, her hand, and so on. This apparently went on for ten or fifteen minutes, until Marija cried out to Marinko: "The Madonna is blackened all over! …[t]here were sinners here who touched her, and as they touched her [,] her robe got darker and darker, until it was black." Marija then told him that they should all go to confession as soon as possible.[419]

Fr Laurentin mentions this incident,[420] but surprisingly makes no comment. It hardly needs stating that the above scenario—the idea that the Blessed Virgin could somehow be contaminated by contact with human beings—is quite absurd. It is absolutely contrary to authentic communications with the Blessed Virgin, as experienced by true mystics and saints, such as St Catherine Labouré, who, as we have seen, was able to put her hands on Our Lady's lap.

This chapter, then, clearly indicates the further problems involved with believing in Medjugorje, including the "apocalyptic" character of some of the messages, which puts them into conflict with the genuine message of Fatima. Similarly, the necessity of being on guard against false prophets does not seem to have been fully realized by many Medjugorje devotees, nor the problems associated with aspects of the spirituality which has developed out of it. In particular, many have been largely oblivious of the potentially very dangerous results of having an excessive desire to see a vision. To a great extent, all of this has happened because of the crisis affecting the Church since the 1960s, which has resulted in many well-meaning Catholics becoming involved with Medjugorje—but tragically, they have not been aware of some of its darker aspects.

21

Medjugorje More Recently

More Recent Developments

What has happened regarding the Medjugorje visionaries and the Franciscans in more recent years? It seems that it is still being claimed that the visions continue, and that those involved still draw the crowds wherever they go. Laurette Elsberry attended a Medjugorje conference in Sacramento, from 25-27 August, 2000. She described how it was "so sad to see so many people being taken in by the tour operators, the religious goods peddlers and a vaude-villian cast of characters intent on making the Mother of God into someone who traipses all around the world following the 'visionaries' and hawking 'pilgrimages'."

But what particularly appalled her was a joke told by one of the visionaries, Marija Pavlovic, who was there with her husband. This joke was taped and the following is an edited transcription:

> Jesus was in Paradise. The Apostles were a bit bored being in Paradise for such a long time, ...[and so] Jesus said, 'Let's go for a tour on the earth'. ... So they went [to the Holy Land] and they decided to have a barbecue on the beach, on the lake, with fresh fish. ... And since they were in Paradise where they had no more faith but they were completely sure about what they could do ...they were all walking on the water. And so also Jesus went on the water but he started to go down— to sink. So he starts thinking to himself: 'What's wrong with me? I'm Jesus. This is impossible. I'm sinking.' And then Peter saw him, got close to him and said: 'Rabbi, you forgot, your feet have holes.'

Laurette Elsberry reports the reaction of the nearly two thousand attendees at the conference: "They broke out in loud, raucous laughs and applause." She then goes on to put the question as to how such people, "could have laughed at such a blasphemous and sacrilegious joke, which ridiculed the Sacred Wounds of the Savior."[421]

Indeed, is it possible to imagine a genuine Marian seer acting in such a way?

Bishop Peric's Indictment

This is what Bishop Ratko Peric of Mostar had to say about Medjugorje, at a confirmation homily, given in the village itself, in July 2000:

> [A] true believer can only remain amazed at the talk that here in Medjugorje, for almost twenty years now, day by day, Mary has been presumably "appearing" for five, ten or fifteen minutes to so-called "seers"; that she is presumably handing something over: in the form of so-called "messages", or "ten secrets", it's not sure if there are exactly ten, if each person has received the same number, or if there are six times more, meaning that each person received a different amount. Does this mean that this "apparition" up until this time has appeared 6,940 times (19 years multiplied by 365/6 days)? And that constantly, every day, she is speaking, and that only once in a month she leaves a "message", and thanks the so-called "seers" for responding to her call? And this has been going on for almost twenty years now, and could keep on going another ten, twenty or even more years? The official statements of the Church, starting from the local Bishop up to the Bishops' Conference has not in this case recognized a single "apparition" as authentic. The Church has clearly declared that it is impossible to affirm that these events involve supernatural apparitions."[422]

There could hardly be a more solid indictment of Medjugorje.

Meanwhile, the death of Fr Slavko Barbaric was reported in December 2000. It appears that he died while climbing Mount Krizevac, and was actually in Medjugorje contrary to the wishes of Bishop Peric, who had withdrawn his faculties for hearing confessions the previous February. As might be expected, some of the Medjugorje visionaries claimed that the Blessed Virgin had appeared to them to inform them that Fr Barbaric was in heaven. It is worth noting that Bishop Peric personally came to conduct the funeral, despite all the problems the deceased had caused in the diocese.[423]

But if Fr Barbaric was dead, his example of disobedience lived on: on 28 May 2001, the Vicar General of the diocese of Mostar-Duvno issued a communiqué regarding an imposter bishop and illicit confirmations. As in the case of previous incidents of this kind, the latter had taken place at various Franciscan parishes in the diocese: these included Capljina, where Frs Boniface Barbaric and Bozo Rados were still ensconced although they had been dismissed from the Order. A certain "Bishop" Srecko Franjo Novak had performed the confirmations, but it turned out that he had been expelled from the regular Catholic seminary, only to join the "Old Catholics" where he was, at most, a deacon.[424]

The French Bishops and Medjugorje

In January 2001, during an assembly of the French bishops, Msgr Henri Brincard, Bishop of Puy-en-Velay, responded in writing to the following question put by a member of the conference: "Is there an authorised and official position of the Church concerning the events which motivate pilgrimages to Medjugorje?" Msgr Brincard replied by outlining the official Church position on this subject, that it belongs to the local Ordinary of the diocese to investigate such events, as the 1978 Congregation for the Doctrine of the Faith instruction made clear, and that Bishop Zanic had acted correctly in carrying out his own investigations between 1982 and 1986. In other words, he had set up commissions as required, and had likewise provided general guidance for the faithful by indicating his own position. Following advice from the Congregation, he had agreed that the Yugoslav Episcopal conference should study the dossier which had been compiled on Medjugorje, given that it was having an effect well beyond his own diocese.

Msgr Brincard then pointed out that: "The Holy Father never intervenes directly in affairs of this kind," and that the Congregation had expressed its appreciation of "the work accomplished by the diocesan commission, under the responsibility of Bishop Zanic." When on 26 April 1986, he had delivered to Cardinal Ratzinger an outline of the expected negative judgment which the commission would reach, the Cardinal asked Bishop Zanic to delay the publication of any definitive judgment. On 2 May 1986, the commission voted against recognizing any supernatural character in the events at Medjugorje, and on 15 May 1986, Bishop Zanic informed the Congregation about the negative findings of the commission. Msgr Brincard was at pains to point out that it was "not correct to state that Bishop Zanic was relieved of the dossier," as some Medjugorje supporters had claimed. The Yugoslav Episcopal Conference of Yugoslavia then undertook its own study of the dossier on Medjugorje, by means of a new commission, and this ultimately resulted in the Zadar declaration of 10 April 1991.[425]

Role of Local Bishop Crucial

Summing up all these developments, Msgr Brincard stated quite clearly that: "Up to this day, only the bishops of Mostar—Bishop Zanic, then Bishop Peric—and the Yugoslav Episcopal Conference (dissolved *de facto* by the partition of the country after the war) have expressed a judgement on the events of Medjugorje. The Congregation for the Doctrine of the Faith, on the other hand, has never issued an official judgement. It has only given directives of a pastoral order." Msgr Brincard then went on to state that in previous cases dealing with apparitions: "Rome always remits ... [finally] to the authority and the competence of the local Ordinary." To illustrate this he mentioned several approved apparitions including those at La Salette, Beauraing, and Banneux, where the local bishops were able to issue official pronouncements despite difficulties.[426]

On the vexed question of pilgrimages, Msgr Brincard was content to reiterate the advice, detailed above, which was given by Vatican officials, in particular Archbishops Bovone and Bertone, to the effect that official pilgrimages to Medjugorje should be discouraged. Regarding private pilgrimages, however, he makes the following pertinent point: "How, in fact, ...[can one] organise a private pilgrimage without it being motivated by the conviction that the events of Medjugorje are of a supernatural origin?"

Regarding the question of the fruits which are supposed to have arisen from Medjugorje, Msgr Brincard pointed out that according to the 1978 CDF document, the alleged supernatural events themselves must first be evaluated before there can be any question of examining the fruits. And he emphasized this by saying: "When this order is not respected errors of judgment can arise." Moreover, he went on to make the following observations:

> If we examine the events of Medjugorje in the light of the fruits, what do we observe? It is first of all undeniable that at Medjugorje there are returns to God and "spiritual" healings. It is no less evident that the sacramental life there is regular and the prayer fervent. One could not deny these good fruits *in situ*. We should even rejoice in them. But can we say that they continue in our parishes? Difficult question, for we must note unfortunately that the susceptibility, even aggressiveness, of some partisans of Medjugorje towards those who do not share their enthusiasm is such that in some places it provokes serious tensions which attack the unity of the People of God.

Finally, he looked at the fruits in the lives of the visionaries, focusing particularly on the question of their obedience to the Bishop of Mostar. He was forced to conclude that many problems existed in this area. The importance of Msgr Brincard's response can hardly be overstated since it was made at the request of the permanent council of the French Episcopal Conference, in January 2001, and published in their official bulletin.[427]

Warnings from Prominent Churchmen

The divisive nature of the activities of some Bosnia-Herzegovina Franciscans was noted by Cardinal Vinko Puljic of Sarajevo, at the Synod of Bishops in Rome, in October 2001. He spoke of how:

> certain members of the Order of Franciscan Friars Minor and those expelled try to impose their own points of view in the individual Dioceses, substituting the authentic charisms of their Institute with pseudo-charisms, a serious threat for the Church and for her organizational and doctrinal unity. Suffice it to recall the sad events last summer when the protagonists of the aforementioned Order and a self-declared bishop: an old style Catholic deacon expelled from his community, or a systematic disobedience to the same religious persons who for years have been in the Diocese of Mostar-Duvno [sic].[428]

Cardinal Pell of Sydney refused to allow Vicka Mijatovic-Ivankovic, one of the six alleged Medjugorje visionaries, now married, to speak in any Church building during a visit to his diocese. He feared that if he allowed her to address Catholics from Church property he would be giving official sanction to claims that were rejected by Mrs Mijatovic-Ivankovic's local bishop, whose function it was to determine their authenticity.[429]

In late 2002, Fr Zovko was refused permission to celebrate Mass at the Immaculate Conception national shrine in Washington. Msgr Michael J. Bransfield, the Rector, had written to Bishop Peric asking him to clarify the juridical status of the Franciscan. The bishop responded, in a letter dated 18 November, that Fr Zovko's disobedience had led to his faculties and canonical mission being revoked by Bishop Zanic on 23 August 1989, and that as his successor he had upheld this decision.[430]

As for Fr Vlasic, at the time of writing, he is said to be dividing his time between various communities and houses in Italy, Austria, and Medjugorje.

Visions and Secrets: The Current Situation

According to a recent Medjugorje author, writing in 2002, the situation as regards the visionaries and their secrets is as follows. Having ceased to receive daily visions in December 1982, Mirjana is now claiming visions on the second day of each month, with an annual one on her birthday. In addition, she claims to have received all ten secrets. Ivanka supposedly stopped receiving daily visions in May 1985, though she too has an annual vision on 24 June, and has received the full complement of secrets. Jakov, likewise, has received all ten secrets, and ceased having daily visions in 1998. Marija, Vicka, and Ivan all claim to continue to have daily visions, and similarly all claim they have received nine secrets.[431]

Bishop Peric delivered an address at Maynooth College in Ireland, on 17 February 2004, in which he outlined the present situation regarding Medjugorje. He itemized the number of total claimed visions, which varied between about 770 for Ivanka, to over 8,000 for Vicka, Marija, and Ivan, with a grand total for all the visionaries of over 33,000! As he notes, the Church has not accepted a single one of these visions as authentic.[432] This is what the Bishop had to say about the various secrets confided to the visionaries, and the "sign":

> Those who have daily "visions" have received nine secrets, while those who have "apparitions" once a year, have ten secrets. It is not clear if

nine or ten secrets have been given and are known to each of the "seers", or if each of the "seers" has his/her own number of secrets which differ from the rest. If we compare this to the authentic apparitions, then one can see that at Lourdes there were no secrets for the world, while at Fatima one secret was divided into three parts. Yet at Medjugorje till now there have been 9 or 10, or even 57 possible secrets, which have been divided by three "seers" who have received 10 and another three who have received 9. To this day not a single secret has been revealed. In the first years there was apocalyptic talk about a "great sign" to happen, yet to this day this "great sign" has not occurred, and the expectation of a sign has diminished.

In February 2006, Bishop Peric made his *ad limina* visitation to Pope Benedict VVI, and discussed the state of affairs in his diocese with the Pontiff. He was able to note that there had been some progress as regards the Franciscan problem, although there were still a number of examples of disobedience. He also discussed Medjugorje with the Pope, who intimated that for some time now, the Congregation for the Doctrine of the Faith had been skeptical as regards the claims of daily visions made by some of the visionaries. Bishop Peric confirmed that nothing had happened in the intervening period to affect the findings of the Bishops' conference of ex-Yugoslavia, the Zadar declaration, made in 1991. He then reiterated his own position as regards the non-supernaturality of the visions, before continuing:

> The numerous absurd messages, insincerities, falsehoods and disobedience associated with the events and "apparitions" of Medjugorje from the very outset, all disprove any claims of authenticity. Much pressure through appeals has been made to force the recognition of the authenticity of private revelations, yet not through convincing arguments based upon the truth, but through the self-praise of personal conversions and by statements such as one "feels good". How can this ever be taken as proof of the authenticity of apparitions?

At the conclusion of the meeting, Pope Benedict said the feeling at the Congregation had been that priests should be available to deal with the sacramental needs of pilgrims, but that this was to leave aside "the question of the authenticity of the apparitions".[433]

22

The Importance of Fatima

Pope John Paul II and the Consecration of 1984

Pope John Paul II's formal association with Fatima stems from the attempt made on his life in Rome on 13 May 1981, the anniversary of the first apparition at Fatima, when he was shot in St Peter's square. Providentially, the bullet wounds were not fatal, and while in hospital recovering, the Pope apparently reviewed all the documents on Fatima. He certainly felt that the Blessed Virgin's intercession had saved his life, and his reading apparently convinced him that the consecration of Russia to Mary's Immaculate Heart was an absolute necessity if the world was to be saved from war and atheism.

Consequently, on 13 May 1982, exactly a year after the assassination attempt, John Paul II went to Fatima, both to thank the Blessed Virgin for saving his life, and also to carry out a public act of consecration of the whole world, including Russia, to her Immaculate Heart. After this was accomplished, however, it became apparent that many of the world's bishops had not been informed in time. Thus, this consecration had not fulfilled the condition of collegiality asked for by Mary at Fatima, that is, that the Pope, in union with the bishops of the world, should consecrate Russia to her Immaculate Heart. Sr Lucia, still living in the Carmelite convent at Coimbra, apparently later made this known to the Apostolic Nuncio in Portugal.

Interestingly, in this 1982 consecration, John Paul II specifically described Fatima as a place "chosen" by the Blessed Virgin, thus indicating official confirmation of its status and intimating that we are to understand it as the major "prophecy" of modern times, a prophecy whose urgent message cannot be ignored. During his homily, the Pope made the following remarks:

> If the Church has accepted the message of Fatima, it is above all because that message contains a truth and a call whose basic content is the truth and call of the Gospel itself. "Repent, and believe in the Gospel" (Mk 1:15). These are the first words of the Messiah addressed to humanity. The message of Fatima is, in its basic nucleus, a call to conversion and repentance, as in the Gospel. This call was uttered at the beginning of the twentieth century, and it was thus addressed particularly to this present century. The Lady of the message seems to have read with special insight the "signs of the times," the signs of our time.

John Paul II also spoke of Fatima during this homily in these significant terms: "The appeal of the Lady of the message of Fatima is so deeply rooted in the Gospel and the whole of Tradition that the Church feels that the message imposes a commitment on her."

The Pope decided to renew the consecration in March 1984, with letters being sent to all the world's bishops in good time, including the Orthodox, asking them to join him in this action. On 25 March 1984, the feast of the Annunciation, John Paul II duly renewed the act of consecration in St Peter's Basilica in Rome, before the statue of Mary from the site of the apparitions at Fatima, which was specially brought over for the occasion. Although the text used did not mention Russia, the Pope did specifically recall the acts of consecration made by Pope Pius XII in 1942 and 1952, the latter being essentially concerned with Russia. It also appears that John Paul II paused during the ceremony, and, according to the then bishop of Leiria-Fatima, Alberto Cosme do Amaral, quietly included Russia in the consecration. This action is understandable, given the delicate political situation, and, it has been argued, with the understanding that God was leaving the Pope, as head of the Church on earth, to decide the precise form the act should take.

Certainly, Russia was in the Pope's mind in the following reference; "in a special way we entrust and consecrate to you those individuals and nations which particularly need to be thus entrusted and consecrated." Although not all the world's bishops joined in the act of consecration, it appears that a "moral totality" did, thus satisfying the request of the Blessed Virgin. Following this consecration, Sr Lucia was again visited by the Apostolic Nuncio; this time, she told him that the consecration of Russia had indeed been accomplished, and that God had accepted it. Thus, after nearly seventy years, the act of collegial consecration had finally been carried out.[434]

The Collapse of Communism

It's hard not to see a connection between the consecration made in 1984 and the rise to power of Mikhail Gorbachev in Russia, in March 1985, when he became General Secretary of the Communist Party. Realizing the dangerous situation of the Soviet Union, he began a program of reform based on restructuring and openness. This led to greater democratization in Russia, a more tolerant attitude to religious believers, and fruitful arms reductions talks with the United States; but also, ultimately, to the collapse of Communism in Russia.

This, however, was for the future; and, from 1988, Gorbachev was able to introduce major political changes, including a democratic Russian parliament. At the same time, he began to ease restrictions on religion, on the pragmatic basis that the country needed the energies of believers if it was to rebuild itself. This was also probably an acknowledgment of the fact that Communism had been unable to crush Christianity, despite exercising total control over it for more than eighty years. Meanwhile, popular unrest in Eastern Europe, in protest at Communist rule, led to the end of the Warsaw Pact, in 1989, as Gorbachev made it clear that Russia was not going to intervene to repress emerging democratic movements in countries such as Poland. In December 1989, President Gorbachev met the Pope at the Vatican, surely an unbelievable scenario just a few years previously.[435]

Further Fatima Developments

Fatima had received further papal support when, earlier in the year, on 13 May 1989, Pope John Paul II had declared Jacinta and Francisco "Venerable," the first stage in the canonization process. In May 1991, a decade after the assassination attempt, the Pope returned to Fatima to give thanks to the Blessed Virgin for the marvelous fruits of the 1984 consecration and for saving his life. But he warned that, although Marxism was losing its influence, there was a danger of its being replaced by another form of atheism equally hostile to Christian morality, a reference to Western materialism. Later in the same year, in August 1991, an attempted coup against President Gorbachev failed, and the Soviet Union as a belligerent world power began to collapse. Given Russia's military might, this dissolution was far more peaceful than had been feared.

These massive changes in Russia and Eastern Europe support the view that the consecration of 1984 was carried out largely in accordance with Mary's wishes. The Blessed Virgin promised the conversion of Russia if her wishes were complied with, but she did not say that this would happen overnight. Seventy years of Communist misrule could not be put right in a few years. The conversion of the Roman Empire took centuries to fully accomplish, although the decisive blow was struck by Constantine early in the fourth century at the battle of the Milvian bridge—but only after three hundred years of persecution for the early Church. If it took that long to convert the Roman Empire—despite the tremendous graces poured out as a result of Christ's crucifixion and resurrection, to say nothing of all the sufferings of the early martyrs—then there is surely a need to be cautious about demanding quick results with regard to Russia's conversion.

The Conversion of Russia

Comparisons have been made between what happened in Mexico after Guadalupe in 1531, when there were mass conversions to Catholicism within a few decades, and the lack of a like process in Russia in recent years. But this is to lose sight of the fact that the apparitions, and the miraculous *tilma* which resulted from them, were common knowledge in the country. In addition, the evangelization of Mexico was greatly helped by the presence of Franciscan missionaries who were able to minister to the people. Regarding Fatima, too, the apparitions, and in particular the miracle of the sun, were common knowledge in Portugal, and it was essentially a matter of reinvigorating the Catholic sentiments of the people, who had been adversely affected by vicious governmental persecution.

But in the case of Russia, the situation is completely different. Not only was there no great public miracle in Russia either in 1917 or 1984, but in addition the Catholic population of Russia is tiny, and equally crucially, there are very few priests or missionaries available for evangelization.

There is no case in history of a large country being converted without either some sort of miraculous intervention in the country itself, or intense missionary activity—with the latter preferably accompanied by miracles. Neither of these conditions was or is present in Russia, and so its conversion looks like being a long drawn out process, one which will require either a much larger Catholic presence in the country, or the renewal/conversion of the Russian Orthodox Church.

There is still much to be done, but it is difficult to argue that there have not been huge changes in Russia in recent years. Russian society is by no means tranquil, there is a great deal of corruption and the threat of a return to some form of authoritarian government, but at least the vicious persecutions of the past are over, and there is an opportunity for a new beginning.[436]

Fatima and Medjugorje Contrasted

It is clear, then, that the contrast between Fatima and Medjugorje could hardly be greater. As we have seen, the course of the Fatima apparitions from May to October 1917 is radically different from the early events at Medjugorje. Portugal was completely transformed as its people lived out the message of Fatima, while by contrast, following the alleged visions at Medjugorje, there was no lasting spiritual revival amongst the people living in the surrounding areas. Indeed, it could be said that those followers of Medjugorje who became embroiled in the cause of Croatian nationalism were a strong contributory factor towards the violence which erupted during the 1990s. In particular, elements from the July 1917 Fatima secret have been shown to have come true over the course of time, in contrast to the supposed "secrets" of Medjugorje, while the Fatima miracle of the sun, in October 1917, dwarfs any other claimed "miracles" at Medjugorje.

The later apparitions to Sr Lucia, which developed the important link between the consecration of Russia and the Five First

Saturdays devotion, likewise indicate how crucial this devotion is, and why it is necessary that it should become much better known throughout the Church. Unfortunately, one of the reasons why this is not happening is the popularity of Medjugorje, which has little practical emphasis on this important devotion.

The consecrations of Portugal to Mary's Immaculate Heart by the Portuguese bishops during the 1930s were instrumental in keeping the country out of both the Spanish Civil War and World War II, whereas Medjugorje was unable to prevent Yugoslavia, during the early nineties, from becoming the scene of the bitterest fighting in Europe for decades.

Finally, the profound power and impact of Fatima is shown by the fact that the consecration of the world to Mary's Immaculate Heart made by Pius XII in 1942 was able to shorten the Second World War, while Pope John Paul II's collegial consecration in 1984 led to the virtually peaceful collapse of Communism in the Soviet Union and Eastern Europe.

What can Medjugorje possibly offer in comparison with this unique association of Fatima with the papacy, which has been of such deep significance for the world? Not only has Medjugorje failed to gain any tangible support from the See of Rome; it has not even been accepted by the successive bishops of Mostar.

Some Questions for Medjugorje Supporters

Thus, supporters of Medjugorje have to ask themselves some crucial questions.

Why, for example, having warned about the "errors of Russia" at Fatima, did the Gospa at Medjugorje not warn about the threat presented by Communism to the salvation of the local people? Or why, if Mary really was appearing at Medjugorje, did it take the Pope's consecration to Our Lady of Fatima in 1984 to bring an end to the Communist persecution of the Church in Eastern Europe? If Medjugorje was the continuation and fulfillment of Fatima—"the last apparition on earth"—why didn't the Gospa perform a great public miracle like the miracle of the sun at Fatima?

But if there was no great miracle at Medjugorje, the results of the Pope's act of consecration to the Immaculate Heart of Mary in 1984, that is, the virtually peaceful collapse of Communism in the

Soviet Union and Eastern Europe, are quite plain. There is now a great burgeoning of vocations in the countries of Central and Eastern Europe, where there are many thousands of seminarians presently studying for ordination. Tragically, in the West, where there has been minimal compliance with the requests of the Blessed Virgin at Fatima, congregations are falling and seminaries are being closed because vocations are drying up.

So how does one explain the ongoing crisis of faith in the Church in the West, if Mary did in truth begin to appear at Med-jugorje as recently as 1981, and Medjugorje is supposed to have far surpassed Fatima in its efficacy and power? Millions of people have visited Medjugorje and a vast amount of information about it has been circulated throughout the Church, but where are the concrete results of all this activity which stand comparison with those effected in Portugal after 1917, and in Central and Eastern Europe after John Paul II's consecration in 1984? Where is the evidence, in the words of the Zadar declaration, for a "healthy devotion toward the Blessed Virgin Mary" which has had a real effect in solving the problems of Bosnia-Herzegovina—including the religious problem relating to the Franciscans—or the rest of ex-Yugoslavia for that matter?

In sum, why is Medjugorje still a subject of ongoing doubt, dispute and disagreement in the Church, whereas, as detailed above, Fatima brought about a marvelous and harmonious spiritual renewal of the Church throughout Portugal, and today Our Lady's message is welcomed in many dioceses throughout the world, where it contributes to the authentic spiritual renewal of many Catholics? These are some of the questions which any convinced supporter of Medjugorje needs to answer, but meanwhile it is clear that the spiritual effects of Medjugorje have been minimal in comparison with the great blessings bestowed on the Church through the message of Fatima.

More Recent Fatima Developments

In 1999, it was announced that Pope John Paul would beatify Francisco and Jacinta in Fatima on 13 May 2000. On the evening of 12 May, a crowd of 650,000 greeted the Holy Father as he arrived at the Cova da Iria on his third pilgrimage to the shrine as Pope.

The next morning, the Pope returned to the Cova for the Beatification Mass, stopping off at the Basilica to meet privately with 93-
year-old Sr Lucia. This Mass was concelebrated before the vast
crowd, by a large number of bishops in front of the Basilica. During
the Mass, the Holy Father read out the text of beatification, which
allows the celebration of a local feast for the two children on 20
February each year, the anniversary of Jacinta's death in 1920.
Assuming they are eventually canonized, this will become a feast of
the universal Church and they will have the title of Saint.

Towards the end of the Mass, Cardinal Sodano, the Vatican
Secretary of State, unexpectedly announced, at the Pope's behest,
the imminent publication of the third part of the secret of Fatima
along with an official commentary. He revealed, too, that part of
the text dealt with the Holy Father, and described it as a "prophetic
vision similar to those found in Sacred Scripture," which had to be
interpreted in symbolic terms. He further described the contents as
being concerned with the persecutions suffered by the Church and
successive Popes during the twentieth century, and particularly that
"the bishop clothed in white," who the children witnessed being
shot, was Pope John Paul II. A little over a month later, the full
text of the third part of the secret, originally set down by Sr Lucia
in the 1940s, was released by the Holy See, along with a commentary by Cardinal Joseph Ratzinger.

The importance of Fatima in the life of the Church was further
confirmed by the act of the Holy Father, on 8 October 2000, of
entrusting the third millennium to Mary. The statue of Our Lady of
Fatima at the Capelinha was again specially brought to Rome for
the occasion, a move of particular symbolic importance in the
Jubilee Year. As in the case of the 1984 collegial consecration, all
the bishops of the world were encouraged to join in this new act of
entrustment. Thus these developments, the beatifications, the
revelation of the third part of the secret, and the dedication of the
third millennium to Our Lady, indicate that Fatima has assumed a
position of center-stage in the life of the Church in the first years of
the new century, a position which can only grow in strength.

It is clear that the message of Fatima was not confined to one
period of time, as in the case of other apparitions, but rather has
continued to develop over the course of the twentieth century, and,

indeed, it is not complete yet. The implications of the message of Fatima still have to be taken up by the Church as a whole.[437]

Medjugorje a Continuation of Fatima?

Some Medjugorje supporters have claimed that it is a continuation of Fatima.[438] But if this is the case why has there been virtually no mention of Mary's Immaculate Heart in the messages? This was the devotion which God wished to establish in the world, as Our Lady told Lucia at Fatima on 13 July 1917. The reality is that there can only be one continuation of Fatima, and that is voluntary compliance with Our Lady's requests, according to the teaching, acts, and example of John Paul II—and now Benedict XVI—until the world experiences the triumph of her Immaculate Heart, which she promised would finally come.

It is certainly true that the Medjugorje messages do give a cursory mention to some of the more important themes from Fatima, including the necessity of saying the rosary. But essentials like this are buried in the sheer profusion of questionable, banal, and endlessly repetitive messages. Thus, it is quite incorrect to regard Medjugorje as having any sort of genuine link with Fatima.

In illustration of this, a Dutch woman, Mrs Hildegard Alles, concerned about reports that Sr Lucia was receiving messages from Our Lady about what she was allegedly doing in Medjugorje, wrote to the Bishop of Fatima, in 1998, requesting a clarification. This letter was passed on to Dr Luciano Cristino, the director of SESDI [Department of Studies and Publications] at the Fatima Sanctuary, who replied saying that such an allegation was "completely false."

This point, that Sr Lucia was not receiving any heavenly revelations, whether regarding Medjugorje or otherwise, was further emphasized in December 2001. It was then revealed, in connection with the release of the third part of the Fatima secret, that Sr Lucia had met Archbishop Bertone, the secretary of the Congregation for the Doctrine of the Faith, and amongst other things had said. "If I had received new revelations, I would have told no one, but I would have communicated them directly to the Holy Father".[439]

However, it does seem that some time after the collegial consecration of 1984, Sr Lucia *did* receive a direct revelation from heaven confirming that the consecration had been carried out correctly. In a recent interview, the Archbishop, now a cardinal, spoke of an "apparition in which the Virgin showed Sr Lucia that she accepted and was pleased with John Paul II's consecration of the world and Russia to her Immaculate Heart." Indeed, in the 2001 meeting referred to above, Sr Lucia herself stated that: "I have already said that the consecration that Our Lady desired was accomplished in 1984, and was accepted in heaven." The Cardinal also reaffirmed the point—questioned by some—that the complete text of the third part of the secret of Fatima had been revealed in 2000, saying: "I completely deny that the full secret has not been revealed ... I brought the text to Sr. Lucia ...and [she] exclaimed, 'This is my text, these are my pages, this is my envelope and this is my writing. There is nothing else.' "[440]

The following Medjugorje message, which explicitly mentions Fatima, is dated 25 August 1991: "Dear Children ... I want you to make sacrifices for nine days so that, with your help, all that I mean to carry out through the secrets which I started giving at Fatima may be achieved ...Thank you for your response to my call!"[441]

This message, of itself, is a strong indication that Medjugorje is false. We just don't find any explicit reference to the other apparitions in the approved, genuine, historical Marian apparitions.

The Five First Saturdays Devotion

It is important to note that as early as the July 1917 apparition at Fatima, the Blessed Virgin was jointly linking the consecration of Russia to Mary's Immaculate Heart and the Five First Saturdays devotion of reparation, as being amongst the means by which manifold evils would be undone and peace brought to the world. Having mentioned all the problems facing the Church in the world, she explicitly said: "To prevent this, I shall come to ask for the consecration of Russia to my Immaculate Heart, and the Communion of Reparation on the First Saturdays."

We have looked at the incident in which the Blessed Virgin appeared to Sr Lucia in December 1925, and spoke to her about the Five First Saturdays devotion, which involved her promise to "assist at the hour of death, with all the graces necessary for salvation, all those who, on the first Saturday of five consecutive months go to confession and receive Holy Communion, recite five decades of the

Rosary and keep me company for a quarter of an hour while meditating on the mysteries of the Rosary, with the intention of making reparation to me."

There is also the letter Sr Lucia wrote to her confessor in 1930, in which she said:

> If I am not mistaken, Our Dear Lord God promises to end the persecu-
> tion of Russia, if the Holy Father condescends to make, and likewise
> ordains the Bishops of the Catholic World to make, a solemn and
> public act of reparation and consecration of Russia to the Most Holy
> Hearts of Jesus and Mary. In response to the ending of this persecution,
> His Holiness is to promise to approve of and recommend the practice
> of the already mentioned devotion of reparation.[442]

It is extremely important to note the explicit link between the consecration of Russia and the Five First Saturdays devotion, but it does not seem as though many in the Church are really aware of this. The active persecution of Christians in Russia is over now, although no-one is pretending that life there is easy, or that there are not human rights abuses—but as a state-sponsored activity, such persecution has ceased.

It seems, then, that the full conversion of Russia promised by Our Lady may well not happen until this First Saturdays devotion of reparation is widely known and practised. John Paul II gave us an example by fulfilling Our Lady's requests to a quite unprecedented extent, and now it would appear that a response is required from the whole Church.

If the Five First Saturdays devotion was properly implemented throughout the Church, with full backing from the Pope and all the Bishops, it would have a profound impact. Not only would it be a great encouragement to frequent reception of the sacraments, the primary sources of grace, but it would also give Catholics an assurance of eternal salvation through its promise of the grace of final perseverance. Great graces that are being held in store for the Church by God would undoubtedly be released *if* large numbers of Catholics really took this devotion to heart. Would it be too much to believe that, just as the collegial consecration led to the downfall of Communism in Russia, so also the widespread implementation of the First Saturdays devotion could lead to both the conversion of Russia, *and* a great revival for the Church in the West?

Whereas the Five First Saturdays devotion is particularly in-tended to call for a response from priests and laity, the collegial consecration was specifically directed to the Pope and the bishops in union with him. Both aspects together, then, invite the whole people of God to play their respective parts in fulfilling the requests of Our Lady of Fatima.

Thus, the Five First Saturdays devotion of reparation is one of the "missing links" in the message of Fatima, and its adoption would appear to be far more important than has hitherto been realized. In fact, what is needed is nothing less than a worldwide movement to promote this devotion, along the lines of the Divine Mercy movement. But instead of this happening, the energies of great numbers of well-meaning Catholics have been diverted into promoting Medjugorje, which has thus become a serious stumbling block to a genuine renewal of the whole Church.

During the June 1917 apparition, Lucia was told by Our Lady that unlike Jacinta and Francisco, who would shortly be going to heaven, she would have to remain behind for "some time to come." The reason for this was that Jesus wanted to establish devotion to Mary's Immaculate Heart throughout the world. The Blessed Mother then continued: "I promise salvation to whoever embraces it; these souls will be dear to God, like flowers put by me to adorn his throne."

This promise of salvation is for everyone without exception, and as indicated above the Five First Saturdays devotion forms an integral part of the Fatima message, one which the Church, principally in the persons of her priests and laity, now needs to enthusiastically accept and promote. If this is done, then we can expect a new Marian era and a wonderful rebirth for the Church, all of which will eventually lead to the long-awaited triumph of Mary's Immaculate Heart.

23

Medjugorje: An Ongoing Problem for the Church

Some Conclusions

We have looked, then, at the historical background to Medjugorje, and seen how the long-running dispute between the Franciscans and the local bishops in Bosnia-Herzegovina is one of the keys to understanding why Medjugorje has become such a problem for the Church. In addition, we have seen how the link between the Charismatic Movement and the visions has facilitated their acceptance by many Catholics, despite the fact that there has been no Church approval for Medjugorje. Similarly, we have analyzed the crucial role that Fr René Laurentin played in the promotion of the visions, as well as the effect of the numerous books supportive of Medjugorje. This combination of factors has assured Medjugorje its present high profile, despite the serious problems involved in accepting it as genuine.

We have also seen that both the contents of the visions themselves, and the activities of the visionaries, have been far from satisfactory. The early accounts about Medjugorje were mostly based on late interviews, whereas the primary source material, the very revealing tapes made during the first week or so of the visions, has been largely ignored. These tapes indicate that whatever the visionaries saw during this period it was *not* the Blessed Mother. Moreover, they also reveal that there was no real message from the Gospa, and that the visions were supposed to end very quickly.

It has been demonstrated that the arguments often put forward in support of the visions are without serious foundation, and that the wordy and repetitive messages bear almost no relation to what the Blessed Virgin has previously said during her approved apparitions. Similarly, the evidence for miraculous healings and other allegedly supernatural events at Medjugorje has been assessed and found wanting. The activities of some of the Franciscans involved in Medjugorje have been sadly disedifying, while the horrific inter-clan violence which took place in Medjugorje in the early nineties—when pilgrims were mostly absent—surely could not have taken place if Our Lady had truly been appearing there.

While acknowledging that there have been some good fruits arising from Medjugorje, it has been shown that these cannot be used as the sole criteria for assessing the truth of the visions. Likewise, the fact that Medjugorje has been accepted by so many Catholics is not of itself an argument in favor of authenticity. We are still living through the upheavals which have been affecting the Church since the sixties, and it is against this confused and troubled background that the popularity of Medjugorje must be judged.

Mary Craig tells us that on 30 June 1981, a week after the visions began, Fr Zovko made the following admission to Frs Tomislav Pervan and Ivan Dugandzic, saying that it would be "awful" if in the future, "newspaper headlines proclaim that twenty, thirty, maybe even fifty thousand people have been the victims of a hoax on our bleak and barren hillside."[443]

The reality is that, twenty-five years later, Fr Zovko's warning has apparently been borne out—except that he greatly underestimated the numbers involved.

The Church in Crisis

This, then, is the situation which confronts the Church, and the papacy, twenty-five years after the beginning of the visions in 1981. As we have seen, nothing in the official pronouncements of the Church gives any suggestion of approval for Medjugorje, rather it has been regarded as an ongoing problem, one which has been reluctantly tolerated.

The Church in the West has still not recovered from the aftermath of the cultural revolution which, in the wake of Vatican II, threatened to overwhelm it. Catechesis has largely collapsed, and the result has been large numbers of ill-formed Catholics, who have turned out to be easy prey for those involved in promoting suspect visions. Similarly, the loss of a sense of the sacred which followed the changes in the liturgy has left many Catholics looking for spiritual solace elsewhere. In addition, influential theologians have played a large part in giving questionable visions like Medjugorje a degree of respectability and mass appeal. These are probably the main reasons why Medjugorje has had such an impact on the Church, and they indicate the difficulties faced by the Holy See in formulating a policy to deal with it.

Pope John Paul II's Position

Indeed, Pope John Paul found himself in a situation very like that outlined by Christ in the parable of the wheat and the weeds. (Matt 13:24–30)

> The kingdom of heaven may be compared to a man who sowed good seed in his field; but while men were sleeping, his enemy came and sowed weeds among the wheat, and went away. So when the plants came up and bore grain, then the weeds appeared also. And the servants of the householder came and said to him, "Sir, did you not sow good seed in your field? How then has it weeds?" He said to them, "An enemy has done this." The servants said to him, "Then do you want us to go and gather them?" But he said, "No; lest in gathering the weeds you root up the wheat along with them. Let both grow together until the harvest; and at harvest time I will tell the reapers, Gather the weeds first and bind them in bundles to be burned, but gather the wheat into my barn."

Pope John Paul II was the householder who had to tolerate the Medjugorje "weeds" which were sowed in the field of the Church. The point of the parable is that in the beginning, when both the weeds and the wheat sprout, they are very difficult to distinguish. In the same way, at the beginning, many of the signs associated with Medjugorje seemed good. Thus it had to be given time to develop. But, having been given that time, it is now quite clear that the weeds are largely just that, weeds. They have grown up and are threatening to overwhelm the good seed, that is, the message of Fatima. Unfortunately, Medjugorje is proving to be a long-lasting plant, and it does not look as though it will wither away by itself; rather some sort of negative declaration coming from the highest levels of the Church will be necessary. But the "harvest" is surely approaching, the time when Medjugorje will have to be uprooted from the Church, regardless of the difficulties this will involve.

As Michael Davies puts it:

> It would seem that the Vatican is delaying its announcement that nothing supernatural has occurred at Medjugorje, for fear of the reaction among its devotees, but the longer it delays the announcement, which must inevitably come, the greater will be the number of those devotees and the greater their disillusionment. When the announcement comes, many souls will be lost to the Church, as they will prefer the authority of spurious messages to the authority of the Magisterium. [444]

At the same time, the good seed must be protected and promoted, that is, the message of Fatima must be proclaimed much more strongly throughout the Church. While sites of alleged visions such as Medjugorje continue to attract large crowds, rank and file Catholics are neglecting Fatima, despite the fact that it has attracted unprecedented approval from the Church.

The Truth of Fatima: The Problems with Medjugorje

As we have seen above, the truth and power of the Fatima message have become quite clear over the years. But despite all this, and the complete lack of any official backing for Medjugorje, the latter has mysteriously maintained a very high level of support among Catholics.

If Medjugorje was nothing more than a series of false visions, then the Church is resilient enough to cope with that. There have been false visions and false visionaries throughout Church history, but sooner or later they become manifest and remedial action is taken. It is true that for a quarter of a century, millions of people have been misled into believing in Medjugorje in good faith, but in a pastoral sense, over time, that damage can be undone. But Medjugorje is much more than a passing difficulty which can be shrugged off with little in the way of ill effects. The truth is that it has played a very damaging role in diverting Catholics from Fatima. The reader might ask: is Fatima really that crucial? And the answer

most certainly is "Yes," it is that vital. It represents an unprecedented intervention on the part of the Blessed Virgin in order to
bring back to Christ a world which is increasingly denying and
rejecting the Gospel of eternal salvation precisely as she warned us
at Fatima. Its effects are still being worked out nearly a century after
the original apparitions, and its message will be of great importance
for many decades to come.

During the July 1917 apparition, Our Lady, as part of the secret,
told the children that: "In the end, my Immaculate Heart will
triumph. ... and a period of peace will be granted to the world."
This is an extremely complex subject,[445] but suffice to say that the
most realistic interpretation of these words involves seeing in them
a prophecy of a great worldwide triumph for the Church, and a time
of global peace. We only have to look around us to see how many
conflicts are raging, conflicts which often have deep historical roots
and which do not seem, humanly speaking, to be capable of
resolution. The threat of further violence is ever present, and it is
difficult to see how there can be genuine peace in the world unless
there is a major change in the present way of thinking. Just as the
growth of Christendom was an imperfect example of the way that a
society based on Catholicism could be lived out, so also we need to
look forward to a new Christendom, a new "Civilization of Love," a
worldwide civilization based on the teaching of the Church, as
Pope John Paul II proclaimed throughout his pontificate.

Triumph of the Immaculate Heart of Mary

If the triumph of Mary's Immaculate Heart is nothing more than a
patching up of the present system so that it can creak along, then it
will be a very poor triumph. We are talking here of a radical
transformation of the world—otherwise the use of the word
"triumph" is completely inappropriate. And it should be obvious,
too, that such a triumph is not going to happen overnight. The
deep-seated problems presently convulsing the world are not, it
would seem, going to be solved in a decade or two.

This idea, that the triumph of Mary's Immaculate Heart is going
to be of worldwide importance, is clearly present in the writings of
some well-known Marian saints.

St Louis de Montfort, author of the famous *True Devotion to Mary,* wrote, in the early eighteenth century, of the "great saints of the latter times," who by their word and example, "shall draw the *whole world* to true devotion to Mary." He also described how they would, "imbued with the spirit of Mary, ... work great wonders in the world, so as to destroy sin and to establish the Kingdom of Jesus Christ, her Son, upon the ruins of the kingdom of this corrupt world."[446]

This prophecy, incidentally, only emphasizes the point made above about the conversion of Russia, that is, that this will not happen until there are sufficient apostolic workers on the ground to bring it about, perhaps even to the extent of their working miracles to this end—Russia will certainly not be converted in a religious vacuum. St Louis indeed said that the *whole world* would be drawn to Mary, but also that this would not happen without a great deal of heroic evangelizing work.

Before her death in 1876, St Catherine Labouré, the seer of the Rue du Bac in Paris, made the following fascinating prediction, one which certainly seems to equate with Mary's words at Fatima: "Oh, how wonderful it will be to hear, 'Mary is Queen of the Universe ...' It will be a time of peace, joy and good fortune that will last long; she will be carried as a banner and she will make a tour of the world."[447]

Similarly, one of St John Bosco's most famous prophetic dreams apparently casts light on the triumph of Mary's Immaculate Heart. This famous nineteenth-century educator, the founder of the Salesian Order, quite often told his pupils the details of his mysterious dreams, one of which apparently concerned the future of the papacy and the Church. He saw the Catholic Church as a great ship, with a future Pope as its captain in the midst of storms, being increasingly attacked by irreligious forces, as other boats, representing persecutions of all sorts, seemed about to destroy it. But at the last moment, the Pope managed to steer his ship towards two great columns, one representing the Eucharist and the other the Blessed Virgin, and a great period of peace then descended on the Church and the world. This prophecy ties in very well with the message of Fatima, that, following persecutions and the recognition of Mary's importance and her association with the Eucharist, the world will be given a period of peace.[448]

More recently, St Maximilian Kolbe, the great martyr of Auschwitz, summed up the situation succinctly when he said that mankind "will find true happiness only when Mary Immaculate reigns over the whole world."[449]

And indeed, Pope John Paul II himself said in *Crossing the Threshold of Hope:* "Christ will conquer through [Mary], because he wants the Church's victories now and in the future to be linked to her."[450]

Fatima is the Answer

Thus, genuine Marian devotion, as contained in the message of Fatima, in reality provides a blueprint for the whole Church for the foreseeable future, and particularly, as we have seen, in regard of the promotion of the Five First Saturdays devotion. For that reason alone it is of enormous importance. This is not to say, though, that Fatima is some sort of panacea for all the problems in the Church— rather its message is meant be seen as part of a complete renewal of Catholicism, one involving evangelization, catechesis, and so on. But factors in this renewal, such as the importance of the Five First Saturdays devotion, have certainly been seriously underrated.

For the good of the Church, then, it is necessary that a genuine and properly regulated Marian piety and practice once more become part of normal Catholic life. This is precisely what the Second Vatican Council intended by means of the teaching about Our Lady in chapter eight of *Lumen Gentium*, which clearly indicates the importance of her place in the Church. And the unprecedented Marian teachings of Pope John Paul II likewise indicate that the Church should be much more focused on the role of Mary.

Thus the genuine enthusiasm and any real achievements attached to Medjugorje, where these exist, should be integrated into mainstream Marian Catholicism. This means that the apparently genuine conversions and spiritual good points coming from Medjugorje—for example, the large numbers involved in receiving the Sacraments—somehow need to be harnessed to the ordinary

Marian "channels" which exist in the Church, particularly those involving Fatima.

For if this kind of integration does not happen, then the Medjugorje movement will continue to divert the faithful away from Fatima, and thus risk their becoming even more estranged from the true life of the Church. There are signs to indicate this is already happening, particularly in terms of disobedience to lawful Episcopal authority. Either the "good fruits" of Medjugorje are properly appropriated, or there is a danger that they will evaporate in an excess of enthusiasm, or worse lead to the formation of schismatic or even heretical groups. It has certainly been the case in the past that groups which have started out with the best of intentions have deviated from normality and ended up in opposition to the Church, so this is not a far-fetched scenario.

Heavenly Visions or Religious Illusion?

If you are a Medjugorje supporter, and you have stayed with the book this far, you may be feeling rather upset that you have not previously been informed about the questionable activities that have been described above, and which have gone on for so long and caused so many problems for the Church. It is painful to have to face the fact that someone or something has led us astray. We feel cheated. It is easy, once a person realizes that Medjugorje is not genuine, particularly if they have invested a lot of spiritual capital in the visions, to become somewhat bitter and resentful. But if you are inclined to feel that way, I would urge you rather to turn towards Our Lady as she has revealed herself at Fatima. There, contrary to the situation regarding Medjugorje, you can have complete moral certainty that the message of Fatima is good, truthful, and life-giving, and in total harmony with the Church and the Gospel.

As Mary herself told us in June 1917, her Immaculate Heart will be our refuge on our journey, and the secure and trustworthy way to lead us to God. If we truly live the message of Fatima, she will save us from being deceived. Given this, our task is to do all we can to help bring about the triumph of Mary's Immaculate Heart, by complying unreservedly with her requests, following the sublime example of Francisco, Jacinta and Lucia.

Thus, all those genuinely devoted to the Blessed Virgin should examine their position, and look at the Church's approach to both Fatima and Medjugorje. It has given the fullest possible support to the former, whereas it has given no official support whatsoever to the latter. To continue to support Medjugorje means to continue on a misguided quest for "signs and wonders," to continue on a doubtful path that will probably end in disappointment and quite possibly disaster. This book has sought to give readers a real understanding of Medjugorje, and while we can definitely affirm that Fatima is of heavenly origin, sadly, the only rational conclusion about Medjugorje is that it has turned out to be a vast, if captivating, religious illusion.

Select Bibliography

Apolito, Paolo, *Apparitions of the Madonna at Oliveto Citra: Local Visions and Cosmic Drama*, trans. W. Christian, (Pennsylvania State University Press, Pennsylvania, 1998).

_____, *The Internet and the Madonna: Religious Visionary Experience on the Web,* trans. A. Shugaar, (The University of Chicago Press, Chicago, 2005).

Aumann Fr Jordan, OP, *Spiritual Theology,* (Sheed and Ward, London, 1995).

Bax, Mart, *Medjugorje: Religion, Politics, and Violence in Rural Bosnia,* (VU Uitgeverij, Amsterdam, 1995).

Bouflet, Joachim, *Medjugorje, ou la fabrication du surnaturel,* (Éditions Salvator, Paris, 1999).

Claverie, Élisabeth, *Les guerres de la Vierge,* (Gallimard, 2003).

Craig, Mary, *Spark from Heaven: The Mystery of the Madonna of Medjugorje,* (Spire, London, 1991).

Davies, Michael, *Medjugorje After Fifteen Years: The Message and the Meaning,* (The Remnant Press, St Paul, 1998).

_____, *Medjugorje after Twenty-One Years, 1981–2002: The Definitive History,* (available as an internet download from: www.mdaviesonmedj.com).

Farges, Msgr Albert, *Mystical Phenomena,* trans., S. P. Jacques, (Burns, Oates & Washbourne Ltd., London, 1926).

Franken, Fr Rudo, *A Journey to Medjugorje: Objections to the Apparitions,* (Roggel en Neer, 1999).

Guerrera, Rev Vittorio, *Medjugorje: A Closer Look,* (Maryheart Crusaders, Meriden, 1995).

Horvath, Agnes, & Arpad Szakolczai, *The Dissolution of Communist Power: The Case of Hungary,* (Routledge, London, 1992).

John of the Cross, St., *The Complete Works of Saint John of the Cross*, 3 vols, trans., E. Allison Peers, (Burns Oates, London, 1943).

_____, *The Collected Works of Saint John of the Cross*, trans., Kavanagh & Rodriguez, (ICS Publications, Washington, 1991).

Johnson, Kevin Orlin, *Twenty Questions About Medjugorje: What Rome Really Said*, (Pangaeus Press, Dallas, 1999).

_____, *Apparitions: Mystic Phenomena And What They Mean*, (Pangaeus Press, Dallas, 1995).

Jones, E. Michael, *Medjugorje: The Untold Story*, (Fidelity Press, South Bend, 1993).

_____, *The Medjugorje Deception: Queen of Peace, Ethnic Cleansing, Ruined Lives*, (Fidelity Press, South Bend, 1998).

Klanac, Daria, *Aux Sources de Medjugorje*, (Éditions Sciences et Culture, Montréal, 1998).

_____, *Medjugorje, Réponses aux objections*, (Le Sarment, 2001).

Kondor, Fr Louis, ed., *Fatima in Lucia's own words*, (Postulation Centre, Fatima, 1976).

Kraljevic, Svetozar, OFM, *The Apparitions of Our Lady at Medjugorje*, ed. M. Scanlan, (Franciscan Herald Press, Chicago, 1984).

Laurentin, René, *Bernadette of Lourdes*, trans. J. Drury, (Darton, Longman & Todd, London, 1980).

_____, *The Life of Catherine Labouré*, trans., P. Inwood, (Collins, London, 1983).

_____, *Medjugorje Testament: Hostility Abounds, Grace Superabounds*, (Ave Maria Press, Toronto, 1999).

Laurentin, René & Ljudevit Rupcic, trans. F. Martin, *Is the Virgin Mary Appearing at Medjugorje?* (The Word Among Us Press, Gaithersburg, 1988).

Laurentin, René & René Lejeune, *Messages and Teachings of Mary at Medjugorje: Chronological Corpus of the Messages*, (The Riehle Foundation, Milford, 1988).

Nolan, Denis, *Medjugorje: A Time for Truth and a Time for Action*, (Queenship Publishing, Santa Barbara, 1993).

O'Carroll, Fr Michael, CSSp, *Medjugorje: Facts, Documents, Theology*, (Veritas, Dublin, 1986).

Pelletier, Fr Joseph, *Our Lady Comes to Garabandal*, (Assumption Publications, Worcester, 1971).

Peric, Msgr Ratko, *Criteria for Discerning Apparitions: Regarding the Events of Medjugorje*, (Mostar, 1995).

Ratzinger, Joseph Cardinal with Vittorio Messori, *The Ratzinger Report: An Exclusive Interview on the State of the Church*, (Fowler Wright Books, Leominster, 1985).

Rooney, Lucy & Robert Faricy, *Mary Queen of Peace: Is the Mother of God Appearing in Medjugorje?* (Fowler Wright, Leominster, 1984).

_____, *Medjugorje Journal: Mary Speaks to the World*, (McCrimmons, Great Wakering, 1987).

Sanchez-Ventura y Pascual, F., *The Apparitions of Garabandal*, trans. A de Bertodano, (San Miguel Publishing Co., Detroit, 1976).

Sivric, Ivo, OFM, *The Hidden Side of Medjugorje, Vol. I*, ed., L. Bélanger, trans. S. Rini, (Psilog Inc., Saint-François-du-Lac, 1989).

_____, *La face cachée de Medjugorje, tome I*, (Éditions Psilog, Saint-François-du-Lac, 1988).

Sullivan, Randall, *The Miracle Detective: An Investigation of Holy Visions*, (Little Brown, London, 2004).

Verdery, Katherine, *What was Socialism, and What Comes Next?* (Princeton University Press, Princeton, 1996).

Volken, Fr Laurent, *Visions, Revelations, and the Church*, trans. E. Gallaher,(P. J. Kenedy & Sons, New York, 1963).

Weible, Wayne, *The Final Harvest: Medjugorje at the End of the Century*, (Paraclete Press, Brewster, 1999).

Videos

All I Need Is a Miracle, Bounty Hill Media Productions, 1991.

Cover Up: The Hidden Agenda, 1 hour 20 min., Network 5 International, 1998.

Marian Apparitions of the 20[h] Century, Marian Communications Ltd., 1991, P.O. Box 8, Lima, Pennsylvania 19037.

Visions on Demand: The Medjugorje Conspiracy, 60 min., Network 5 International, 1997.

Notes

[1] E. Michael Jones, *The Medjugorje Deception: Queen of Peace, Ethnic Cleansing, Ruined Lives,* (Fidelity Press, South Bend, 1998), pp. 309–310; cf. *Visions on Demand: The Medjugorje Conspiracy,* 60 min., Network 5 International, 1997, video.

[2] Jones, *The Medjugorje Deception,* pp. 304, 308–309.

[3] Ivo Sivric, OFM, *The Hidden Side of Medjugorje, Vol. I,* ed., L Bélanger, trans. S. Rini, (Psilog Inc., Saint-François-du-Lac, 1989), p. 195 n. 214.

[4] Mart Bax, *Medjugorje: Religion, Politics, and Violence in Rural Bosnia,* (VU Uitgeverij, Amsterdam, 1995), pp. 68–70.

[5] Sivric, *The Hidden Side of Medjugorje, Vol. I,* p. 117; Bax, *Medjugorje: Religion, Politics, and Violence,* pp. 10, 70, 84, 85–90.

[6] Bax, *Medjugorje: Religion, Politics, and Violence,* pp. 70–73.

[7] Jones, *The Medjugorje Deception,* pp. 2, 68; Bax, *Medjugorje: Religion, Politics, and Violence,* pp. 73–75, 91, 92, 93–94, 105–106, 122–23; Marcus Tanner, *Croatia: A Nation Forged in War,* (Yale University Press, New Haven, 1997), pp. 152, 179.

[8] Jones, *The Medjugorje Deception,* pp. 25–26, 54–55, 74; Sivric, *The Hidden Side of Medjugorje, Vol. I,* pp. 115–16, 117–18.

[9] Jones, *The Medjugorje Deception,* pp. 60–62; Daria Klanac, *Medjugorje, Réponses aux objections,* (Le Sarment, 2001), pp. 26–27.

[10] Jones, *The Medjugorje Deception,* pp. 43–46; Sivric, *The Hidden Side of Medjugorje, Vol. I,* p. 105; cf. Klanac, *Medjugorje, Réponses aux objections,* p. 46.

[11] Jones, *The Medjugorje Deception,* pp. 43–47; Mary Craig, *Spark from Heaven: The Mystery of the Madonna of Medjugorje,* (Spire, London, 1991), p. 56; cf. *Visions on Demand* video.

[12] René Laurentin, *Medjugorje Testament: Hostility Abounds, Grace Superabounds,* (Ave Maria Press, Toronto, 1999), pp. 93, 214.

[13] Jones, *The Medjugorje Deception,* pp. 50–52.

[14] Ibid., pp. 53–54.

[15] Denis Nolan, *Medjugorje: A Time for Truth and a Time for Action,* (Queenship Publishing, Santa Barbara, 1993), p. 24; see also p. 181.

[16] For sources dealing with concerns about the Charismatic renewal see: www.catholicculture.org/docs/doc_view.cfm?recnum=2798; www.cwnews.com/news/viewstory.cfm?recnum=16816; www.cwnews.com/news/viewstory.cfm?recnum=16795

[17] Dates of birth from: Élisabeth Claverie, *Les guerres de la Vierge,* (Gallimard, 2003), pp. 371–72. Other sources give variations on these dates.

[18] Sivric, *The Hidden Side of Medjugorje,* Vol. I, pp. 32, 35, 36; cf. Bax, *Medjugorje: Religion, Politics, and Violence,* p. 75.

[19] Agnes Horvath & Arpad Szakolczai, *The Dissolution of Communist Power: The Case of Hungary,* (Routledge, London, 1992), pp. xiii, 1, 216, 217, 220.

[20] Katherine Verdery, *What was Socialism, and What Comes Next?* (Princeton University Press, Princeton, 1996), pp. 21–27.

[21] L. Rooney & R. Faricy, *Mary Queen of Peace. Is the Mother of God Appearing in Medjugorje?* (Fowler Wright, Leominster, 1984), pp. 28–29.

[22] Sivric, *The Hidden Side of Medjugorje, Vol. I,* pp. 105–106, (n. 183). The correct spelling is "Tardif." Cf. *Visions on Demand* video.

[23] Wayne Weible, *The Final Harvest: Medjugorje at the End of the Century,* (Paraclete Press, Brewster, 1999), p. 4; *emphasis added.*

[24] Fr Rudo Franken, *A Journey to Medjugorje: Objections to the Apparitions,* (Roggel en Neer, 1999), p. 49; René Laurentin & Ljudevit Rupcic, trans. F. Martin, *Is the Virgin Mary Appearing at Medjugorje?* (The Word Among Us Press, Gaithersburg, 1988), pp. 20–21.

[25] Laurentin & Rupcic, *Is the Virgin Mary Appearing at Medjugorje?* pp. 97–98.

[26] Morton T. Kelsey, *Tongue Speaking: The History and Meaning of Charismatic Experience,* (Crossroad, New York, 1981), pp. 55–58, 60–65.

[27] Kelsey, *Tongue Speaking,* pp. xii-xiii; Walter Hollenweger, *The Pentecostals,* (SCM Press Ltd, London, 1972), pp. 8–9.

[28] René Laurentin, *Catholic Pentecostalism,* (Darton, Longman and Todd, London, 1977), pp. 12–13.

[29] Laurentin, *Catholic Pentecostalism,* pp. 107–110.

[30] Kelsey, *Tongue Speaking,* pp. xiii-xvi, 208.

[31] Kelsey, *Tongue Speaking,* pp. 223–25, 231.

[32] Laurentin, *Catholic Pentecostalism,* p. 9; Laurentin & Rupcic, *Is the Virgin Mary Appearing at Medjugorje?* p. 3.

[33] Laurentin & Rupcic, *Is the Virgin Mary Appearing at Medjugorje?* p. 21.

[34] Jones, *The Medjugorje Deception,* pp. 83–84; Daria Klanac, *Aux Sources de Medjugorje,* (Éditions Sciences et Culture, Montréal, 1998), p. 178; Sivric, *The Hidden Side of Medjugorje, Vol. I,* p. 102. However, it is true that both the children of La Salette, and to a lesser extent St Bernadette, also had less than ideal family backgrounds, so this factor is not necessarily decisive even though it does have to be taken into account.

[35] Svetozar Kraljevic, OFM, *The Apparitions of Our Lady at Medjugorje,* ed. M. Scanlan, (Franciscan Herald Press, Chicago, 1984), p. 152; *emphasis added.*

[36] Craig, *Spark from Heaven,* p. 119.

[37] Claverie, *Les guerres de la Vierge,* p. 154.

[38] Jones, *The Medjugorje Deception,* pp. 84–86, 350–51, 353.

[39] Edited by Fr Louis Kondor, published by Secretariado dos Pastorinhos, Fatima, Portugal, 1999.

[40] Craig, *Spark from Heaven,* pp. 57–58, 59, 75; Fr Michael O'Carroll, *Medjugorje: Facts, Documents, Theology,* (Veritas, Dublin, 1986), p. 34.

[41] Sivric, *The Hidden Side of Medjugorje, Vol. I,* pp. 55–56, 59, 87.

[42] Klanac, *Aux Sources de Medjugorje,* pp. 11–12.

[43] Ibid., p. 68.

[44] Cf. Fr Ivo Sivric, *La face cachée de Medjugorje, tome I,* (Éditions Psilog, Saint-François-du-Lac, 1988), pp. 303–309, and Klanac, *Aux Sources de Medjugorje,* pp. 127–31.

[45] Cf. Klanac, *Aux Sources de Medjugorje,* pp. 69–81, and Sivric, *La face cachée de Medjugorje,* pp. 247–51.

[46] Cf. Klanac, *Aux Sources de Medjugorje,* pp. 97–100, and Sivric, *La face cachée de Medjugorje,* pp. 267–68.

[47] Klanac, *Aux Sources de Medjugorje,* pp. 93–95.

[48] Ibid., p. 83.

[49] Klanac, *Aux Sources de Medjugorje,* pp. 168, 176, 178, 179, 181, 183.

[50] Fr Ljudevit Rupcic & Dr Viktor Nuic, in *Once Again The Truth about Medjugorje,* (K. Kresmir, Zagreb, 2002), pp. 61–62, 79.

[51] Claverie, *Les guerres de la Vierge,* p. 375.

[52] Jones, *The Medjugorje Deception,* pp. 73–75; Laurentin & Rupcic, *Is the Virgin Mary Appearing at Medjugorje?* p. 38; Craig, *Spark from Heaven,* pp. 20–21.

[53] Sivric, *The Hidden Side of Medjugorje, Vol. I,* pp. 220–21.

[54] Msgr Albert Farges, *Mystical Phenomena,* trans. S. P. Jacques, (Burns, Oates & Washbourne Ltd., London, 1926), pp. 330–31. This book

received an approbation from Pope Benedict XV; Sivric, *The Hidden Side of Medjugorje, Vol. I,* p. 224.

[55] Sivric, *The Hidden Side of Medjugorje, Vol. I,* pp. 243–44, 286.

[56] Ibid., pp. 205–206.

[57] René Laurentin, & René Lejeune, *Messages and Teachings of Mary at Medjugorje: Chronological Corpus of the Messages,* (The Riehle Foundation, Milford, 1988), pp. ix, 20.

[58] Laurentin, *Medjugorje Testament,* p. 81.

[59] Weible, *The Final Harvest,* p. 11.

[60] F. Sanchez-Ventura y Pascual, *The Apparitions of Garabandal,* trans. A de Bertodano, (San Miguel Publishing Co., Detroit, 1976), pp. 32–34.

[61] Sivric, *The Hidden Side of Medjugorje, Vol. I,* p. 271; cf. Klanac, *Aux Sources de Medjugorje,* p. 96.

[62] Craig, *Spark from Heaven,* pp. 58, 60.

[63] Sivric, *The Hidden Side of Medjugorje, Vol. I,* p. 60.

[64] Ibid., p. 254.

[65] Sivric, *The Hidden Side of Medjugorje, Vol. I,* pp. 260, 263; cf. Klanac, *Aux Sources de Medjugorje,* pp. 83–84.

[66] Farges, *Mystical Phenomena,* pp. 336–37.

[67] Sivric, *The Hidden Side of Medjugorje, Vol. I,* p. 214.

[68] Ibid., pp. 209–210.

[69] Fr Robert Fox, *Fatima Today,* (OSV, Huntington, 1982), p. 217; see also Martins & Fox, *Documents on Fatima,* (Fatima Family Apostolate, Alexandria, 1992), pp. 241–42.

[70] Sivric, *The Hidden Side of Medjugorje, Vol. I,* pp. 206, 207, 213, 224, 228, 244.

[71] Sivric, *The Hidden Side of Medjugorje, Vol. I,* pp. 208, 301, 320; Kraljevic, *The Apparitions of Our Lady at Medjugorje,* p. 154.

[72] Sivric, *The Hidden Side of Medjugorje, Vol. I,* p. 211. The square brackets with italicized wording are present in the original texts given by Fr Sivric.

[73] Sivric, *The Hidden Side of Medjugorje, Vol. I,* pp. 59, 211–13, 255–56; cf. Klanac, *Aux Sources de Medjugorje,* pp. 70–71.

[74] Fr Janko Bubalo, *A Thousand Encounters with the Blessed Virgin Mary in Medjugorje,* (Friends of Medjugorje, Chicago, 1996), p. 17.

[75] Sivric, *The Hidden Side of Medjugorje, Vol. I,* pp. 216, 225–27, 228.

[76] Ibid., pp. 231–34, 237, 238.

[77] Ibid., pp. 239–40.

[78] Sivric, *The Hidden Side of Medjugorje, Vol. I,* p. 263; cf. Klanac, *Aux Sources de Medjugorje,* pp. 86–87.

[79] Sivric, *The Hidden Side of Medjugorje*, *Vol. I*, pp. 263–64; cf. Klanac, *Aux Sources de Medjugorje*, p. 87.

[80] Sivric, *The Hidden Side of Medjugorje*, *Vol. I*, pp. 278, 284.

[81] Sivric, *The Hidden Side of Medjugorje*, *Vol. I*, pp. 281–82; cf. Klanac, *Aux Sources de Medjugorje*, pp. 117, 118.

[82] Sivric, *The Hidden Side of Medjugorje*, *Vol. I*, pp. 284, 286; cf. Klanac, *Aux Sources de Medjugorje*, p. 121.

[83] Sivric, *The Hidden Side of Medjugorje*, *Vol. I*, pp. 287–88, 294–95, 312; cf. Klanac, *Aux Sources de Medjugorje*, pp. 102, 122, 130–31.

[84] Sivric, *The Hidden Side of Medjugorje*, *Vol. I*, p. 57.

[85] Klanac, *Aux Sources de Medjugorje*, pp. 123, 125–26; cf. Sivric, *The Hidden Side of Medjugorje*, *Vol. I*, pp. 288–89, 291–92.

[86] Sivric, *The Hidden Side of Medjugorje*, *Vol. I*, p. 304.

[87] Craig, *Spark from Heaven*, pp. 65, 68, 72–73.

[88] Laurentin & Lejeune, *Messages and Teachings of Mary at Medjugorje*, p. 60.

[89] Cited by Frances Parkinson Keyes, "Bernadette and the Beautiful Lady," in J. Delaney, ed., *A Woman Clothed with the Sun*, (Doubleday, New York, 1961), p. 122.

[90] René Laurentin, *The Life of Catherine Labouré*, trans., P. Inwood, (Collins, London, 1983), pp. 73–76.

[91] Fr Jean Jaouen, *A Grace called La Salette*, trans. N. Théroux, (La Salette Publications, Attleboro, 1991), pp. 40–42, 49–50; John Beevers, *The Sun Her Mantle*, (Browne and Nolan Ltd, Dublin, 1954), pp. 26–28.

[92] John de Marchi, I.M.C., *Fatima from the beginning*, trans., I. M. Kingsbury, (Missões Consolata, Fatima, 1983). pp. 50–51.

[93] Kondor, *Fatima in Lucia's own words*, pp. 60–62. Cf. the similar accounts in the *Fourth Memoir* of this volume, pp. 150–53. Some secondary accounts of this incident may give the impression that the Angel only gradually assumed his final appearance before the children, and thus that this would invalidate the argument given above. But clearly, Sr Lucia's memoirs are the primary source for the history of the Fatima apparitions, and thus her account here is not comparable with what happened at Medjugorje.

[94] Farges, *Mystical Phenomena*, pp. 358–59.

[95] Léon Cristiani, *Evidence of Satan in the Modern World*, (TAN, Rockford, 1974), pp. 58–60.

[96] Ingo Swann, *The Great Apparitions of Mary*, (The Crossroad Publishing Company, New York, 2000), pp. 162–63; Yves Chiron, *Enquête sur les Apparitions de la Vierge*, (Éditions J'ai Lu, Paris, 1995), p. 459.

[97] Marlene Maloney, "Necedah Revisited: Anatomy of a Phony Apparition," in *Fidelity Magazine,* February, 1989, p. 22; Kevin Orlin Johnson, *Apparitions: Mystic Phenomena and What They Mean,* (Pangaeus Press, Dallas, 1995), p. 333.

[98] Mark Garvey, *Searching for Mary,* Plume, New York, 1998), p. 42.

[99] Sivric, *The Hidden Side of Medjugorje, Vol. I,* pp. 127, *emphasis added,* 128–31, 297; cf. Klanac, *Aux Sources de Medjugorje,* p. 104.

[100] Rooney & Faricy, *Mary Queen of Peace,* pp. 73–74; Craig, *Spark from Heaven,* p. 108.

[101] Lucy Rooney & Robert Faricy, *Medjugorje Journal: Mary Speaks to the World,* (McCrimmons, Great Wakering, 1987), pp. 93–96. The 1978 CDF document on apparition discernment is available online at: www.theotokos.org.uk/pages/appdisce/cdftexte.html

[102] Joachim Bouflet, *Medjugorje, ou la fabrication du surnaturel,* (Éditions Salvator, Paris, 1998), pp. 204–205, 223–24.

[103] Ljudevit Rupcic, *The Truth about Medjugorje,* (Ljubuski-Humac, 1990), p. 13.

[104] Laurentin, *Medjugorje Testament,* p. 87.

[105] Rupcic & Nuic, *Once Again The Truth about Medjugorje,* pp. 229–32.

[106] Klanac, *Aux Sources de Medjugorje,* pp. 133, 135; cf. Sivric, *The Hidden Side of Medjugorje, Vol. I,* pp. 316–19.

[107] Klanac, *Aux Sources de Medjugorje,* p. 135; cf. Sivric, *The Hidden Side of Medjugorje, Vol. I,* p. 319; Bubalo, *Thousand Encounters,* p. 37.

[108] Laurentin & Lejeune, *Messages and Teachings of Mary at Medjugorje,* p 36; cf. Jones, *The Medjugorje Deception,* pp. 78–79, 152.

[109] Sivric, *The Hidden Side of Medjugorje, Vol. I,* p. 321; cf. Klanac, *Aux Sources de Medjugorje,* p. 137.

[110] Sivric, *The Hidden Side of Medjugorje, Vol. I,* pp. 323, 324; cf. Klanac, *Aux Sources de Medjugorje,* pp. 139, 140.

[111] Sivric, *The Hidden Side of Medjugorje, Vol. I,* pp. 324–25; cf. Klanac, *Aux Sources de Medjugorje,* pp. 140, 141.

[112] Sivric, *The Hidden Side of Medjugorje, Vol. I,* pp. 326–28; cf. Klanac, *Aux Sources de Medjugorje,* p. 141.

[113] Klanac, *Aux Sources de Medjugorje,* p. 147; cf. Sivric, *The Hidden Side of Medjugorje, Vol. I,* pp. 329–31.

[114] Sivric, *The Hidden Side of Medjugorje, Vol. I,* pp. 332–33; cf. Klanac, *Aux Sources de Medjugorje,* pp. 148, 149.

[115] Sivric, *The Hidden Side of Medjugorje, Vol. I,* pp. 336–39.

[116] Klanac, *Aux Sources de Medjugorje*, pp. 155, 156, 158; cf. Sivric, *The Hidden Side of Medjugorje*, Vol. I, pp. 341–44.

[117] Kraljevic, *The Apparitions of Our Lady at Medjugorje*, p. 115.

[118] Sivric, *The Hidden Side of Medjugorje*, Vol. I, pp. 105–106.

[119] Klanac, *Aux Sources de Medjugorje*, pp. 159–160; cf. Sivric, *The Hidden Side of Medjugorje*, Vol. I, pp. 63–64, 345–47, 359–60, 373–74; Bubalo, *Thousand Encounters*, p. 58.

[120] Klanac, *Aux Sources de Medjugorje*, pp. 160, 170; cf. Sivric, *The Hidden Side of Medjugorje*, Vol. I, pp. 347–59.

[121] Sivric, *The Hidden Side of Medjugorje*, Vol. I, pp. 360–61, 371; Craig, *Spark from Heaven*, p. 74; cf. Klanac, *Aux Sources de Medjugorje*, pp. 174, 184.

[122] Bubalo, *Thousand Encounters*, pp. 41–42.

[123] Sivric, *The Hidden Side of Medjugorje*, Vol. I, p. 366; cf. Klanac, *Aux Sources de Medjugorje*, p. 179.

[124] Rupcic & Nuic, *Once Again The Truth about Medjugorje*, pp. 79–80. Some of the footnotes on these two pages are incorrectly numbered.

[125] Ibid., pp. 80–81.

[126] Ibid., p. 82.

[127] Rupcic & Nuic, *Once Again The Truth about Medjugorje*, pp. 85–87; Klanac, *Aux Sources de Medjugorje*, p. 36.

[128] Laurentin, *Medjugorje Testament*, p. 228.

[129] Klanac, *Aux Sources de Medjugorje*, p. 37.

[130] Ibid., p. 184; the original French text is : P. JOZO: Soit! Ceci m'intéresse. Encore trois fois. Donc, quand finissent-elles ces visions? MICA: Ils ont dit: "Tout de suite." Plus tard, ils ont dit: "Ça finit vendredi." P. JOZO: Mais où est-ce que cela va finir vendredi? JAKOV: A l'église. MIRJANA: Si Gospa ne nous le dit pas, peut-être que pour le dernier jour, elle désire que ce soit sur la colline!

[131] Fr Ljudevit Rupcic, *The Great Falsification: The Hidden Face of Medjugorje by Ivo Sivric*, p. 3, cited in Nolan, *Medjugorje: A Time for Truth*, p. 200.

[132] O'Carroll, *Medjugorje: Facts, Documents, Theology*, pp. 103–35.

[133] Sivric, *The Hidden Side of Medjugorje*, Vol. I, p. 26.

[134] Rupcic, *The Great Falsification*, p. 4, cited in Nolan, *Medjugorje: A Time for Truth*, p. 202.

[135] Bubalo, *Thousand Encounters*, pp. 37, 41; Sivric, *The Hidden Side of Medjugorje*, Vol. I, pp. 359–60; cf. Klanac, *Aux Sources de Medjugorje*, pp. 171–72.

[136] Rupcic, *The Great Falsification,* p. 4, cited in Nolan, *Medjugorje: A Time for Truth,* p. 201.

[137] Klanac, *Aux Sources de Medjugorje,* p. 126; cf. Sivric, *The Hidden Side of Medjugorje, Vol. I,* pp. 60, 292.

[138] Klanac, *Aux Sources de Medjugorje,* pp. 136–37; cf. Sivric, *The Hidden Side of Medjugorje, Vol. I,* p. 320.

[139] Sivric, *The Hidden Side of Medjugorje, Vol. I,* pp. 62, 378; cf. Klanac, *Aux Sources de Medjugorje,* p. 190.

[140] Craig, *Spark from Heaven,* p. 71.

[141] Kraljevic, *The Apparitions of Our Lady at Medjugorje,* pp. 41–42.

[142] Jones, *The Medjugorje Deception,* pp. 88–89.

[143] Sivric, *The Hidden Side of Medjugorje, Vol. I,* pp. 67–68.

[144] Rupcic & Nuic, *Once Again The Truth about Medjugorje,* p. 84.

[145] Fr Rupcic, cited in O'Carroll, *Medjugorje: Facts, Documents, Theology,* p. 110.

[146] Kraljevic, *The Apparitions of Our Lady at Medjugorje,* pp. 191–92; Laurentin & Rupcic, *Is the Virgin Mary Appearing at Medjugorje?* pp. 1, 3.

[147] Sivric, *The Hidden Side of Medjugorje, Vol. I,* pp. 68, 176–77, 257, 260; Klanac, *Aux Sources de Medjugorje,* pp. 74–75, 82–83; Kraljevic, *The Apparitions of Our Lady at Medjugorje,* p. 39.

[148] Sivric, *The Hidden Side of Medjugorje, Vol. I,* p. 206.

[149] The situation is somewhat complicated because, according to Fr Laurentin, there were actually only eighteen rather than nineteen apparitions in total at Lourdes. But we are concerned here with popular perceptions, and it is the number of apparitions which the villagers, the visionaries, and Fr Zovko respectively, *believed* had taken place which really matters. See René Laurentin, *Bernadette of Lourdes,* (Darton, Longman, & Todd, London, 1998), pp. 31–90; René Laurentin, *Lourdes: récit authentique des apparitions,* (P. Lethielleux, Paris, 1987), p. 250.

[150] Laurentin & Lejeune, *Messages and Teachings of Mary at Medjugorje,* p. 153.

[151] Sivric, *The Hidden Side of Medjugorje, Vol. I,* p. 177; Laurentin, *Bernadette of Lourdes,* p. 40.

[152] Sivric, *The Hidden Side of Medjugorje, Vol. I,* pp. 178, 324–25.

[153] Ibid., pp. 208, 209–10.

[154] Sanchez-Ventura y Pascual, *The Apparitions of Garabandal,* pp. 46–49; Fr Joseph Pelletier, *Our Lady Comes to Garabandal,* (Assumption Publications, Worcester, 1971), pp. 35–36.

[155] Sanchez-Ventura y Pascual, *The Apparitions of Garabandal*, pp. 67–72; Pelletier, *Our Lady Comes to Garabandal*, p. 67.

[156] Sivric, *The Hidden Side of Medjugorje*, Vol. I, pp. 212–13, 244, 261.

[157] Kraljevic, *The Apparitions of Our Lady at Medjugorje*, p. 12.

[158] Sivric, *The Hidden Side of Medjugorje*, Vol. I, pp. 211–12.

[159] Ibid., pp. 238, 263.

[160] Sivric, *The Hidden Side of Medjugorje*, Vol. I, pp. 286, 294–95; Craig, *Spark from Heaven*, p. 65.

[161] See the relevant chapters of the author's volume, *Marian Apparitions, the Bible, and the Modern World*, (Gracewing, Leominster, 2002), for more details on this point. The actual, and generally very brief, words said by Mary during a number of her approved apparitions, can also be accessed via: www.theotokos.org.uk/pages/approved/approved.html

[162] Robert M. Maloy, "The Virgin of the Poor," in *A Woman clothed with the Sun*, (Doubleday, New York, 1961), pp. 247–62; L. Wuillaume, *Banneux: a message for our time*, (Banneux Shrine, 1995), pp. 3–34.

[163] Kondor, *Fatima in Lucia's own words*, pp. 158–60.

[164] Klanac, *Aux Sources de Medjugorje*, p. 160; Sivric, *The Hidden Side of Medjugorje*, Vol. I, pp. 63–64, 345–47.

[165] Craig, *Spark from Heaven*, p. 70.

[166] Sivric, *The Hidden Side of Medjugorje*, Vol. I, pp. 70–71, 245.

[167] Ibid., p. 73.

[168] Ibid., p. 74.

[169] Rupcic & Nuic, *Once Again The Truth about Medjugorje*, pp. 89–92; Sivric, *The Hidden Side of Medjugorje*, Vol. I, p. 248.

[170] Kondor, ed., *Fatima in Lucia's own words*, p. 161.

[171] Sanchez-Ventura y Pascual, *The Apparitions of Garabandal*, pp. 134–35, 138.

[172] Cf. Pelletier, *Our Lady Comes to Garabandal*, pp. 114–15.

[173] Laurentin & Rupcic, *Is the Virgin Mary Appearing at Medjugorje?*, p. 70.

[174] Jones, *The Medjugorje Deception*, pp. 91–93; Sivric, *The Hidden Side of Medjugorje*, Vol. I, pp. 33, 74.

[175] Jones, *The Medjugorje Deception*, pp. 95, 107; Sivric, *The Hidden Side of Medjugorje*, Vol. I, pp. 58–59.

[176] Jones, *The Medjugorje Deception*, p. 70.

[177] Jones, *The Medjugorje Deception*, p. 94; *Corpus Chronologique Des Messages*, (Paris: OEIL, 1988); Sivric, *The Hidden Side of Medjugorje*, Vol. I, pp. 10–12, 95, 250; Bubalo, *Thousand Encounters*, pp. 90–92.

[178] René Laurentin, *Eight Years,* (The Riehle Foundation, Milford, 1989), p. 38, cited in Nolan, *Medjugorje: A Time for Truth,* p. 328.

[179] Sivric, *The Hidden Side of Medjugorje, Vol. I,* pp. 92–95.

[180] Paolo Apolito, *Apparitions of the Madonna at Oliveto Citra: Local Visions and Cosmic Drama,* trans. W. Christian, (Pennsylvania State University Press, Pennsylvania, 1998), pp. 63–64.

[181] O'Carroll, *Medjugorje: Facts, Documents, Theology,* pp. 159, 165.

[182] Ibid., p. 168.

[183] Laurentin & Lejeune, *Messages and Teachings of Mary at Medjugorje,* p. 189; *emphasis added.*

[184] Ludwig Ott, *Fundamentals of Catholic Dogma,* (TAN Books and Publishers, Rockford, 1974), pp. 489–90.

[185] Laurentin & Lejeune, *Messages and Teachings of Mary at Medjugorje,* p. 191; *emphasis added.*

[186] Cf. Ott, *Fundamentals of Catholic Dogma,* pp. 212–15.

[187] St Louis de Montfort, *The Secret of Mary,* (TAN Books and Publishers, Rockford, 1998), p. 11.

[188] See www.medjugorje.org/olmpage.htm for a list of these messages.

[189] *Cover Up: The Hidden Agenda,* 1 hour 20 min., Network 5 International, 1998, video; Weible, *The Final Harvest,* p. 24.

[190] Fr Jordan Aumann, *Spiritual Theology,* (Sheed and Ward, London, 1995), p. 430.

[191] Bouflet, *Medjugorje, ou la fabrication du surnaturel,* p. 136.

[192] René Laurentin & Henri Joyeux, *Scientific and Medical Studies on the Apparitions of Medjugorje* (Veritas Publications, Dublin, 1987), pp. 77–78, 84.

[193] Bubalo, *Thousand Encounters,* pp. 186–87.

[194] Jones, *The Medjugorje Deception,* p. 65.

[195] Bouflet, *Medjugorje, ou la fabrication du surnaturel,* pp. 201–202.

[196] *Cover Up* video.

[197] E. Michael Jones, *Medjugorje: The Untold Story,* (Fidelity Press, South Bend, 1993), pp. 64–65.

[198] Fr. Karl Rahner, S.J., *Visions and Prophecies,* (Burns & Oates, London, 1963), pp. 31–39, n. 37, 51, n. 47.

[199] Sivric, *The Hidden Side of Medjugorje, Vol. I,* pp. 145–46.

[200] Ibid., pp. 130–131.

[201] Bax, *Medjugorje: Religion, Politics, and Violence,* pp. xv, 36–37.

[202] Ibid., pp. 34–35.

[203] Franken, *A Journey to Medjugorje,* pp. 28–30.

[204] Michael Davies, *Medjugorje After Fifteen Years: The Message and the Meaning*, (The Remnant Press, St Paul, 1998), pp. 62–63.

[205] Weible, *The Final Harvest*, p. 116.

[206] Sivric, *The Hidden Side of Medjugorje, Vol. I*, pp. 136–37.

[207] O'Carroll, *Medjugorje: Facts, Documents, Theology*, pp. 142–43, 144–45.

[208] Davies, *Medjugorje After Fifteen Years*, pp. 24–25.

[209] Jones, *The Medjugorje Deception*, pp. 105–106, 107; Sivric, *The Hidden Side of Medjugorje, Vol. I*, p. 152.

[210] Jones, *The Medjugorje Deception*, pp. 107–108; cf. Sivric, *The Hidden Side of Medjugorje, Vol. I*, p. 129; Laurentin & Rupcic, *Is the Virgin Mary Appearing at Medjugorje?* pp. 142–44.

[211] Donal Anthony Foley, *Marian Apparitions, the Bible, and the Modern World*, (Gracewing, Leominster, 2002), pp. 224–26.

[212] Ibid., pp. 231–33.

[213] Ibid., pp. 234–38.

[214] Ibid., pp. 238–43.

[215] Ibid., pp. 243–50.

[216] Ibid., pp. 250–51.

[217] Ibid., pp. 251, 270–72.

[218] Ibid., pp. 251–52.

[219] Ibid., pp. 304–305.

[220] Ibid., pp. 305–307.

[221] Ibid., pp. 312–15.

[222] Frère Michel de la Sainte Trinité, *Fatima Revealed ... and Discarded*, tr. T. Tindal-Robertson, (Augustine Publishing, Devon, 1988), chapters 2–5, quotations from pp. 11, 45, 48; Francis Johnston, *Fatima: The Great Sign*, (Augustine Publishing, Devon, 1980), pp. 23, 38, 85.

[223] Foley, *Marian Apparitions, the Bible, and the Modern World*, pp. 347, 360.

[224] Jones, *The Medjugorje Deception*, pp. 53–54; Klanac, *Aux Sources de Medjugorje*, p. 9.

[225] O'Carroll, *Medjugorje: Facts, Documents, Theology*, pp. 50–51.

[226] Paolo Apolito, *The Internet and the Madonna: Religious Visionary Experience on the Web*, trans. A. Shugaar, (The University of Chicago Press, Chicago, 2005), pp. 36–37.

[227] Laurentin & Rupcic, *Is the Virgin Mary Appearing at Medjugorje?* p. 77.

[228] O'Carroll, *Medjugorje: Facts, Documents, Theology*, pp. 50, 53; emphasis added in both cases.

[229] Laurentin & Rupcic, *Is the Virgin Mary Appearing at Medjugorje?* p. 7.

[230] Laurentin & Lejeune, *Messages and Teachings of Mary at Medjugorje*, pp. 14–15.

[231] Bernard Billet, et al, *Vraies et Fausses Apparitions dans L'Eglise*, (P. Lethielleux, Paris, 1971), pp. 8–19; *Chiron, Enquête sur les Apparitions de la Vierge*, p. 462.

[232] Apolito, *The Internet and the Madonna*, p. 23.

[233] Laurentin & Rupcic, *Is the Virgin Mary Appearing at Medjugorje?* pp. 3, 106.

[234] Rooney & Faricy, *Medjugorje Journal*, p. 92.

[235] Bouflet, *Medjugorje, ou la fabrication du surnaturel*, pp. 208–209.

[236] Laurentin & Rupcic, *Is the Virgin Mary Appearing at Medjugorje?* pp. 83, 106.

[237] Ibid., p. 83.

[238] Ibid., p. 105.

[239] Ibid., p. 130.

[240] Fr William G. Most, *Mary in Our Life*, (The Mercier Press, Cork, 1955), p. 219.

[241] Laurentin & Rupcic, *Is the Virgin Mary Appearing at Medjugorje?* p. 120.

[242] Kraljevic, *The Apparitions of Our Lady at Medjugorje*, p. 124.

[243] Laurentin & Rupcic, *Is the Virgin Mary Appearing at Medjugorje?* pp. 136–37.

[244] Laurentin & Rupcic, *Is the Virgin Mary Appearing at Medjugorje?* pp. 135–36, 145; O'Carroll, *Medjugorje: Facts, Documents, Theology*, pp. 54–56, 201; Rooney & Faricy, *Mary Queen of Peace*, p. 12.

[245] Msgr Ratko Peric, *Ogledalo Pravde,[Mirror of Justice]*, (Mostar, 2001), p. 55, as cited in "Medjugorje: Secrets, Messages, Vocations, Prayers, Confessions, Commissions," a talk given at Maynooth, Co. Dublin, on February 17, 2004.

[246] It appears that some time after this, Fr von Balthasar withdrew his belief in the genuineness of the ongoing claims for apparitions at Medjugorje. Regrettably, he was less public in his retraction than in his original criticisms. He apparently told a group on retreat under him, around 1987, that he did believe in Medjugorje at one time but no longer. In any event, the result was no positive public statement on Medjugorje from him after this. This information comes from a personal communication to the author from Fr Peter Joseph, who was reliably informed about this at the time.

[247] Laurentin & Rupcic, *Is the Virgin Mary Appearing at Medjugorje?* p. 113.

[248] Ibid., p. 2.

[249] Sivric, *The Hidden Side of Medjugorje, Vol. I*, pp. 53, 141.

[250] Laurentin & Lejeune, *Messages and Teachings of Mary at Medjugorje*, p. 11, *emphasis added.*

[251] O'Carroll, *Medjugorje: Facts, Documents, Theology*, p. 195.

[252] O'Carroll, *Medjugorje: Facts, Documents, Theology*, pp. 191–95; Laurentin & Lejeune, *Messages and Teachings of Mary at Medjugorje*, p. 15.

[253] Rupcic, *The Truth about Medjugorje*, pp. 69–75.

[254] Msgr Ratko Peric, *Criteria for Discerning Apparitions: Regarding the Events of Medjugorje*, (Mostar, 1995), p. 17.

[255] Sivric, *The Hidden Side of Medjugorje, Vol. I*, pp. 91, 270–71, 315; Laurentin & Rupcic, *Is the Virgin Mary Appearing at Medjugorje?* pp. 27, 125, 134; Craig, *Spark from Heaven*, p. 174; Fr Laurent Volken, *Visions, Revelations, and the Church*, trans. E. Gallaher (P. J. Kenedy & Sons, New York, 1963) p. 161.

[256] Laurentin & Joyeux, *Scientific and Medical Studies*, pp. 46–47; Laurentin et al., *Medjugorje Today*, (Franciscan University Press, Steubenville, 1990) p. 53; the 1985 interview in *Paris Match* mentioned below in the text has the word "polygraphy" in brackets in a statement about the experiments carried out, but gives no details, cf. as cited in Nolan, *Medjugorje: A Time for Truth*, p. 136.

[257] Laurentin & Joyeux, *Scientific and Medical Studies*, pp. 13, 20–27, 47.

[258] Ibid., p. 25.

[259] Ibid., p. 24.

[260] Cited in, Nolan, *Medjugorje: A Time for Truth*, p. 141.

[261] See: Laurentin & Joyeux, *Scientific and Medical Studies*, pp. 13, 23, 24, 26, 27.

[262] Ibid., pp. 6–7. The general line of argument against supernaturality for this section, is adapted from: http://skepticfiles.org/think/lucifer1.htm

[263] Laurentin & Joyeux, *Scientific and Medical Studies*, p. 7. Another observer, Dr Lucia Capello, (pp. 14–15), claimed that some of the visions she observed ended with "perfect simultaneity" but it is difficult to reconcile this with Fr Laurentin's testimony, and more generally with the available video footage.

[264] *All I Need Is a Miracle*, Bounty Hill Media Productions, 1991, video.

[265] *Marian Apparitions of the 20ᵗʰ Century,* Marian Communications Ltd., 1991, P.O. Box 8, Lima, Pennsylvania 19037, video.

[266] See "A Literature Review on Reaction Time," by Robert J. Kosinski, at: http://biae.clemson.edu/bpc/bp/Lab/110/reaction.htm

[267] Laurentin & Joyeux, *Scientific and Medical Studies,* p. 7.

[268] Ibid., pp. 26, 28, 70–71, 75–76.

[269] *Visions on Demand* video.

[270] Translated *Il Tempo* interview cited in Nolan, *Medjugorje: A Time for Truth,* p. 144.

[271] Laurentin & Joyeux, *Scientific and Medical Studies,* pp. 29, 36, 52; *emphasis added.*

[272] Sharkey and Debergh, *Our Lady of Beauraing,* (Abbey Press, Indiana, 1973), pp. 132–36.

[273] Laurentin & Joyeux, *Scientific and Medical Studies,* p. 9.

[274] Laurentin, *Bernadette of Lourdes,* p. 34.

[275] Laurentin & Joyeux, *Scientific and Medical Studies,* p. 114.

[276] Laurentin & Rupcic, *Is the Virgin Mary Appearing at Medjugorje?* p. 128; O'Carroll, *Medjugorje: Facts, Documents, Theology,* p. 66.

[277] *All I Need Is a Miracle* video.

[278] See: http://www.medjugorje.org/science3.htm

[279] Medjugorje Messenger interview, cited in Nolan, *Medjugorje: A Time for Truth,* pp. 139–40.

[280] Laurentin, *Medjugorje Testament,* p. 59.

[281] Laurentin, *Medjugorje Testament,* pp. 220–24; see also the information at: http://antipolygraph.org/ and "Polygraph" in Microsoft ® Encarta ® Encyclopedia 2004.

[282] Bax, *Medjugorje: Religion, Politics, and Violence,* p. 31.

[283] Ibid., pp. 32–33.

[284] Kondor, *Fatima in Lucia's own words,* p. 141.

[285] Jones, *Medjugorje: The Untold Story,* pp. 1–3.

[286] Bax, *Medjugorje: Religion, Politics, and Violence,* p. 39.

[287] Ibid., pp. 53–55.

[288] Bax, *Medjugorje: Religion, Politics, and Violence,* pp. 55–57; Adolphe Tanquerey, *The Spiritual Life,* (Desclée & Co., Tournai, 1950), pp. 718–20.

[289] Bax, *Medjugorje: Religion, Politics, and Violence,* pp. 60–61.

[290] Ibid., pp. 75–76.

[291] Craig, *Spark from Heaven,* p. 20.

[292] Bax, *Medjugorje: Religion, Politics, and Violence,* pp. 76–77.

[293] Bax, *Medjugorje: Religion, Politics, and Violence*, pp. 96–97, 98–99, 100 n. 12, 106. Cf. Claverie, *Les guerres de la Vierge*, pp. 119, 136.

[294] Sivric, *The Hidden Side of Medjugorje*, Vol. I, pp. 78–79, 82–84. Mark Waterinckx's evidence was communicated personally to the author.

[295] Craig, *Spark from Heaven*, pp. 255–56.

[296] Sharkey & Debergh, *Our Lady of Beauraing*, p. 74.

[297] St John of the Cross, "Ascent of Mount Carmel," in *Complete Works*, Vol. I, pp. 106–108; St John of the Cross, "Ascent of Mount Carmel," in *Collected Works*, p. 230.

[298] Nolan, *Medjugorje: A Time for Truth*, p. 182.

[299] Maloney, "Necedah Revisited," in *Fidelity Magazine*, February, 1989, p. 18.

[300] Ibid., pp. 18, 21, 23.

[301] Sivric, *The Hidden Side of Medjugorje*, Vol. I, pp. 79–81.

[302] C. Malanga and R. Pinotti, *I fenomeni B.V.M.: Le manifestazioni mariane in una nuova luce*, (Montadori, Milan, 1990), cited in, Apolito, *Apparitions of the Madonna at Oliveto Citra*, pp. 95–96.

[303] Laurentin & Lejeune, *Messages and Teachings of Mary at Medjugorje*, p. 69.

[304] Michael J. Mazza, *The Catholic Church and Medjugorje*, p. 10.

[305] Jones, *Medjugorje: The Untold Story*, pp. 25–26.

[306] Sivric, *The Hidden Side of Medjugorje*, Vol. I, pp. 155–56, 199 n. 311; Rev. Vittorio Guerrera, *Medjugorje: A Closer Look*, (Maryheart Crusaders, Meriden, 1995), p. 66.

[307] Guerrera, *Medjugorje: A Closer Look*, pp. 65–66; Cf. Jones, *Medjugorje: The Untold Story*, p. 22.

[308] Randall Sullivan, *The Miracle Detective: An Investigation of Holy Visions*, (Little Brown, London, 2004), p. 217.

[309] Fr Rupcic cited in O'Carroll, *Medjugorje: Facts, Documents, Theology*, p. 125.

[310] *All I Need Is a Miracle* video.

[311] Jones, *The Medjugorje Deception*, p. 54.

[312] Ibid., p. 65.

[313] Joseph Cardinal Ratzinger, with Vittorio Messori, *The Ratzinger Report: An Exclusive Interview on the State of the Church*, (Fowler Wright Books, Leominster, 1985), pp. 111–12.

[314] O'Carroll, *Medjugorje: Facts, Documents, Theology*, pp. 149–54.

[315] Ratzinger , *The Ratzinger Report*, pp. 111–12.

[316] Jones, *The Medjugorje Deception*, p. 66.

[317] Ibid., pp. 113–14.

[318] Sivric, *The Hidden Side of Medjugorje, Vol. I*, p. 135.

[319] Peric, *Criteria for Discerning Apparitions*, pp. 9–10. From *La Civiltà Cattolica*, 19 October 1985.

[320] Jones, *The Medjugorje Deception*, pp. 124–25; Sivric, *The Hidden Side of Medjugorje, Vol. I*, pp. 53, 187, n. 42.

[321] Sivric, *The Hidden Side of Medjugorje, Vol. I*, p. 141.

[322] Jones, *The Medjugorje Deception*, pp. 125–27.

[323] Cf. Sivric, *The Hidden Side of Medjugorje, Vol. I*, pp. 142–43.

[324] Guerrera, *Medjugorje: A Closer Look*, p. 64, (Prot. No. 909/88/5). A recent report on the web site *Spirit Daily*, (www.spiritdaily.org), dated 19 May 2005, cites written evidence to the effect that John Paul II had some private devotion to Medjugorje—but this clearly did not affect his public stance, which was noncommittal.

[325] Sivric, *The Hidden Side of Medjugorje, Vol. I*, pp. 15–16, 37. See *Dernières Nouvelles ...* (No. 7), 1988.

[326] Sivric, *The Hidden Side of Medjugorje, Vol. I*, pp. 100–101.

[327] Kraljevic, *The Apparitions of Our Lady at Medjugorje*, p. 133.

[328] Kraljevic, *The Apparitions of Our Lady at Medjugorje*, p. 136; Aumann, *Spiritual Theology*, p. 412.

[329] Bubalo, *Thousand Encounters*, p. 17. For other examples of Vicka's irreverent way of answering Fr Bubalo see pp. 10, 15, 17, 18, 28, 31, 39, 42, 64, 78, 93, 152, 177.

[330] Bubalo, *Thousand Encounters*, pp. 215–16; *emphasis added.* Fr Vlasic quote from: Lucy Rooney & Robert Faricy, *Medjugorje Unfolds: Mary Speaks to the World*, (Fowler Wright Books Ltd, Leominster, 1985), p. 55; *All I Need Is a Miracle* video.

[331] Guerrera, *Medjugorje: A Closer Look*, pp. 40–41; Jones, *The Medjugorje Deception*, pp. 117–18; *All I Need Is a Miracle*, video. Daria Klanac claims that on this occasion, Vicka was actually talking about a *previous* vision, but this goes against the explicit videotaped testimony of Louis Bélanger; see Klanac, *Medjugorje, Réponses aux objections*, pp. 77–78, and the above mentioned video.

[332] O'Carroll, *Medjugorje: Facts, Documents, Theology*, p. 205.

[333] Jones, *The Medjugorje Deception*, pp. 101–102; Sivric, *The Hidden Side of Medjugorje, Vol. I*, pp. 53, 74–77.

[334] O'Carroll, *Medjugorje: Facts, Documents, Theology*, p. 206.

[335] Weible, *The Final Harvest*, pp. 98, 164.

[336] Jones, *Medjugorje: The Untold Story*, pp. 89–91; Guerrera, *Medjugorje: A Closer Look*, pp. 68–70; Laurentin & Lejeune, *Messages and Teachings of Mary at Medjugorje*, p. 166; cf. *Visions on Demand* video.

[337] Davies, *Medjugorje After Fifteen Years*, pp. 32–33. Frs Rupcic and Nuic, in their *Once Again The Truth about Medjugorje*, (K. Kresmir, Zagreb, 2002), p. 32, claim that Marija was not speaking about her own messages, but those allegedly received by Agnes Heupel, but it is not clear what they base this idea on.

[338] Weible, *The Final Harvest*, p. 166.

[339] Sivric, *The Hidden Side of Medjugorje, Vol. I*, pp. 96–100; Bouflet, *Medjugorje, ou la fabrication du surnaturel*, p. 178; Craig, *Spark from Heaven*, pp. 240, 299; cf. Bubalo, *Thousand Encounters*, pp. 283–87. Mary Craig, pp. 240–41, also relates how other medical/psychological investigators looked on Vicka's general condition in a more positive light, but, as indicated in chapter 13 of this book, the various tests which were carried out were far from rigorous, and it seems as though some investigators were unduly influenced by the "superstar" status of the visionaries.

[340] Aumann, *Spiritual Theology*, p. 430.

[341] Bubalo, *Thousand Encounters*, p. 54; Sivric, *The Hidden Side of Medjugorje, Vol. I*, p. 199, n. 317.

[342] For critical evidence see particularly, Jones, *The Medjugorje Deception*, pp. 46–50, 75, 77, 84, 96, 114; cf. also *Visions on Demand* video. For the opposite point of view see: Nolan, *Medjugorje: A Time for Truth*, pp. 183, 245–248, 320–27, & Klanac, *Medjugorje, Réponses aux objections*, pp. 49–53.

[343] Jones, *The Medjugorje Deception*, pp. 147, 164–65, 370; Laurentin & Lejeune, *Messages and Teachings of Mary at Medjugorje*, p. 168. Laurentin, *Dernières Nouvelles de Medjugorje*, Nr. 15, June 1996, p. 34. Mark Waterinckx gives explicit testimony about the allegations concerning Fr Zovko on the *Cover Up* video, with this being based on his own first hand experiences as a former close friend of Fr Zovko over many years. Furthermore, these details have been personally confirmed to the author by Mark Waterinckx. The details of the suspensions of Fr Zovko are contained in the Mostar Chancery documents numbers 622/89 and 423/94. Cf. also *Cover Up* video.

[344] Letter from Bishop Peric to Fr Rudo Franken, 7 February 2000, cited in Michael Davies, *Medjugorje after Twenty-One Years, 1981–2002: The Definitive History*, pp. 148–49. At the time of writing, this text is only available as a download from: www.mdaviesonmedj.com, although a printed version is also apparently planned.

[345] Jones, *The Medjugorje Deception*, pp. 167–74.

[346] Davies, *Medjugorje after Twenty-One Years, 1981–2002*, p. 86.

[347] Jones, *The Medjugorje Deception*, pp. 184–86. According to Jones, the details of the Zadar declaration had been leaked to reporters from the CNS in "late 1990." So it was obviously finalized by that date, and thus Cardinal Ratzinger would have been aware of the decision of the Yugoslav bishops before it was officially issued, in April 1991.

[348] From the Introduction in Janice T. Connell's, *The Visions of the Children*, (St Martin's Press, New York, 1992), p. xv.

[349] *30 DAYS*, March 1991, p. 55.

[350] Jones, *The Medjugorje Deception*, pp. 188–89, 191; Jones, *Medjugorje: The Untold Story*, p. 124.

[351] Jones, *The Medjugorje Deception*, pp. 189–91, 192, 194.

[352] Ibid., pp. 233, 235–38.

[353] Bax, *Medjugorje: Religion, Politics, and Violence*, pp. xvi, xvii, xviii.

[354] Ibid., pp. 101–102, 106–107, 108–11. Bax comments that it is difficult to give exact figures because of the destruction of records caused by the war, p. 116. n. 2.

[355] Ibid., pp. 111–14, 118, n. 19.

[356] Jones, *The Medjugorje Deception*, pp. 246–247, 267; Bax, *Medjugorje: Religion, Politics, and Violence*, p. 78.

[357] Jones, *The Medjugorje Deception*, pp. 200–201; for further information on Cardinal Ratzinger's letter, see the EWTN website, as follows: www.ewtn.com/expert/answers/poem_of_the_man.htm

[358] Elliot Miller & Kenneth R. Samples, *The Cult of the Virgin: Catholic Mariology and the Apparitions of Mary*, (Baker Book House, Grand Rapids, 1994), pp. 150, 177.

[359] Jones, *The Medjugorje Deception*, p. 240.

[360] Ibid., p. 295.

[361] Jones, *The Medjugorje Deception*, pp. xvii, xix, 297, 304, 309–10; cf. *Visions on Demand* video.

[362] Laurentin, *Medjugorje Testament*, p. 96.

[363] See: Davies, *Medjugorje after Fifteen Years*, p. 78.

[364] Aumann, *Spiritual Theology*, pp. 420–21.

[365] Ibid., pp. 402–403.

[366] Ibid., pp. 403, 412.

[367] Johnson, *Apparitions: Mystic Phenomena and what they mean*, pp. 286–88; Rev. Michael Walsh, *The Apparition at Knock*, (St Jarlath's College, Tuam, 1959), p. 10.

[368] *De Servorum Dei*, III, 53, xxii, II.

[369] Most, *Mary in our Life*, p. 217.

[370] Joseph de Sainte-Marie, OCD, *Reflections on the Act of Consecration at Fatima of Pope John Paul II on 13th May 1982,* trans, W. Lawson, (Augustine Publishing Company, Devon, 1983), pp. 23–24; see also Ranwez, "The Value of the Episcopal Declarations concerning the events at Beauraing," in *Marian Library Studies,* 96, pp. 3–4.

[371] Augustin Poulain, *The Graces of Interior Prayer,* (Kegan Paul, London, 1912), pp. 349–50.

[372] Walsh, *The Apparition at Knock,* pp. 13–14; Louis Lochet, *Apparitions of Our Lady: Their Place in the Life of the Church,* (Herder, Freiburg, 1960), pp. 34–35.

[373] Davies, *Medjugorje After Fifteen Years,* pp. 85–88.

[374] Jones, *The Medjugorje Deception,* p. 362.

[375] Ibid., p. 368.

[376] Davies, *Medjugorje After Fifteen Years,* pp. 89–91.

[377] Davies, *Medjugorje After Fifteen Years,* pp. 97–99; Laurentin, *Medjugorje Testament,* p. 99.

[378] Davies, *Medjugorje after Twenty-One Years,* pp. 111–12, (Prot. No. 32343/97 & Prot. No. 32344/97).

[379] Kevin Orlin Johnson, *Twenty Questions About Medjugorje: What Rome Really Said,* (Pangaeus Press, Dallas, 1999), pp. 6–8.

[380] Johnson, *Twenty Questions About Medjugorje,* pp. 8–12.

[381] Sivric, *The Hidden Side of Medjugorje, Vol. I,* pp. 71–72, 156.

[382] Rooney & Faricy, *Mary Queen of Peace,* pp. 32, 75.

[383] Maloney, "Necedah Revisited" in *Fidelity Magazine,* February, 1989, pp. 21, 22–23.

[384] O'Carroll, *Medjugorje: Facts, Documents, Theology,* pp. x, 13.

[385] Laurentin & Lejeune, *Messages and Teachings of Mary at Medjugorje,* p. 27.

[386] Sivric, *The Hidden Side of Medjugorje, Vol. I,* pp. 156–57, 158. The information about quarrelling came via a personal communication to the author from Mark Waterinckx.

[387] Rooney & Faricy, *Medjugorje Journal,* pp. 101, 107.

[388] Craig, *Spark from Heaven,* p. 164.

[389] Weible, *The Final Harvest,* pp. 155–56.

[390] Moira Noonan, *Ransomed from Darkness,* (North Bay Books, El Sobrante, 2005), pp. 55–96.

[391] David Baldwin, *Medjugorje,* (CTS, London, 2002), p. 75; Gina Hutchings, *Youth 2000,* (CTS, London, 2001), pp. 4, 8–10, 70.

[392] Craig, *Spark from Heaven,* pp. 178–79.

[393] Johnson, *Twenty Questions About Medjugorje*, pp. 13–14; Davies, *Medjugorje After Fifteen Years*, pp. 67–69.

[394] Weible, *The Final Harvest*, p. 125.

[395] Cf. Apolito, *The Internet and the Madonna*, pp. 3, 4.

[396] Nolan, *Medjugorje: A Time for Truth*, p. 161.

[397] O'Carroll, *Medjugorje: Facts, Documents, Theology*, pp. 145–46.

[398] Sanchez-Ventura y Pascual, *The Apparitions of Garabandal*, pp. 88, 92.

[399] Johnson, *Twenty Questions About Medjugorje*, pp. 14–16; cf. Apolito, *The Internet and the Madonna*, pp. 30, 44–45, 46–47.

[400] Volken, *Visions, Revelations, and the Church*, p. 166.

[401] Chiron, *Enquête sur les Apparitions de la Vierge*, pp. 462–64.

[402] Fr René Laurentin, *The Apparitions of the Blessed Virgin Mary Today*, (Veritas Publications, Dublin 1991), pp. 141–46.

[403] Jones, *The Medjugorje Deception*, p. xiv. The information about Fr Sivric was passed on to the author by Mary Broome, who knew him personally when he lived in St Louis, Missouri.

[404] Nolan, *Medjugorje: A Time for Truth*, p. 182.

[405] Weible, *The Final Harvest*, pp. 155–56.

[406] Bouflet, *Medjugorje, ou la fabrication du surnaturel*, pp. 185–88.

[407] Jones, *The Medjugorje Deception*, pp. xviii, 352, 359.

[408] *The Sunday Times*, 29 December 2002, "Village grows rich on Virgin visions", by Tom Walker, Medjugorje, Bosnia.

[409] See: http://www.medjugorje.org/ivanse.htm

[410] Johnson, *Twenty Questions About Medjugorje*, pp. 3–4.

[411] Ibid., pp. 4–6.

[412] Nolan, *Medjugorje: A Time for Truth*, pp. 109–22.

[413] Johnson, *Twenty Questions About Medjugorje*, p. 19; Donovan, "Bayside Unveiled", in *Fidelity Magazine*, March, 1988, pp. 34–35; Davies, *Medjugorje after Twenty-One Years, 1981–2002*, p. 86.

[414] St John of the Cross, "Ascent of Mount Carmel," in *Collected Works*, p. 226.

[415] Noonan, *Ransomed from Darkness*, pp. 51–53.

[416] Kraljevic, *The Apparitions of Our Lady at Medjugorje*, pp. 125–26.

[417] Although such incidents were not unknown in the lives of saints such as Padre Pio, such persons are clearly in a different category to the Medjugorje visionaries.

[418] Kondor, *Fatima in Lucia's own words*, pp. 137–38.

[419] Kraljevic, *The Apparitions of Our Lady at Medjugorje*, pp. 156–57.

[420] Laurentin & Lejeune, *Messages and Teachings of Mary at Medjugorje*, pp. 38, 157.

[421] *Homiletic and Pastoral Review Magazine*, (letter to the editor), pp. 5–6, July 2002.

[422] Davies, *Medjugorje after Twenty-One Years, 1981–2002*, p. 151; the full text of the homily by Bishop Peric is at: www.theotokos.org.uk/pages/unapprov/medjugor/bpperic3.html

[423] Davies, *Medjugorje after Twenty-One Years, 1981–2002*, pp. 152–53.

[424] Ibid., pp. 159–63.

[425] Ibid., pp. 138–42.

[426] Ibid., pp. 142–43.

[427] Ibid., pp. 138, 143–46.

[428] *L'Osservatore Romano,* Vatican, October 17, 2001. See also www.catholicculture.org/docs/doc_view.cfm?recnum=3977, and CWNews.com–Vatican, October 10, 2001, ref. 16570. The ungrammatical nature of the latter part of this text is present in the original.

[429] *The Catholic Weekly* (Australia), 14 July 2002: www.catholicweekly.com.au/02/jul/14/08.html

[430] *The Catholic Herald*, 29 November 2002.

[431] Baldwin, *Medjugorje,* pp. 43–44.

[432] "Medjugorje: Secrets, Messages, Vocations, Prayers, Confessions, Commissions," a talk given at Maynooth, Co. Dublin, on February 17, 2004. This is available at Bishop Peric's website: http://www.cbismo.hr/

[433] From the interview with Msgr. Ratko Peric, Bishop of Mostar-Duvno, released to the "Crkva na kamenu" (The Church on the Rock), monthly pastoral bulletin of the Dioceses of Mostar-Duvno and Trebinje-Mrkan, nr. 4/2006, pp. 22-24, after his "visitatio Ad Limina" from 23-28 February 2006. To see the complete document, please visit : www.theotokos.org.uk/pages/unapprov/medjugor/adlimina.html

[434] Foley, *Marian Apparitions, the Bible, and the Modern World*, pp. 350–51. For a discussion on the validity of the collegial consecration, see pages 352–56.

[435] Ibid., pp. 360–61.

[436] Ibid., pp. 361–62.

[437] Ibid., pp. 362–66.

[438] For example, see: Nolan, *Medjugorje: A Time for Truth,* passim.

[439] SESDI, 1J5.1/11.209, 1998 11 10, 5938; CWNews.com, Vatican, 20 December 2001.

[440] *Inside the Vatican,* December 2004, p. 39; CWNews.com, Vatican, 20 December 2001.

[441] *Medjugorje: All Our Lady's Messages*, (Edizioni Martini, n.d.), p. 88; Also available at: www.medjugorje.org/olmpage.htm

[442] Martins & Fox, *Documents on Fatima*, p. 246.

[443] Craig, *Spark from Heaven*, p. 71.

[444] Davies, *Medjugorje after Fifteen Years*, p. 69.

[445] See, for example, Johnston, *Fatima: The Great Sign*, for more details on this subject.

[446] St Louis de Montfort, *True Devotion to Mary*, (TAN Books and Publishers, Rockford, 1985), p. 27, *emphasis added*; de Montfort, *The Secret of Mary*, p. 45.

[447] Dirvin, Joseph, C.M., *Saint Catherine Labouré of the Miraculous Medal*, (TAN Books and Publishers, Rockford, 1984), p. 208.

[448] See E. M Brown, ed., *Dream, Visions and Prophecies of Don Bosco*, (Don Bosco Publications, New Rochelle, 1986), pp. 105–108, for details of this dream.

[449] St Maximilian Kolbe, *The Crusade of Mary Immaculate*, (Crusade of Mary Immaculate Press, Manchester, 2000), p. 66.

[450] *Crossing the Threshold of Hope*, (Jonathan Cape, London, 1994), p. 221.

Index

Recommended Fatima Books

Fatima in Lucia's own words I, edited by Fr Louis Kondor

This book contains the four memoirs written by Sr Lucia at the request of the original bishop of Fatima. They give a profound insight into the life of the Fatima seers, and into the real message of Fatima—which is about allowing Our Lady complete freedom to lead us to God.

Fatima: the Great Sign, by Francis Johnston

Still one of the best books on Fatima, it looks at the central role of Fatima in the Church, as expounded by popes, bishops and eminent theologians, and indicates how we can best respond to Our Lady's message.

What Happened at Fatima by Leo Madigan

An up-to-date and beautifully told account of the events at Fatima, which really brings them to life.

The Children of Fatima, by Leo Madigan

Now for the first time the complete story of Blessed Francisco and Jacinta Marto has been revealed in a full-length book. Marked by poignant, intimate details, and a captivating writing style, this moving biography of two extraordinary children has become an instant classic.

The Fatima Prayer Book contains many of the Prayers, Masses, Devotions and Hymns which express the Fatima message—a beautiful gift.

All of the above books are available via: www.theotokos.org.uk

By the same author

Marian Apparitions, the Bible, and the Modern World

Foreword by Fr Aidan Nichols OP

Imprimatur from Bishop McMahon of Nottingham, England

ISBN 0852443137 - 374pp - £19.99

This is an in depth investigation into the major Marian apparitions that have occurred during the last five centuries. It relates them to secular happenings and important revolutionary events in Western history including the Reformation and the French and Russian Revolutions. It also argues that the major apparitions are not random or historically inconsequential events, but actually seem to follow a preordained plan, one intimately linked with the biblical Marian typology explored by the Church Fathers. In particular, this books looks at the importance of Fatima in the life of the Church, its links with the papacy, and its continuing relevance for the Third Millennium.

"With his Marian Apparitions, the Bible, and the Modern World, *Donal Foley has made a very important contribution to our under-standing and appreciation of private revelations, in particular those of Our Lady. ... Not only ... scholars and believers, but the general public will find this volume informative and inspirational."*
- Fr. Peter M. Fehlner, F.I.

"Donal Foley has written a book with an extraordinary message."
- Fr Aidan Nichols OP

To order please visit:
www.theotokos.org.uk/pages/books/mariapps/mariapps.html

or: www.amazon.co.uk/exec/obidos/ASIN/0852443137/theotokoscath-21

or you can order via other online booksellers or through your local bookseller.

Printed in the United States
95882LV00001B/214/A

9 780955 074608